Success In On-line Learning

Success In On-line Learning

Candice Kramer

DELMAR

THOMSON LEARNING ™

Australia Canada Mexico Singapore Spain United Kingdom United States

Success in On-line Learning
Candice Kramer

Business Unit Director: Susan L. Simpfenderfer	Executive Production Manager: Wendy A. Troeger	Executive Marketing Manager: Donna J. Lewis
Executive Editor: Marlene McHugh Pratt	Production Manager: Carolyn Miller	Channel Manager: Wendy E. Mapstone
Acquisitions Editor: Zina M. Lawrence	Production Editor: Kathryn B. Kucharek	Cover Images: PhotoDisc
Editorial Assistant: Elizabeth Gallagher		Cover Design: Eve Siegel

For permission to use material from this text or product, contact us by
Tel   (800) 730-2214
Fax   (800) 730-2215
www.thomsonrights.com

Library of Congress Cataloging-in-Publication Data

Kramer, Candice,
  Success in On-line Learning / Candice Kramer.
    p. cm.
  Includes bibliographical references (p.) and index.
  1. Distance education—United States. 2. Internet in education—United States. 3. Adult education—United States.
  I. Title.
  LC5805.K72 2001

374'.4'0973—dc21   00-065835

NOTICE TO THE READER

This book is dedicated to the memory of my mother, who encouraged me always to "keep learning."

CONTENTS

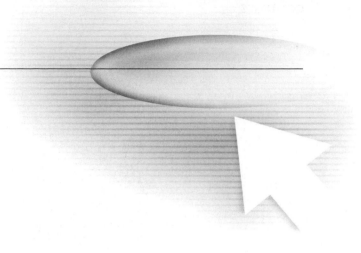

Section IV   Get It Done—Managing the Educational Project

Section V   A Look into the Future

Preface

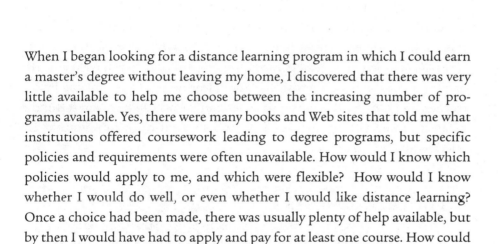

When I began looking for a distance learning program in which I could earn a master's degree without leaving my home, I discovered that there was very little available to help me choose between the increasing number of programs available. Yes, there were many books and Web sites that told me what institutions offered coursework leading to degree programs, but specific policies and requirements were often unavailable. How would I know which policies would apply to me, and which were flexible? How would I know whether I would do well, or even whether I would like distance learning? Once a choice had been made, there was usually plenty of help available, but by then I would have had to apply and pay for at least one course. How could I—or anyone—be sure to save time and money and make the right choice?

As an adult educator and academic support professional, I at least knew what questions to ask. I had been helping adults succeed in their educational endeavors for many years, and had learned where the pitfalls were. As a classroom teacher and trainer, I had helped many different kinds of people learn in many different ways. As an adult learner myself, I had overcome the barriers to achievement in classroom learning. I knew what it was like to rush home from work in time to feed the family and dash off to class; and I knew the discipline required to study and master unfamiliar material.

By asking the right questions, I found the program that worked for me. As I worked through it, I communicated with others who had been through the same search as I had. I became curious about how others had found distance learning options that worked for them. Through these informal interviews and personal experience, the idea for this book was born: a guide to help you succeed in your distance learning experiences.

In this guide, you will find advice from professionals and from learners just like you who have already succeeded through distance learning. Through their stories (names have been changed to protect their privacy), you will see how they have managed to fit learning into their busy lives, and the impact that learning has continued to have on them. But that is not all.

In addition to the assistance you will find here in choosing and completing your desired learning experience, On-line Resources are available to help you find what you need, when you need it. The Online Resources Web site contains specific information to help you personalize your distance learning experiences. Information will be updated regularly, providing you with the most current intelligence available. In addition, a bulletin board will provide access to other learners with whom you can discuss your mutual learning goals. Here, you can also ask me any questions that the text prompts you to ask. The Online Resources icon appears at the end of each chapter to prompt you to go on-line and take advantage of the many features provided. You can find the Online Resources at <www.delmar.com>.

You may have seen other distance learning guides, written by teachers, administrators, or combinations of the two groups. You may wonder how this guide is different. The difference is this: *This is the only guide that is written about adult learners by an adult learner.* It is designed to help you overcome the habits you might associate with classroom learning that is regulated by the teacher, and take control of your own learning. This can help you fulfill the greatest promise of distance learning and shape it to fit in ways that are relevant and useful to you.

I have written it for you, and I wish you success!

ACKNOWLEDGEMENTS

Without the support and assistance of many people, the completion of this book would not have been possible. I would like to thank my degree mentor, Sybil McClary, for her guidance during completion of the thesis project on which this book is based. I am indebted to my friend and colleague, Fred Antico, for his role as a sounding board and facilitator.

Many thanks to my editor, Zina Lawrence, her outstanding assistant, Elizabeth Gallagher, and the entire Delmar publication team. I also owe a debt of gratitude to the many colleagues and learners who helped to make this publication a reality, including, but not limited to, Gloria John, Rich Douglas, and the good people at Capella University. I would also be remiss if I did not include my thanks to the hundreds of students it has been my privilege to learn from and with over the years. Without them and their constant pursuit of personal fulfillment and excellence, this book would never have been undertaken.

Most of all, I would like to thank my husband, Richard, and my son, Jesse, for their relentless support and encouragement, without which this quest would have remained a dream.

ABOUT THE AUTHOR

Candice Kramer has over 20 years of experience as a teacher and trainer of adult learners, including 10 years of experience as an academic advisor and prior learning assessment counselor. A learner and educator both on-line and off, she coaches others to help them achieve the goals they have set for themselves, and consults to institutions and organizations in effective learning design for adults.

Photo courtesy of Jill A. Bochicchio, Bochicchio Photography

In addition to public school teaching credentials and doctoral study, Candice holds two master's degrees, one of which was completed entirely on-line. The inspiration for *Success in On-Line Learning* grew out of her own searches for a comprehensive support resource for adults interested in on-line learning. Unable to find such a resource, she decided to write one. Combining her experience in adult student support and academic advising with knowledge gleaned from studies and interviews with fellow distance learners, *Success in On-Line Learning* became a reality.

Based in suburban Washington, D.C., Candice continues to teach, write, and consult.

Introduction and Orientation

This introduction will acquaint you with what is available in the world of learning at a distance. It will also explain how this text and its companion Online Resources can help *you* become a successful distance learner.

"I hear and I forget. I see and I remember. I do and I understand."

—*Confucius*

The chapters in this section are:

Chapter 1 - A World of Learning at Your Fingertips

Chapter 2 - How to Use This Guide

A World of Learning at Your Fingertips

"Two fundamental characteristics of a modern society are complexity and change. Together, these characteristics put increasing demands on the education needed for the citizens to cope with their life in the society."

—Erling Ljoså

Welcome! By choosing this book, you have taken the first steps toward an exciting new learning experience called distance learning. Does learning in your home, at your convenience, and on your own schedule sound wonderful? Well, you are not alone in feeling that it does. The National Center for Educational Statistics has estimated that by 2002, over 2.5 million new adult learners will seek education or training, and many of them want, and need, their learning delivered when it is most convenient. Like you, they need to fit new skills and education into a busy schedule. Between work, child and elder care, community service, and recreational activities, they need to find the time to learn. There is no time to waste.

With the Internet, access to education has become possible for literally millions of adults who were previously unable to fit education into their lives. But access has not necessarily led to success, because distance learners must possess important skills and characteristics to become successful distance learners. *Success in On-Line Learning* identifies those crucial skills and characteristics and provides new distance learners with the step-by-step processes to learn how to learn in an information society. By combining information with student services and adding resources through the flexible medium of the Web-based companion, Online Resources, *Success in On-Line Learning* helps the on-line learner to make choices and undertake learning experiences that are appropriate, regardless of age, educational level, or purpose for returning to lifelong learning.

UNIVERSAL ACCESS TO LIFELONG LEARNING IS AT HAND

You know that the world is changing; the way people learn is changing, too. Learning is becoming more flexible, more of a lifelong endeavor. Many people just like you have realized that they need to learn new things to remain competitive and current in their chosen fields or to change careers. They have realized that they will need to continue to learn throughout their lifetimes and that learning must become a regular part of their lives.

Educational providers are realizing this too. Many are adjusting to the needs of working adults and offering flexible options geared toward those needs. Educational providers from colleges to training centers are entering this market on a daily basis. Why? Because they realize that the projections of increased educational enrollment are just the beginning of a huge market, the market for your educational investment.

According to a Merrill Lynch report, the total value of Web-based education will top $740 billion by 2003. These educational providers want you to choose what *they* offer, so they are marketing strongly to the need their demographic experts have identified: Adult learners like you. How will you know which claims can be trusted and which cannot? This book will help you learn how to separate hard facts from wishful thinking before you make the first excursion in your distance learning journey.

Distance Learning, a Background

Distance learning as a method of study has really been around for some time. Over a hundred years ago, correspondence courses became available to allow students who lived in remote areas to complete course objectives by mail, reading assignments and completing papers and tests that were graded by professors miles away. These isolated endeavors were not without their problems, with intervals of weeks or months between correspondence being the norm. With these forced limits on responsiveness, it is easy to understand why many students found it difficult to complete their correspondence studies.

More recently, distance learning has taken the form of mailed videotapes, in which students could watch taped lectures and complete workbook or text assignments to mail or fax to a professor. Although the response time could often be cut in half, many felt it was still a poor substitute for the face-to-face interaction

"College students represent the single largest nongender-based on-line demographic, constituting 24% of the total number of adult Internet users."

—Merrill-Lynch
Knowledge Web report

The 'hint' icon, which looks like this will let you know about a tip or strategy to help you become a more effective online learner.

The 'pitfall' icon, which looks like this will caution you to watch out for those little things that can sneak up on you when you are distracted and create problems. With these items in mind, your success will be in your own hands!

"Distance learning is now a key component of our new learning society, in which learners must take increased responsibility for control and direction of the learning process." —American Council of Education website <www.acenet.edu/calec/dist_learning/home.html>.

that is an intrinsic part of the classroom setting. But the technology to overcome these limitations has been progressing steadily.

As technology has progressed, so have its educational applications and opportunities. However, the numbers of learners undertaking distance options has thus far represented a small minority of total learners. The reasons for this are complex, but they are partly due to the limitations of the technology and partly due to the real needs of the average learner.

Few people feel comfortable learning on their own, as most distance learning methods have essentially required until very recently. Combinations of delivery methods have been tried with varying degrees of success, from one-to-one mentorships using the telephone to pre-Internet e-mail instruction. Moreover, the number of people undertaking these technologically enhanced methods of learning have not reached the kind of critical mass that is necessary to impel the curious to action. That, too, is changing.

Within the previous two decades, many institutions have undertaken the expense of providing regional media learning centers at which students can interact with teachers and other learners through **synchronous video,** essentially a closed-circuit live televised learning event. This distance learning option provides video transmission of classes to students at remote locations, usually via satellite, as they occur from the home campus. This allows students to interact with professors and at least the students in their group. (Some systems allow interaction with students at multiple locations, as well.)

For the first time, synchronous video permitted distance learners to see and interact with each other while the class was meeting. Technology could finally provide a level of **interactive media** that allowed for two-way exchange of ideas and information that had been lacking in the distance education realm. Still, many learners who desperately wanted to add to their knowledge and increase their career potential were unable to meet a regularly scheduled class, even if it was in a convenient location, until the advent of the World Wide Web.

Most people think of the **Internet** and the **World Wide Web** as the same thing, yet one is part of the other. Very simply, the term Internet actually refers to the vast network of inter-connected computers around the world. Its precursor, ARPANET, was designed to allow scientists and academicians from all over the world to interact on one or several large mainframe computers, connecting via modems between them by dialing a number. With the Internet, all of the computers in this network became connected one with the other, so that information could flow easily in multiple directions at one time. This yielded a system that was lightning fast, but limited only to text and accessed through telephone wires.

The World Wide Web (WWW), on the other hand, was begun in 1990 and is that part of the Internet that allows web pages to be viewed with software called browsers, like Netscape® or Internet Explorer®. Web browsers, as you probably know, allow you to view images and interactive text that may be physically located anywhere. This is possible because of a standardized technical advancement called

Key terms are shown in **boldface** and explained the first time they are used. These terms and their definitions are also included in the glossary at the end of this book, and as a searchable document in the Online Resources Web site, located on-line at <www.delmar.com>.

hypertext transfer protocol (http), which is the agreed-upon standard for Web-site addresses. With the use of a standard technical **protocol** for reading and exchanging data, remembering arcane codes was no longer required. Suddenly, people without special training or technical skills were able to connect to remote servers and access diverse information. It is this advancement in technology—the World Wide Web—that has had such an impact on the conduct of our lives and on the practices of education. Technology has opened a door to learning for anyone who wants it.

Developments in Internet-based Learning

If there were any doubt in even the recent past that there was an interest in the general public in an ability to connect to other people, obtain information, and communicate at any time, from anywhere, the explosive growth of the Internet has removed it. Emblematic of that growth is the mushrooming membership in one of the first **Internet service providers (ISPs)** to become available, America Online™ (AOL).

In August of 1999, Reuters news service reported that AOL's total worldwide membership exceeded 20 million users. Further, membership climbed from 17 million to 18 million members in 125 days, compared with the previous summer, when it took 133 days to add one million members to reach 13 million. You may be one of those millions.

The World Wide Web and Internet browsers like Netscape® and Microsoft Explorer® have made the Internet a user-friendly environment. Web pages offer the ability to integrate graphics, text, and sound into a single tool that is accessible to even novice learners. Pairing this graphical utility with the interactivity of e-mail allows learners to effectively participate in educational activities **asynchronously,** that is, without having to be in direct contact at the same time. With education provided **on-line** (over the Internet), students can physically be *anywhere* and complete course requirements without ever stepping foot in a classroom. One of these students could be you.

It may be called distance education, distance learning, computer-mediated education, distributed learning, asynchronous, or on-line learning. But whatever it is called, learning anywhere and anytime through the medium of your home or office computer holds the promise of access to learning that has never been available before. The U.S. Distance Learning Association <www.usdla.org> states that

> "In higher education, distance learning is providing undergraduate and advanced degrees to students in offices, at community colleges, and at various receive sites. Students for whom convenience may be a crucial factor in receiving college credit are earning degrees by satellite, audio, and over the Internet."

You may have noticed that more and more educational institutions are marketing aggressively to the adult learner. If you have opened a newspaper or general interest magazine lately, you have probably seen advertisements for new and 'redeveloped' programs to complete a degree or earn certification without leaving the comfort of your home or office. Perhaps you were intrigued by what you read. One thing is sure, as more institutions enter the distance arena, the marketing greeting their arrival will only become more strident. Until learning at a distance becomes commonplace—and it will—speculations about its effectiveness and usability will sound like the claims of so many political candidates. How are you, the learner, to decide where to cast your educational vote? This book can assist you in becoming an informed educational consumer. But it can also do much more.

"There is little doubt that the Web is the most phenomenally successful educational tool to have appeared in a long time"

—*Robin Mason,*
in Globalising Education;
Trends and Applications

"Faced with retraining 50 million American workers, corporate America is using distance learning, both internally and externally, for all aspects of training. Many major corporations save millions of dollars each year using distance learning to train employees more effectively and more efficiently than with conventional methods."

—*Source, U.S. Distance*
Learning Association
<www.usdla.org>

WHAT YOU CAN EXPECT FROM THIS BOOK

Like anything that is new, learning at a distance over the Internet also presents many questions. You are probably asking many of the questions yourself: What is it like? Will it be as effective as learning in a classroom? Will I like it? How do I tell the difference between marketing hype and actual experience? Is there help available? How do I choose? Is it for me? This book can provide the answers to these questions and give you the support you need to be a successful on-line distance learner. Beyond that, it can help you learn how to be an effective and efficient learner both on-line and off, so that learning can become a lifelong habit.

You may have a desire to learn something new, change careers, enhance your present skills, or simply try a different method of learning. You may be interested in beginning a certificate program or completing an advanced degree. You may have wonderful study skills and be an excellent writer, or need some skills strengthening to become a more effective learner. Whatever your reasons for investigating distance learning, this resource can help you to lay the necessary groundwork *before* you choose the program that is best for you and provide the resources you need to complete it. This text is geared primarily toward those who:

- have *basic* e-mail and Internet skills*,
- want to learn more about on-line learning before trying it out, and
- want to do as much as possible to assure their own success.

This text will *not* tell you what to study, but it will help you learn how to make those decisions, as well as how and where to find information that you want and need. You will learn what questions you should ask, as well as what you can expect of on-line learning providers, so that problems can be minimized and a successful experience assured from the outset.

Learning on-line is not the same as learning in a classroom, but it is not so different, either. Like any other method of instructional delivery, the importance is on the learning process, which is a process that you *can* master. In the course of mastering it, you will gain powerful skills and abilities that will make you successful in other areas of your life, now and into the future. Skills such as critical thinking, which can help you separate concrete facts from marketing claims. Abilities such as conducting research effectively, so that you can ask questions that provide worthwhile answers. These are skills and abilities you will *need* in the future.

According to Robert B. Reich, former secretary of labor,

> "The intellectual equipment needed for the job of the future is an ability to define problems, quickly assimilate relevant data, conceptualize and reorganize the information, make deductive and inductive leaps with it, ask hard questions about it, discuss findings with colleagues, work collaboratively to find solutions, and then convince others."

*Basic Internet skills include the ability to access the Internet, move from site to site by entering addresses (called **URLs,** or Uniform Resource Locators) and clicking on hotlinks, navigate around websites using a mouse and scrollbar, and exit the connection.

These are the very skills and abilities that you can practice and learn through engaging in on-line learning activities. After you have become proficient in the safe learning environment, you will be able to apply these skills in your career. In the supportive environment of learning with your peers, you can safely experiment with new ideas and behaviors and reflect on what you have learned, with the additional support of this guide.

To help you meet your goals, this book is organized into **three major sections,** prefaced by an introductory section.

- Know Yourself
- Know the Possibilities
- Get It Done

Section II, "Know Yourself," will help you discover your needs and strengths, so that you can choose experiences that work best for you. Section III, "Know the Possibilities," will help you understand the many choices available to you. In Section IV, "Get It Done," you will find concrete assistance in progressing successfully to the completion of the educational choice you have made and celebration of that success. You will also take a brief glimpse into the future in Section V.

This guide will present the skills and information you need to become a successful learner. Here, you will find advice from professionals and from learners just like you who have already succeeded in on-line distance learning. You will read their stories and come to understand the impact that their learning experiences have had, and continue to have, on the way they view themselves and the world around them. Through their experiences, you will see how they have used technology to successfully fit learning into their busy lives. But, again, that is not all.

The Online Resources Interactive Companion

In addition to the assistance you will find here in choosing and completing your desired learning experience, the Online Resources Web site will furnish specific information to personalize the acquisition of knowledge to your own needs. With the Online Resources, you can find what you need, when you need it, all in one place.

The Online Resources Web site is designed to be your consistent, one-stop connection to distance learning developments and information. The data on the Online Resources Web site will be amended regularly, providing you with the most current intelligence available. You will also be able to interact with other distance learners, with whom you can discuss your mutual learning goals, ask questions of other learners or of the author, and find the distance learning information you need to be successful. The Internet address for the Online Resources site is <www.delmar.com>. This Web site address is also listed at the end of this, and every, chapter.

You could also think of this text and Online Resources as the blueprint for your own "house of learning." Before you can furnish your house with specific topics, facts, and ideas, you must build a solid foundation and a comfortable floor plan so that the learning you choose will work effectively with your lifestyle and help you attain the goals you desire. Other texts exist to help you furnish your "house of learning," and many of these texts are noted in these pages and on the Online Resources Web site. *This* text will help assure your success by giving you solid information and skills to build a foundation for becoming an effective and efficient distance learner.

Whether you are interested in improving your skills and marketability, seek to complete a long-postponed degree goal, or are simply curious about how distance learning is done, you have come to the right place. Many other texts are available to help you find the program you want when you have finally decided to pursue it. That information is also available, updated regularly, at the Online Resources Web site. Unlike those other texts, this is an interactive guide and record of your personal learning journey, where you can record your thoughts, ideas, and reactions to what you learn as you become aware of them.

ADULT LEARNERS ARE DIFFERENT LEARNERS

Much has been made in recent years about the differences between the ways that children and adults learn. Specialists in adult learning contend that adult learners learn most effectively when certain conditions are present. Adults need to

- understand why something is important for them to learn;
- understand their relationship to what is being learned;
- integrate the new information into what they already know;
- be motivated and ready to learn;
- overcome barriers like fears, behaviors, and perceptions about learning.

As adults, we have learned to become practical, but we are also often so busy and have so much going on that the only material we remember is that which makes a connection to our lives. And certainly, it makes sense that our past educational experiences can have a great impact on our ability to learn. But are we really that different from our children in the way that we learn new things? Many educators are beginning to think that there are more similarities than differences.

Do you remember wondering what a succession of dates or mathematical formulas had to do with you and your future? Perhaps, as many are beginning to think, the only major difference that *age* plays in learning is in the nature and amount of experience the student brings to the learning experience. Of course, children have less knowledge and past experience to organize in their minds than adults do. They also have fewer memories, fond or otherwise, of their educational experiences.

This Book Is Not Just for Distance Learners!

Many of the tips and resources provided here can also be used by adults who choose to pursue education in a more traditional manner, such as classroom or group training opportunities. As numerous studies have shown, there is little difference in quality and effectiveness between classroom-based and distance learning; what does make a difference are the expectations and abilities of learners. This text will tell you what to expect and help you make the most of your abilities. You will discover what to expect from academic institutions and what instructors expect from you. You will ascertain the processes involved in receiving credit for your experiential learning and the value of those courses you took "ages ago."

To return to an earlier analogy, we all—both children and adults—build our own unique houses of learning. Younger students start, perhaps, with a location on which they construct a new structure. Their more mature counterparts, on the other hand, are engaged in a remodeling project, sometimes constantly. As an adult learner, you might choose merely to update an outmoded kitchen, or you might undertake a massive renovation and addition. Either way, the foundation and unique character of the 'house' remains. How will you choose to renovate your 'house of learning'?

Keeping Up With Advancements in Learning

Because of the rapidly evolving nature of the distance education marketplace, books on distance learning are often out of date by the time they are published. And, until learners have decided on an educational provider, they may not have access to the fine tutorials and advising that many schools and training institutes provide. So, how can a new on-line learner like yourself obtain the information necessary to make informed choices, ask pertinent questions, and avoid problems and mistakes *before* they occur? Here is the answer: Your personal journal to on-line learning and its paired Online Resources Web site. With these paired tools, you can document your learning journey and obtain access to information as it becomes available. You can obtain the information you need to make informed decisions about choosing and carrying out your own learning plans without wasting precious time.

As Lao Tse said, every journey begins with a single step. Take the first step. Even if you are not interested in pursuing a degree right now, remember that things change. The degree that does not interest you today may be tomorrow's goal. The sections in this text are somewhat like a map and provide different routes and information for helping you to arrive at your educational destination. Some of the routes may not interest you or be important to you now, but they are there for later exploration and discovery. For your personal journey, then, this resource will serve as a roadmap, helping you to chart the best course for your on-line learning experiences. In that way, if you do choose to continue through a degree program (or several!), you will have a record of both your steps and the paths you have taken.

PREVIEW OF COMING ATTRACTIONS

The next chapter, How to Use This Guide, offers suggestions on how to use the combined text and Online Resources most effectively. Of course, you may choose to use all or just a few of the parts of this text or the Web site. After all, it is *your* journal.

The information provided in this guide will help you to know what questions to ask and give you a place to document both the answers and the questions that are important to you. As you learn more about yourself and your subject, this

Scan the table of contents to find and mark areas that particularly interest you. Consider dating your notes to keep track of your explorations.

guide will remind you where you were and how far you have come. Like a photo album, it will chronicle your lifelong learning.

Please take a moment now to review the contents and skim through the text, noting those areas that you will want to devote more time to later. You can make your notes here:

_____

_____

_____

To Sum Up. . . .

With this guide, you will build a learning journal unique to you. In conjunction with the Online Resources Web site, this guide will give you access to timely information on educational opportunities and advancements and other developing educational support tools as they are unveiled. Information will be provided here to help you choose learning providers wisely, learn effectively and efficiently, and use your new knowledge consciously. You will find tips and strategies to manage your time, maximize your learning style, and build and maintain your on-line community. You will learn what you need to know to avoid the mistakes others have experienced and find the resources others have discovered. And, in the event that you are seeking something you just can not find, a message can be left on the Online Resources Web site for a personalized response.

The Online Resources Web site support to *Success in On-Line Learning* can be found by accessing the following URL, or website address: <http://www.delmar.com/companions/kramer/index.html>.

The Online Resources Web site is a restricted area that requires a username and password to gain access. You will find your username and password information below. You will need these to enter the restricted area, and you must enter the username and password exactly as they appear.

username: pr n45m92

password: success22

Let your learning journey begin!

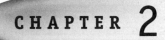

CHAPTER 2

How to Use
This Guide

The purpose of this book is to provide a framework of general information and exercises to support your learning endeavors and assure your educational success. Specific materials, including self-assessments, educational opportunities, tutorials, and other varied and valuable information, are provided at the Online Resources Web site, <www.delmar.com>. Together, this book and the Web site are designed so that you can combine the text and Web-based portions to personalize your progress and create a learning journal unique to you.

THE LEARNING JOURNAL

"What is a **learning journal**?" you might ask. A learning journal, which can also be called a learning log, is a personal document that provides an account of your thoughts, ideas, and conclusions about your interactions in a class or any other learning experience. It can chronicle one class or an entire degree program or, in the case of this book, serve as a record of your experiences and choices in distance learning.

A learning journal can include your opinions, questions that come up while you are reading, your experiences and reflections about the material, or anything else that relates to the class or study. You may have been asked to keep a learning journal as a part of courses you have already taken. Many teachers are now using learning journals as an integral and required part of their courses, because it has been shown that writing about the responses to class materials helps students to connect personally to what they are learning. This personal connection gives learning meaning, and that makes it both more effective and more satisfying.

Throughout this book, you will have opportunities to record your feelings, opinions, and reactions to what you have read and experienced. By using these opportunities, you will create a lasting personal document of the learning you acquire. You will be able to return to it later and reflect further on the changes you

> "We don't receive wisdom;
> we must discover it for
> ourselves after a journey
> that no one can take for
> us or spare us."
>
> —*Marcel Proust*

13

have made. In a time of rapid change, your journal will 'freeze' the moment of discovery. In this way, you will be able to return to what you have recorded and know how far you have come.

In addition to reflection and activity opportunities presented in this text, you will also find a *Learning Journal Template* in the appendix. This template can be customized and used to enhance learning in any educational experiences you choose. It will help you get the most out of your learning while providing crucial documentation to support subsequent study and refresh recollection. The Learning Journal Template and ways of using it to intensify your education are discussed further in Section III.

WHAT TO EXPECT

This text is structured to help you organize your approach to on-line study and assure its success. In each section, functional worksheets have been provided to help you find the best ways to meet your own needs, with additional space for notes and reminders. These worksheets, which may be photocopied as your situation and goals change, are also included for your convenience in a separate section in the appendix.

Of course, not every section will apply equally to every person who reads this book. It has been designed to help many different learners at many different levels. You should take some time to review the contents and scan specific sections to find areas that are of particular relevance or importance.

Be alert, too, for tips and hints that might provide help later in your learning journey. You will see tips to which you should pay special attention highlighted throughout the text.

STRUCTURE OF THE TEXT

You already know that every section in this book may not apply to your situation. However, the text is arranged to follow a linear process. In other words, it is developed along a step-by-step pattern beginning with self-assessment and progressing forward by building on each step that has gone before. This approach will allow you to begin your distance learning experiences at a level that matches your needs and help you to reach your educational goals.

In order to attain those goals, you will need to focus on three major areas: yourself, the possibilities available to choose from, and the skills and abilities needed to accomplish the goals you have chosen. These three areas are divided here into sections, each composed of several chapters.

It is important to begin your search for education with self-assessment. After all, if you do not know what you are capable of, it is difficult to decide what you can accomplish. As you learn what your educational needs are, you will also discover the best methods required to attain your goals. You can then begin to look for options that meet your needs.

In Section II, "Know Yourself" (Chapters 3 through 6), you will find information that will help you determine the skills and abilities needed to be successful at distance learning, and the strategies you can use to make those skills and abilities your own. Included in this section is information to help you discover your own learning style and understand what kinds of programs and teaching styles will best serve your needs. You will also learn what constitutes a self-reliant learner, why it is important to be one, and how to increase your own effectiveness. This section will conclude with specific requirements and skills for using the Internet to both access and complete the education you seek.

Section III, "Know the Possibilities" (Chapters 7 through 11), provides information on both distance and tradition classroom education and explains the degree-earning process. Chapters are devoted to answering the questions common to learners who are new to college, as well as those who are returning to school after a break. Here, you will become acquainted with the terms and concepts needed to choose and negotiate your learning experiences wisely, whether in a classroom or on-line.

You will learn what you need to ask to avoid problems before they occur, how the credit-for-experience process works, and strategies for financing your learning journey. Worksheets are provided to help you every step of the way. They will help keep track of your progress and the information you gather. For maximum utility, these worksheets are available in the text, in the appendix, and on the Online Resources Web site, where even more resources reside.

In Section IV, "Get it Done" (Chapters 12 through 17), you will be given the tools and resources to manage your educational project, from goal setting to maintaining motivation to creating a learning community. You will be given study and research tips and reproducible forms to help you organize and manage your education. As always, the forms will be available both in your text and on the Online Resources site, so you can download as many as you need.

This section will conclude with suggestions for celebrating your achievement and putting your learning to practical use. With suggestions for continuing activities, Chapter 17 helps to reinforce your new learning habits. By consolidating the changes you have made in taking responsibility for your own learning, you will start the learning cycle anew.

There is no doubt that what we have come to think of as 'school' will undergo a drastic change. Section V, the final section (Chapter 18) explores the changes that will inevitably come to the process and business of lifelong learning, and the ways that emerging technologies could help us all become more effective learners. We will look at some of the predictions for the educational choices to come and review where we have been. This glimpse of the future may help you to make long-range plans of your own so that you will *always* be a successful learner.

THE ONLINE RESOURCES WEB SITE

Throughout the text, you will be directed to the Online Resources Web site for specific, concrete information after you have read about general concepts. In other words, whereas the book provides a context for learning about the process of distance learning, the Online Resources Web site provides specific tools for choosing the best means for you to complete the process successfully. The Web site URL and relevant pages are listed at the end of each chapter and elsewhere throughout the text.

When you navigate to the Online Resources home page, shown in Figure 2–1, you will find a wealth of information and links to sites. On the home page, for example, you will find references to support sites, forms you can download to help you make decisions and keep yourself organized, an electronic **bulletin board service (BBS)** on which you can post questions to other learners or the author, and many other resources. These links and other materials are designed to help you make the most of this text and the time you have devoted to learning, and to provide current information as it becomes available in the rapidly changing field of distance learning. Pair them for maximum results.

The Online Resources site page corresponding to Section II, also called "Know Yourself," will provide information and links to assessments, tutorials, and other resources that you can use to personalize your educational choices to your academic needs. In other words, to help you choose options that work for you. Figure 2–2 is what you will see when you navigate your Internet browser to the Online Resources page to help you "Know Yourself."

FIGURE 2-1

The Online Resources home page, your start page for learning about distance learning.

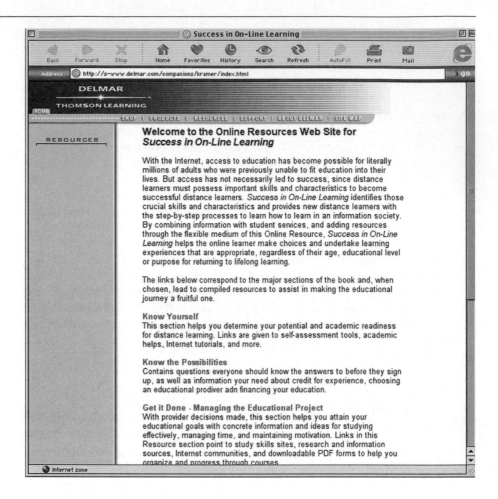

Interact to Learn

Successful learners have found that achievement comes more easily with the encouragement of concerned friends, who understand your desire and share your triumphs. We know that this is especially true for novices, so we have provided an interactive support group in the form of a bulletin board forum right on the Online Resources Web site. Here, you will become a member of the *Success in On-Line Learning* community. By using the bulletin board, you will be able to connect with and exchange messages with other readers, as well as the author. You will also be able to make comments on the text and suggest additions for the site. The Online Resources bulletin board is your forum, and will look somewhat like Figure 2–3.

Hope to meet you there!

To Sum Up. . . .

Success in On-Line Learning is an integrated answer to the question "How do I find and use distance learning options that work for me?" Providing both support and information, this interactive guide-Web site combination will help you navigate your personal learning journey through the ever increasing wealth of global educational opportunities accessible from your desktop. With this guide and support, success is easily attainable.

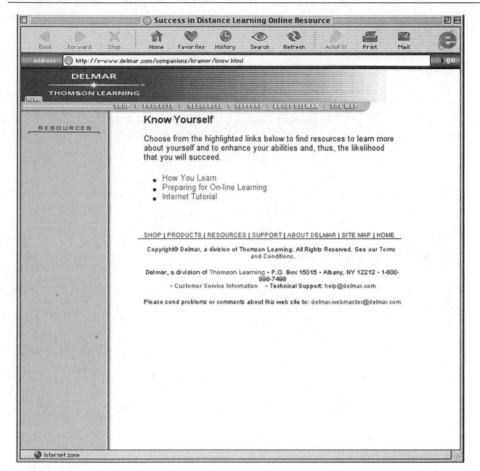

FIGURE 2-2

One of many pages of resources, the 'Know Yourself' section helps you learn how you can use distance learning to your best advantage.

Why not try visiting the Online Resource home page right now? Point your browser to <www.delmar.com>.

Notes to Yourself

Make any notes and preliminary questions here:

_____

_____

_____

_____

_____

_____

FIGURE 2-3

Connect with other distance learners or talk to the author on the Online Resources bulletin board.

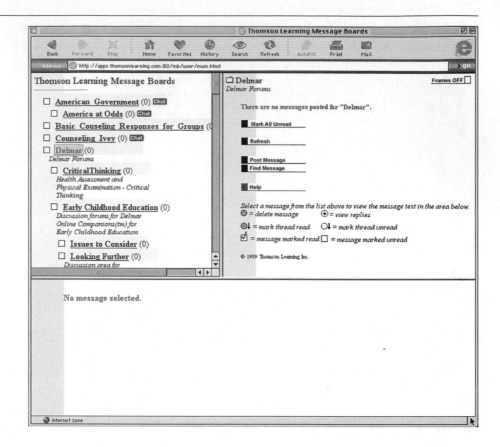

Know Yourself

This section focuses on information that will help you determine the skills and abilities you need to be successful at distance learning.

The chapters in this section are:

Chapter 3 - Is On-line Learning for You?

Chapter 4 - Discovering Your Learning Style

Chapter 5 - Of Course You Are Self-reliant . . . Right?

Chapter 6 - The Technical Connection—Requirements and Skills for Distance Learning

PREVIEW

In this section, you will explore the ways to learn at a distance and discern if this method of educational delivery is for you. In Chapter 3, "Is On-line Learning for you?", information and self-assessments will be offered to help you determine if on-line learning, in particular, may help you to reach your educational goals.

Chapter 4, "Discovering Your Learning Style," will help you to understand why *how* you learn can have a major impact on *what* you learn. We will review the major learning theories and the strategies that teachers use to make learning effective for all.

In Chapter 5, "Of Course You Are Self-reliant . . . Right?", you will come to understand what teachers of adult learners expect and how you can meet those expectations. You will discover how learners can often sabotage themselves, despite their best efforts to succeed. You will meet a trio of distance learners with very different stories and goals, learners whose stories will continue throughout this book.

Finally, you will find out, in Chapter 6, "The Technical Connection—Requirements and Skills for Distance Learning," just what equipment you need to take advantage of the on-line learning revolution. Further, you will find tips and advice on utilizing the technology to assure your educational accomplishment.

Throughout the chapters ahead, you will be directed to the Online Resources Web site for up-to-the-minute information that you can use to become a powerful on-line learner. The Web site is accessible by going to <www.delmar.com>.

Now, turn to the next page to begin your educational exploration!

CHAPTER 3

Is On-line Learning for You?

A speaker at a recent seminar announced that the average person spends more time on researching the purchase of a car than they do on the investment of education. Whether that is actually true or not, it is not hard to understand why. First, information about automobiles is easier to access and understand than is information about education. If you do not believe that, compare the number of car commercials to the number of educational services commercials you see the next time you watch television! Second, cars are concrete objects. Your vehicle, beyond being a means of transportation, may mean many things to you and can express your wishes and dreams. But there it is, sitting in your driveway. You can always point to it and say, "That's my car." It is a little more difficult to do that with your education or training.

You can compare the decision when choosing an educational provider to shopping for a car in several respects. If you know what you want and need to get from your learning, as well as the features that are the most important to you, you can make an informed educational purchase. Just as with a car, there are considerations beyond price and options. If you know the kinds of teaching methods that work best for you and have an understanding of the ways you incorporate new knowledge into your life, you will make a more satisfying investment. If not, it is more likely that you will be swayed by marketing and base your decision on what is important to the providers, not what is important to *you.*

"Today, if you are not confused, you are just not thinking clearly."

—U. Peter

WHAT IS DISTANCE LEARNING?

It may surprise you to learn that even the experts in distance education cannot come to concrete agreement on a definition of distance learning, so if you are confused, you are not alone. For our purposes, distance education is defined as *a system and a process that connects learners with learning resources in the same electronic space, without the constrictions of time.* This means that individuals can overcome the barriers of space and time to learn anytime and anyplace.

You may have noticed that no mention is made in this definition about how learning or learning resources are any different from traditional, campus-based educational delivery. There are, of course, differences between individual courses and learners' levels of satisfaction with those courses. But did you know that many studies have confirmed that there is no significant difference in the *effectiveness* of learning between classroom-based and distance learning? That is because education is education, plain and simple.

Individual learners must have the characteristics and skills that enable them to be individually effective, whether they learn in a classroom or on their home PC. The Internet is making postsecondary education accessible to literally millions of people who previously did not have the time or inclination to take advantage of it. So, learning using this method of delivery is viewed as something new. It is also a method that suddenly makes knowledge more accessible to more people—people who may not be well prepared to utilize it successfully.

As an educational option, distance learning has actually been around for over a hundred years. It was, and still is, referred to as **correspondence study.** As you are probably aware, correspondence learners do not attend regularly scheduled classes, but complete assignments and submit them to a remote instructor, usually by mail. They then wait for the mail to reach the instructor, wait for the instructor to grade the assignment, and wait for the graded assignment to be returned. Then, the time-consuming process begins again.

Within the past 20 years, a number of institutions supplemented their correspondence learning activities by using videotapes of instructor lectures from classes that occurred on campus. Although this enhanced the instruction by providing remote learners with visual cues and the ability to replay, the problem of mailing and waiting, as well as the lack of interactivity between teacher and learners, remained.

Beginning in the recent past, the interactivity problem was addressed with the use of **teleconferencing** and **audiographics.** In teleconferencing, classes are transmitted to remote locations so that learners who cannot attend classes at the "host" institution can participate in educational offerings, able to see and interact with the teacher and other students. Learners still have to travel at least as far as a specially equipped community-based center to participate in these classes. However, the use of teleconferencing technology has made a significant impact on the ability of remote learners to access college courses.

Audiographics technology typically allows participants to view the same still-frame pictures while communicating in a variety of ways: verbally over telephone

Distance learning falls into two categories: **synchronous** and **asynchronous.** Synchronous learning indicates that all of the members of a class—teacher, students, and any others—are interacting all at the same time. Only distance separates the people involved. Asynchronous learning, on the other hand, allows all participants to interact on their own schedules, making it possible to learn *anytime, anywhere.*

lines or by writing or drawing on a screen. This technology is usually used to en-hance another form of teleconference, where it is crucial that images are clear. Connections are made using telephone or digital communications lines, but is not Internet based. Because the equipment needs are less expensive than tele-course technology, audiographics can be utilized at sites with compatible software and a dial-up connection.

Other ways of interacting using technology have also been used in education and training. One such technology is the use of a telephone bridge, which is basi-cally a conference call. The difference is that, in a conference call, each person has to be dialed and linked separately. In a telephone bridge, however, individuals call one central number at a previously arranged time. This technology requires that only one person (the one with the phone number to be called) have specialized equipment and knowledge to facilitate the communication.

Internet telephony is experiencing increasing usage in connecting individu-als, as well. **Internet telephony** uses your Internet connection to place a voice call either from your computer to a telephone or to another person's computer. Because the connection utilizes the Internet connection, there are no additional long distance fees, making this a very economical way to complete a vocal con-nection. Currently, connections can be made only between two numbers, but this technology will likely increase in usage for personal and business connections as well as educational applications.

These educational delivery methods can be a very effective way of delivering educational content and minimizing the barriers imposed by distance, but they are synchronous. For many adults who want to pursue further education, regular attendance, no matter how conveniently located, is incompatible with business travel needs, childcare demands, and other time-sensitive responsibilities. Their schedule is anything but regular.

With the arrival of the Internet in many homes and businesses, the time taken up by mail is compressed to an eye blink. Suddenly, people anywhere can access a wealth of information at their convenience. With this one development, learning has become accessible and manageable to countless people who need it. Still, dis-tance learning—or any learning, for that matter—is not without its challenges.

Challenges of Distance Learning

For many, the removal of mailing time and increase in accessibility creates the per-ception of ease. However, although distance learning may be easy to access, it is anything but easy to complete successfully. Learning at a distance is a challenging task requiring motivation, planning, and ability. In an on-line learning situation, learning is more complex because:

- Most learners interested in on-line learning are older and have many re-sponsibilities that influence their study.
- On-line learners have many reasons to take courses, from upgrading skills to broadening knowledge.
- Learners seldom have face-to-face contact with other learners and teachers, requiring adjustments on all sides.
- Without face-to-face contact, it takes longer for rapport to develop, leading to possible discomfort or misunderstandings.
- Members of distance classes are more likely to be different from one another than those who attend classroom-based courses.
- In on-line learning, information transfer always uses some form of technol-ogy, so those uncomfortable with the use of technology can be inhibited at the outset.

Despite these challenges, thousands of learners have already tried on-line study. And, like many people who try something new, they have often had to fend for themselves. Many have found that it is the best learning medium they have ever experienced, allowing them to meet their work and family obligations and providing opportunities to not only learn new things, but to learn them in the company of new and interesting people.

On-line learning has been available in one form or another at some institutions for several years. Research studies of on-line learners have been conducted that make the advantages and disadvantages clear. According to some of these studies, in comparing traditional classroom learning to the on-line experience, on-line students:

- are nervous about what is expected;
- procrastinated more—"out of sight, out of mind";
- learned as much as, or more than, in traditional courses; and
- found that collaborative [on-line] learning works.

These studies also found that 80 percent of students liked on-line learning, but 20 percent felt uncomfortable in this nontraditional setting, so it is possible that distance learning is *not* for you. By the time you have finished this section, you will have the tools to decide whether you want to try it immediately, commit to skill building before you dive in, or wait for a while.

Distance learning on-line is not for everyone. To determine whether it is for you will require an honest self-evaluation of your strengths and possible deficiencies in two areas: your habits and your expectations.

DETERMINING YOUR POTENTIAL

As with many endeavors, successful participation in on-line learning requires personal project management skills. If you are the kind of person who has difficulty identifying goals and finishing projects or if you seem never to have enough time to do everything, taking on distance learning without strengthening your skills in time and project management is an invitation to frustration and failure.

The good news is that goal-setting and time-management skills can be strengthened, and many of the tools you will need to increase your personal man-

By the time you have finished this section, you will have the tools to decide whether you want to try it immediately, commit to skill building before you dive in, or wait for a while.

"Students come to college for various reasons. They could be interested in changing careers or they might simply want to expand their knowledge base for work or personal reasons. They might want to expand their cultural background, learn a new language, or start a degree program that was postponed due to family or career needs.

Their main reason for choosing distance education as a delivery method is that they want to learn at their own pace, and at a time and location that is convenient to them."

—ITC Web site <www.itc.org>

agement skills are readily available, including the planning worksheets included in this text. These worksheets are also available at the companion Online Resources site, from which you can download and customize them to your specific needs.

Taking the time now to organize yourself will yield benefits in other areas of your life as well. Even if your earlier experiences included pulling "all-nighters" to finish papers, chances are you have more responsibilities now than you did then. Staying up all night to finish a project or paper is no longer a viable option (even if you could do it!). If you make regular reorganization a habit, you will experience less of the stress that accompanies running to meet deadlines. In addition, you will gain a sense of self-control and increased self-esteem, as well as the satisfying knowledge that you *can* attain your goals.

Characteristics for Success

The people that have already been successful in the medium of distance learning possess additional characteristics that make success likely in any endeavor. These attributes are not necessarily required for *your* success, but have been shown to be traits that successful distance learners possess. Just knowing that these characteristics contributed to the achievement of others can help encourage your own development. These successful learners were:

- highly motivated to achieve (motivation, as you know, can take many forms);
- independent, and did not need someone telling them what to do;
- active learners who took part in learning instead of sitting back and absorbing it;
- disciplined enough to study without constant reminders; and
- adaptable to changes and new ways of doing things.

It might sound as though success has as much to do with attitude as with ability, and this is true, as well. Most successful distance learners *assume that they will do well* and make the effort necessary to confirm that assumption. They are assertive and know when to ask for help or clarification, taking personal responsibility for their performance.

> "Success is where preparation and opportunity meet."
>
> —Bobby Unser

Skills for Success

Successful participation in education and training is also dependent in a large part on adequate skills in reading, writing, and critical thinking. Trends in on-line learning design continue to move toward incorporating more graphical material to the explanation of content, but the absence of face-to-face interaction means that most of the learning material is still text intensive. Good reading skills are a basic requirement.

Successful participation in education and training provided by computer—at least at this point in technological development—is especially dependent on your ability to express yourself in writing and to comprehend difficult material well. A lack of competence in reading and writing can, therefore, have a proportionately greater impact on the learning experience.

Paradoxically, those who believe their skills need improvement usually have at least an adequate mastery. It is those who believe that their skills are "good enough" that often do not do well, become overwhelmed and frustrated, and quit. Yet these same people would realize the absurdity of trying to run a marathon without training for it. There is a correlation between marathon running and distance learning, especially if you will be trying to fit learning into an already busy lifestyle. Adequate preparation will make a huge difference in your level of accomplishment.

You may wonder why writing and reading are so important that you should invest time in sharpening your skills. Well, it has been shown that students who are lacking skills in these areas tend to contribute less to on-line discussions. As a result, others interact with them less often. People who have trouble writing clearly, or understanding what has been written, often respond in ways that are confusing to others, when they respond at all. Subsequently, their on-line relationships tend to be shallow. They are not motivated to take full advantage of either the learning process or the learning community that is such a vital part of the on-line experience.

These underprepared learners come to the conclusion that learning is less satisfying or interesting than they have been led to believe, and often give up in disgust. Tragically, they may label themselves "stupid" and avoid any further learning opportunities. Presumably, avoiding this outcome is one reason that you chose this book!

Finding Skill-building Resources

Maybe you are not sure whether you are ready. How do you know whether your reading or writing skills are equal to the task of college-level work? Being unsure of your skills is not a reason to avoid further learning—quite the opposite! As with anything else, practice leads to improvement, and distance learning provides ample practice. If you already have access to the Internet, you might want to jump right in and try it. There are ample resources for free noncredit learning on-line already, with more added every day.

Some for-credit institutions also offer free trial courses to give you an idea of what is in store for you. Take a trial course in a topic you find interesting and challenging, and you will begin to have some feeling for what is required. A listing of some of these providers is available on the Online Resources page. Try to find a course that allows interaction with others, as this is often an integral part of credit-based offerings.

Keep in mind that noncredit training is often different from academic work. In a typical academic class, you will be required to think about and question ideas, do research, and relate concepts to practice. Do not let this frighten you, though. These are things you probably do already, whether in your work or in other parts of your life. There are many rigorous training programs that include requirements similar to academic work; the line between what is considered "education" and what is labeled "training" is sometimes a blurry one. A skills-training program, like computer certification, can require high-level analysis and provide practice in completing assignments and taking tests. Those are useful skills in many careers.

If you are not able or do not feel ready to jump in and try distance learning, and you want to evaluate your writing and reading skills, there are several approaches you might take. Perhaps you have already compiled a report on, say, competitors in your market to support your ideas for strategic planning. Think about it now. How effective was your report? You might ask a colleague whose writing ability you admire to give you an appraisal of your own skills (do not choose someone who reports directly to you, though).

If you do not have anything prepared already, you could write a summary of a meeting and offer it to someone who was there, asking them to appraise your interpretation of the proceedings. Certainly, there are many books on the subject of writing improvement, but you should first have an idea where you need to focus before trying to wade through an overwhelming amount of information, much of which may not be relevant.

If these choices are not available to you, others are. Sources for reading and writing improvement are at least as close as your neighborhood library, and perhaps right in your own home. At the library, look for practice texts for the SAT (*Scholastic Achievement Test*) and ACT entrance examinations taken by high school juniors and seniors. (By the way, these standardized tests are not usually required before college admission if you have been out of high school for more than five years.) Practice texts for the GED (*General Educational Development*) can also be helpful. These texts have reading comprehension sections that can help diagnose areas of difficulty before they become a problem in your studies. Ask the librarian for other recommendations also.

If you have children in middle school or high school, chances are good that writing and reading texts are part of their curriculum. In addition to helping you understand what is being taught to your own children, these texts can provide helpful refreshers for your own academic enterprises. They also contain lists of bibliographic resources that provide further pointers to helpful materials. You may be surprised how much is available, in fact. If you prefer to keep your interactions completely anonymous, you might consider an on-line tutor. There are several services that, for a small fee, will evaluate your skills and provide suggestions for improvement. The anonymity of this service makes it easier to receive evaluations objectively, and you do not have to worry about who knows. Links to these and other resources can be found on the Online Resources Web site, at <www.delmar.com>.

Learning Problems Solved

It is natural to worry about a new undertaking, especially when history has revealed something worth worrying about. If you are concerned with possible conflicts arising from learning difficulties or anxieties, the best defense is preparation. Many adult learners have been successful despite learning disabilities or physical limitations. In fact, on-line learning is used extensively in helping many learners to deal successfully with the limitations imposed by adherence to the traditional educational system. Some of these resources are included as links at the Online Resources Web site.

Many adult learners also suffer from test anxiety, sometimes to the point of avoiding new learning opportunities altogether. Here is another area in which educational technology has produced favorable results. Some **computer-aided instruction (CAI)** helps to reinforce skills by repetition and building on understanding. On-line tests can be designed that adapt to the level of answer you provide, so you are not forced to answer questions that are beneath your skill level. Some on-line tests allow you to take as much time as you need to finish, though you may not be able to 'open' the test more than once. There are also programs, depending on the topic you are interested in, that do not utilize any form of standardized testing. These rely almost exclusively on what is referred to as **authentic assessment.** Here, the evaluation is based on projects, writings, and other materials you might produce to prove your understanding. It can actually be much more difficult and time consuming than a standardized test. For example, instead of taking a test on what is included in a business plan, you might write one. This practical application of learning is being used increasingly in all subject areas. If a product is more important to you than a score, you might consider looking for a program that requires this kind of assessment.

You can increase your likelihood of success by knowing the teaching and evaluation methods in advance and choosing methods that work well for you. For example, if you read slowly and therefore have had difficulty in the past completing paper and pencil tests in the time allotted, seek out programs that allow untimed tests. You might also add this criteria to your search for an educational provider. Further discussion of your needs and teachers' methods will be found in Chapter 4, so you can have a better idea of what, precisely, works best for you and where you may need to focus further attention.

Once you have enrolled in a class, the opportunities for skill development become a part of the experience. One of the real benefits of on-line asynchronous learning is that you can read and revise your contributions to the class before submitting them. (You may wish that opportunity had been available in 'regular' classes!) People whose opinions you trust can read your work before you allow classmates to "hear" what you have to say, if you wish. In this way, you can gain valuable practice in writing clearly.

In addition if, like many others, you have gotten out of the habit of reading, then examining other learners' contributions and textbook readings will help you acquire greater proficiency in your own reading responsibilities. Further suggestions for increasing your reading, writing, and study skills are located in Section IV, and links to skill improvement resources on the Web are listed on the Online Resources Web site.

INCREASING YOUR POTENTIAL

Improving your communication skills takes time and patience, as well as support from others, but it yields multiple benefits. If you prepare before classes begin, your experience will be that much more enjoyable and effective.

 No matter how good your writing skills are, it is *always* a good idea to have a good writer review your papers before you hand them in!

What can you do to improve writing and reading skills and boost your potential for success? Some on-line learning institutions provide an on-line writing center, so if that is something you are interested in, add it to the list of questions that you ask when requesting information. If institutions that otherwise seem right for you do not provide this service, or if you feel more comfortable with a one-on-one tutor, look for options available right in your community. Some of these options are even free for the asking, and include:

- brush-up courses at your local community college,
- a family member,
- a private tutor.

Check ads in your local paper or contact the writing center at your local community college, where student tutors often post advertisements. Inquire at the adult or continuing education office on the campus, or community adult basic education center.

You may feel that your skills are not so bad that you have to inquire at adult literacy centers. That may be true. But those who work in adult literacy are often part of a larger student services network and may be aware of further resources in your neighborhood. Even your local high school can be a resource, as teachers themselves may provide tutoring services or be able to suggest a student who can be especially helpful, as well as inexpensive! One thing is sure: Any investment in self-improvement will be worth the time devoted, as you increase in ability and confidence.

Why not take a moment now to make notes here about where you might look for further resources in your community. What do you need to do to increase *your* potential for success?

In this chapter, you will find a worksheet (Figure 3–1) that can help you further identify and plan ways that will increase your likelihood of success at the distance learning undertaking that you choose. This worksheet is also available on the Online Resources site and in the appendix at the end of this text.

DETERMINING YOUR DESIRE

There are many reasons that could lead you to consider learning at a distance, but just as many reasons why you have been putting it off. Perhaps you live further away than is convenient from any college campus. Maybe the subject you want to study is not available in your area, or your work schedule is not conducive to attending class locally. Possibly, your childcare or other family responsibilities make it difficult or impossible to commute regularly to attend a class. Maybe you do not know enough about the entire process to feel comfortable with a decision. Whatever your reasons for considering distance learning, the strength of your desire to learn will most likely require that you overcome some hurdles.

Reasons for *not* participating in education can be internal or external, and fall into categories based on your attitude or your situation. For the purposes of this discussion, the reasons that inhibit your educational wishes are categorized as barriers, obstacles, or excuses.

- *Barriers* are events or circumstances that are beyond your control, like a physical disability or the unavailability of a program you are interested in.
- *Obstacles* are circumstances that you can overcome with planning or practice, like improving your writing skills or saving the money to attend school.
- *Excuses* cite circumstances that are easier to overcome, like being tired or unable to study.

Obstacles related to your situation at this time in your life can include lack of time because of home or job responsibilities, lack of support from family or friends, inadequate financial resources to pursue study, or lack of study space. Recognizing and dealing with these obstacles before undertaking any course of study—whether in a classroom or on-line—will help you to overcome them.

Your success also depends on your attitude toward yourself as a learner. Do you think of yourself as having the ability to learn anything you set your mind to? Are you able to find the energy to study even when you have had a busy day? Do you enjoy learning new things? Or are you prone to self-doubt, feel you may be too old to learn, or give up when things get difficult? An honest appraisal of your beliefs about the kind of learner you are should be a crucial piece of your preparation. Motivation to learn should be sustainable, and the way to assure that your

FIGURE 3-1

Online Learning Self-Assessment

Here are questions you should ask yourself about your skills, abilities, and resources before trying computer-based distance learning.

Check off the areas where you feel you could use some help, and you will have a roadmap for skills improvement before you begin, instead of a frustrating experience that is educational in more ways than one!

Do I have good skills in...	Y/N	Skills Good	Need Work
Reading?			
Writing?			
Effective note taking?			
Mathematics?			
Library usage and research?			
Test taking?			
Studying?			
Memory?			
Time management?			
Do I possess the characteristics of. . .			
Self-confidence?			
Patience?			
Persistence?			
Self-motivation?			
Do I have. . . .			
A support network?			
Access to a good library?			
A specific goal that education will meet?			

My educational goal is: _____

My greatest studying strength is: _____

_____

My weaknesses are: _____

Review your responses and list below those areas that need improvement. Then note your plans to increase your abilities in those skills. Be specific. Give yourself deadlines. Visit the Online Resources™ for updated lists of helpful resources.

My plans to improve the weaknesses are:

Skill: _____   Plan:_____

Skill: _____   Plan:_____

Skill: _____   Plan:_____

Skill: _____   Plan:_____

desire will continue to fuel your progress is to know the restrictions you face and have a plan to deal with them.

As you probably are aware, there are forces counteracting your very rational desire to succeed and make the best possible life for you and your loved ones. These barriers, if outside your control, can impede your progress and cause frustration. If the barriers originate from within you, they can cause you to make the same mistakes over and over again, also leading to frustration, but of a kind that is difficult to detect without close self-appraisal. Some of these forces constitute barriers that are particularly important to overcome if you wish to be a successful distance learner. Identifying them is the necessary first step to dealing with them.

Now that you have read about the characteristics that are required for success in distance learning and the restrictions that can impede that success, take a moment now to make a list of your own reasons for not yet undertaking the education you feel interested in pursuing. What are the problems you perceive that might prevent you from being a success at distance learning? Write your reasons

down here: _____

_____

_____

Now look at the reasons you have written down. Are they barriers, obstacles, or excuses? Can you do something about them? What *can* you do about them? What *will* you do about them? Restate your reasons below, followed by the ideas you have for overcoming them.

Perceived Problem	Strategy for Overcoming
_____	_____
_____	_____
_____	_____
_____	_____
_____	_____

Commit to Learning

Consider making your commitment to successful change a public one to help generate the support of others and confirm your feeling of commitment to learning. Tell your family and friends about one or more of the restrictions to success you have identified, and ask for their support in specific ways. For example, you might ask your children to help you make time to study by reminding you of deadlines, ask your coworkers to respect a lunchtime study break, or enlist the support of a close friend as a paper proofreader. You could also simply ask your family for suggestions. As many adults have found, their children and others that are not deeply involved in a problem can have a different perspective and often identify a solution that is so simple it just did not come to mind. For more suggestions on enhancing your support network and subsequently increasing your likelihood of success, see "The Importance of Support" in Chapter 16.

Be Aware of Your Needs

Self-awareness includes understanding how you learn best. Despite the potent lure of convenience that distance learning offers, if you are the kind of person who absolutely must have face-to-face interaction with classmates and teachers to reap benefits from a learning experience, computer-based distance learning may feel lacking. You may, instead, wish to investigate the more visual options for educational delivery, like teleconferencing, which allows you to see the teacher and classmates via television from a remote location. But do not dismiss computer-based delivery methods without reading further, and be sure to check the Online Resources for links to on-line self-assessment tools, so that you can check your self-perception.

It may surprise you to learn that the popular understanding of on-line learning as an isolated endeavor is often just not true. On-line learning can be somewhat like listening to a book on tape—exciting and engaging. What is even more exciting is your ability to interact with others. Imagine a book on tape that allows you to join the story! As you interact with other learners, personalities and "voices" begin to emerge. A willingness to share ideas can create an intensely supportive atmosphere. Many learners have actually found that the depth of interaction in on-line courses, where participants share interests, is far greater than the interaction in a traditional classroom-based course. Because you do not see one another, what each person thinks and what you can learn from one another becomes more important than physical details. So if you think of on-line learning as sitting alone pounding away at a keyboard, you may be entirely wrong! Here is what one distance learner has to say:

> Interaction in my experience is plentiful, and I'm glad of it. Those that think there is none have most likely not set up a system that works. Or reached out to interact themselves. It's hard to help someone who hasn't asked. Online learning is a wonderful medium and helpful to me since I work and I can't take classes which might otherwise interfere with my schedule. I like being able to check in on my own time, and I know that takes some discipline. You have to want to learn to make distance learning work for you.

> —Anonymous e-mail

MOTIVATION, ONCE REMOVED

So far, the discussion has been about self-motivation. But what happens if learning is not your idea? What if you are *told* you need retraining or to obtain a degree before you can receive a raise or promotion? Even worse, what if you are laid off because of a merger or change in the company's direction or fortunes? Your employer may be required to fund skills training as a transitional measure, but you will have many questions to consider. This is not an easy time to make an important decision.

It is difficult to maintain a level head and consider your best course of action in such unsettling circumstances, but it is also necessary. Being forced to become a student or trainee can feel belittling and unfair. In addition to the very real survival issues that may have you reeling, you may suddenly be questioning your self-worth and grieving a way of life that seems about to disappear. It is perfectly natural to feel angry when unexpected changes are forced upon you. It is also crucial that you take time to evaluate your feelings and to collect as much information as you can.

When faced with a policy like "all promotions require a degree," for example, it may help to diffuse any anger you may feel by making lists of the positives and negatives of the situation. List the good aspects of the situation on one side of the page, and the negatives on the other. Discuss these possibilities with your family. Promotions can, of course, lead to a better salary and greater responsibility, but learning takes time away from other pursuits.

If your employer has suggested or offered education, determine the policies that pertain to this benefit. Most employers provide reimbursement toward the cost of coursework, but the amount of reimbursement may be tied to the grade received. Some will pay only for certain courses of study, pay only for credit-bearing courses, or provide money for tuition but not books and fees. There are as many variations on educational benefits from employer to employer as there are on other benefit programs. Be sure that you understand the rationale for the policies and request them in writing. Be sure to ask, as well, whether the policies can be considered on a case-by-case basis. This may be important if the degree you really want to pursue is not on the "official list." You may be able to make a convincing argument that the subject can help you do a better job, even if it does not immediately appear to be related to your position.

If you are one of those who has been laid off, be particularly certain of any regulations regarding retraining that the company is required to provide for. Is this a blessing in disguise? Perhaps you will have the opportunity to change your career direction completely. Involve your family in the deliberations and remember that every new learning experience and acquired skill can build your resume, as well as your character!

Other Benefits of Learning

When you are forced to accept a change you have not sought, it is hard to remember that learning provides opportunities and benefits beyond a credential. A comprehensive academic program can connect separate pieces of your vast knowledge into a more coherent whole, making you more effective at work and in your other pursuits. Through education, you will be exposed to new ideas and methods you might not have found in other ways. Studying in a specific subject area will also increase your access to experts in your field, as well as other learners. These people can all become part of your network for support and success. Consider whether you should take the first steps to begin learning now, before the choice is made for you. Why should you plan now for learning? Because it makes sense.

Our society is moving toward an almost constant need to reskill and to learn new things. The U.S. Department of Labor estimates that adults will experience between five and seven career changes in their lifetime. If that sounds amazing, consider that the American Council of Education estimates that more than half of adults over the age of 40 will require retraining to *maintain* their current employment. You may feel right now that there is no burning reason for you to consider adding to your store of knowledge, but keep in mind that things may change. An unexpected layoff or other change of circumstances may cause you to rethink your life plan. That is when the motivation to change will overtake you. To take control of your future and avoid being a casualty of circumstance, you might want to give a proactive thought to possible future education. You may want to try out a short on-line skills course. Is there something you have wanted to know more about? There are links to free on-line tutorials at the Online Resources Web site. These resources can help you decide if this method of learning is for you.

Certainly, on-line learning is not going to go away. Projections from International Data Corporation (1999) indicate that by 2002:

- The number of college students in all distance learning courses will reach 2.2 million (up from 710,000 in 1998).
- Eighty-five percent of two-year colleges will be offering distance learning courses, up from 58 percent in 1998.
- Eighty-four percent of four-year colleges will be offering distance learning courses (up from 62 percent in 1998).

As you can see, the "distance education revolution" is well underway! Despite the opinions of some to the contrary, it will definitely become a regular feature in the future. Futurist Dr. Art Shostak, a professor of sociology at Drexel University, and an adjunct professor at the AFL-CIO National Labor College predicts that:

"Diplomas may increasingly be of the Sunset variety. Career-long recertification may become normative. Accordingly, the market . . . . should prove enormous, as few employees can afford anything but asynchronous schooling and (VR) testing—whether at work or at home.

Advances in distance learning may increasingly derive from new twenty-first century insights into how we learn, relearn, and retain our learning."

This vision of the future in which learning occurs throughout the lifetime is gaining proponents from all areas of endeavor. This vision and its realization are being driven by an economy with an increasing demand for workers with a college education. It has already helped to change the demographics of college campuses. According to the National Center for Educational Statistics, four out of every 10 students entering college in the fall of 2000 were over the age of 25. In 1970, the number of college students over 25 was only 28 percent. By 2003, the number of adults in college is projected to be well over 50 percent. Will you be one of them?

FITTING LEARNING INTO YOUR LIFE

One of the most difficult factors to consider before undertaking a learning program is how it will fit into your life. As an adult, you have many responsibilities. Work, family, and community commitments fill your busy schedule. Can you find time and adjust your schedule to meet the requirements of an educational program? Just because you have the ability to connect from your home after work does not mean you have time to do the coursework. (Remember this part, it is important!) You must still plan time for studying, thinking, researching, and writing.

Many learners have discovered that learning on-line can easily take *more* time than traditional classes, although it is often a richer experience. They find that they become so interested in what others are thinking about the subject that they spend far longer learning and sharing than they expected to. For some, it is the first time that 'learning' and 'fun' are part of the same sentence! But that engagement in learning can take time. If you already work more than 70 hours a week and do not remember what your kids look like, the added stress may be too much right now, or you may have to rethink your priorities. Take a long, realistic look at your schedule and your goals.

FIGURE 3-2

Time and Activity Analysis Worksheet

Fill in the blanks below to determine how much time you spend now on the many tasks of daily living and how much time you can make available for learning. Feel free to make multiple copies to compare different ways of allocating your available time resources. Share this worksheet with your family and others when discussing how priorities may change.

	M	T	W	Th	F	Sa	Su	Total
WORK TIME								
Time at Work								
Commuting								
At-home work tasks								
Total Work Time								
LEISURE TIME								
Socializing								
Hobbies/crafts								
Movies, cultural events								
Travel/vacation								
Fitness/outdoor								
Spiritual								
Volunteer/community								
Other								
Total Leisure Time								
LIVING TIME								
Relationship time								
Cooking/eating								
Shopping								
Sleeping								
Personal grooming								
Housekeeping								
Home/car maintenance								
Managing finances/taxes								
Childcare								
Other								
Total Living Time								
TOTAL TIME NEEDED								

Figure 3–2, the Time and Activity Analysis Worksheet (also on the Online Resources Web site and in the Appendix, as well) is provided to help you decide where your time is currently allocated. The worksheet will help you decide what responsibilities you have, as well as provide a graphic representation of the time you use. It can help show where to make adjustments so that you can include learning in your life. The concrete picture of where your time goes may surprise you! The worksheet can be photocopied or downloaded directly from the Online

Resources Web site, so as changes occur in your life and your dreams, you can make the appropriate alterations. Later in the text, you will find tips and techniques for managing and making the most of the time you have devoted to learning and to improving yourself.

As you examine your priorities, goals, and dreams, the critical need for a support system becomes clearer. The decision to undertake learning is not a decision to keep to yourself. In fact, successful on-line learners have discovered that reliance on a supportive group of family and friends is instrumental to successful learning. In addition to providing encouragement through your educational task, your network of supporters will be able help you celebrate your achievements. In Section III, we will explore ways of building and maintaining a good support network, but believe it: If no one around you supports your desire to learn, change, and grow, your task will be doubly difficult.

Only *you* can decide whether on-line learning is for you. To make that decision, you must assess your abilities and the responsibilities you face. Once you have decided to undertake an educational program, you *can* succeed if you want to. Help is at hand. You are holding a resource that can help assure your success. By answering the questions and providing insights and tips to make the task of on-line learning less overwhelming, you have an ally in the effort to continue a lifetime of learning.

To Sum Up . . .

In this chapter, we have examined the history and challenges of learning at a distance. We reviewed the characteristics that have made previous distance learners successful and explored options for increasing your own likelihood of success. This, we found, requires an honest self-appraisal of our strengths and liabilities and the willingness to commit to a course of action that will pay off with multiple benefits. We know that it may not be easy to find the time and sustain the motivation necessary to succeed, but the tools to assist you are all around you. Be sure to visit the Online Resources Web site at <www.delmar.com> for additional assistance.

Notes to Yourself

How do you feel so far? Are there any specific questions you have before you try on-line learning? Notes you want to make to yourself? Put them here:

_____

_____

_____

_____

CHAPTER 4

Discovering Your Learning Style

There is increasing evidence that the effectiveness of learning can be determined by the methods used to teach. In other words, the way material is presented has an effect on how well you understand and remember it. This may seem like common sense, but traditional teaching methods have continued to emphasize rote learning, in which meaning is separated from knowledge and the teacher is in control of its distribution. This has been referred to as 'banking' education, in which educators treat students as empty vessels. Their job was to 'deposit' the learning into the empty containers. This idea has persisted for several hundred years—until recently.

A single instructional method no longer worked as it had (or seemed to) for generations of students. The world had become more intense, students were more diverse, and the historic teaching practices no longer held attention or seemed relevant. Learning was not interesting or inspiring. More students became lost and turned away from an educational system that seemed to care little for them. Yet historical practices went on, although innovative educators began trying methods that were different but seemed to engage students.

The crisis in education, with students graduating from high school unable to read and devoid of the basic skills necessary to obtain and maintain employment, had cast a questioning eye on the methods used to 'teach' the young. Educators knew there was something wrong, but a single culprit could not be identified. The truth is that there was no single reason, but many. Patterns emerged. Theories were formed. During years of practical and clinical research, groups of educators and psychologists began to understand that individuals can have fundamentally different ways of learning. That is, the way that one person perceives, organizes, and remembers can vary greatly from another's learning processes.

These researches have found that the differences in the ways people learn is likely to be based on how we physically experience the world and construct meanings based on those experiences. Learning is further determined by the ways that

"Spoon feeding in the long run teaches us nothing but the shape of the spoon."

—*E. M. Forster*

each person's brain works, and is further subject to the adaptations each of us has been forced to make to the real or perceived barriers in our lives. There are many explanations offered, taking in many points of view. Each exploration uncovers new information.

The research will continue. Whether one theory will prove to be more precise than another in explaining how learning occurs has yet to be determined. Perhaps an answer will be found in a synthesis of further research. But whereas the final answers may still be unclear, one thing is certain: The more you know about your own strengths and preferences, the better prepared you will be to undertake your own learning expedition.

HOW YOU LEARN CAN DETERMINE WHAT YOU LEARN

Knowledge is power, as the saying goes. This is also true of yourself, particularly in the area of learning. You may have heard about learning styles and wondered what the fuss was about. It seems like common sense that people should have different ways of learning. Yet there are many potential areas of confusion, compounded by a glut of recent media attention. Perhaps well-intended, the stories about learning styles in the popular media have often been misleading and confusing. Often, theories have been mixed up or blended, making a complex subject unintelligible. Because learning is a subject that can be addressed from many different points of view, often using words that can be interpreted in a variety of ways, conflicts and inconsistencies can occur.

The theory of learning styles is one of many that falls under the larger category of learning theories. These will be discussed further later in this section. Following the learning style section, other major learning theories will be briefly discussed, followed by commonly used teaching methods and strategies that are the instructional expression of learning theories.

Armed with this information, you will be able to determine the possible reasons for difficulties you might have in a particular learning situation. You will then be able to correct or avoid them. You will gain information to help you understand the way your own mind works, as well as the ways you like to have new learning presented. This will help you to choose learning experiences that are best suited to your personal needs, or to challenge yourself to learn in new and unfamiliar ways. Either way, you win!

What "Learning Styles" Means

Educators who subscribe to learning style theory believe that students who know how they learn are better able to control their learning experiences and, therefore, assume responsibility for them. **Learning styles** refers to the strengths and preferences that people exhibit in the ways they take in and process information. You have already developed a distinctive learning style, which includes how your brain processes, stores, and retrieves information, your study environment preferences, how you look at things, and other details that contribute to your ability to learn and use what you have learned.

People prefer to learn in different ways, much as they prefer or have become accustomed to engaging in any activity, from problem solving to eating. Think about the ways you learn best and how they may be different from the ways others around you learn. You may need absolute quiet to read and remember, whereas your teenager may need to have lots of noise to focus her mind. You may be more comfortable being provided with a clearly written outline in which detail is filled in an orderly fashion, whereas your classmate may prefer to hear everything at once in what seems like a jumble to you, and make his own outline from what he has heard. You may prefer to work alone on one problem at a time, whereas your coworker might be more effective working on several tasks at a time. You can see that the way you learn can have an effect on the way that you work with others and how effectively you work in general.

Learning style also affects the way that you complete tasks and in this way is related to your behavior. Think about the last time you had to put something together—perhaps a bicycle or a piece of office furniture. Did you read the instructions from beginning to end before starting, or just dive right in? Do you have less trouble when you are given a picture of what the final outcome is expected to look like, or do you feel most competent when you can work completely from a diagram instead of written instructions?

The ways that you perceive the steps that need to be taken to complete a job are a direct reflection of your learning style and what is often referred to by educators as **instructional preferences.** These preferences include whether you like to learn as an observer in a team or on your own through trial and error; whether you like a quiet study area with all study aids at hand or would rather listen to your textbooks on tape while you drive to work. Learning styles also can take into account other behaviors, like the way you approach research, how you take notes, or the way you organize your learning tasks.

Efficient learners find ways to learn that work for them, even if they seem unusual to others. Greg, one of the profiled learners you will meet later, for example, reads his textbooks into a tape recorder and listens to himself while he eats lunch or while he walks the dog. He has found that he remembers things best if he reads or hears while doing some physical activity. He jokes that he needs to get oxygen to his brain to remember, although that view may not be a joke at all. It indicates that Greg is a strongly *kinetic* learner.

Different learning styles are associated with groups of identifiable characteristics, which can help in recognizing a particular preference or style. Educational theorists, among others, have developed frameworks and assessment instruments that can help educators identify students' learning styles. They, in turn, can help those students learn in ways that are appropriate and most effective for them, as well as challenging them to learn in ways that are initially uncomfortable. In fact, helping students to build their skills in different ways of learning is one objective of higher education. It is beneficial to find different ways of learning, because different methods can help you see things in different ways, and can also expand your understanding of others.

Thinking about *how* you think can make your learning more effective. There is even a name for it: metacognition.

Why Learning Styles Are Important to You

Whereas the information age is becoming a greater part of our ingrained culture, so is a shift in educational practice from teacher directed to a learner focussed. This shift requires learners who can take control of the mountain of information that is available and use it to advantage. We cannot expect to analyze and synthesize so much information if we continue to rely only on others to determine what we should learn and how we should learn it. We cannot expect to master technology and gain competitive advantage by relying on old learning habits. To succeed, we must unlearn our reliance on teachers and direct our own learning. Knowing how you learn best is the first step.

When you know how you learn, you are able to make the most of your study time. You can recognize when you are faced with tasks that require you to work a little harder or a little differently. Looking at your own learning objectively also helps to focus your attention on practices that can contribute to your own success. It helps you see yourself as a capable problem solver instead of a helpless victim.

When you can recognize the teaching methods and strategies an instructor uses, you are able to adjust to the methods rather than focussing on the person using them. You can focus on your own abilities and not feel unfairly pressured. Understanding your own attributes will help you to choose the opportunities that best match your preferred style(s) or challenge yourself to choose strategies that increase your development as a learner.

 Be sure not to label yourself. You can not learn if your mind is closed.

Understanding that people learn differently can have other benefits, as well. For example, if you know how your *children* learn most effectively, you can advocate for them and support their educational development, directly assisting them in attaining success. If you are aware of your coworkers', employees', and employer's learning styles, you can collaborate with them more effectively, overcome common misunderstandings more easily, and enjoy a more productive work life.

You may not yet be aware of how your style has affected your past experiences, or that there are ways to enhance your ability to learn. Have you ever really thought about it? For instance, are you more comfortable focussing on facts, data, and algorithms, or do you prefer theories and mathematical models? Some learners process information best when they can physically manipulate learning materials in a trial-and-error fashion; others want to be shown the 'right' way first. Some people learn best when they interact with others; some prefer to think and work individually. Which preferences describe you best?

Research on learning styles indicates that 60 percent of adults prefer to learn visually, which means that they remember best when the information is presented in the form of pictures, diagrams, and schematics. It has also been found that our preferences often change as we age, so what may work for us now may not work as well in the future. It may surprise you to learn that only 30 percent of learners prefer verbal forms such as written and spoken explanations, *although this is the dominant teaching method most of us have been exposed to.* This overreliance on one teaching method has been cited as a reason why so many students have failed to perform to expectations, both historically and currently. The combination of rigid teaching methods and lack of alternatives contributed to this failure. One result of this traditional teaching approach is that many adults who have an urgent need to learn lack the skills to do so.

There are many reasons to learn how to function in ways that do not come naturally to us, and as the world becomes more complex, the need to be able to function well in many intellectual areas becomes even more imperative. To function well in a professional capacity, in particular, requires working well in many styles. Because information comes to us in a variety of ways, from pictures, sounds, models, and the like, it makes sense that the better you are at processing information in different ways, the more effective your learning and functioning will become. And, as more people of different social and cultural experiences join the workforce, competence in these "soft skills" is increasingly important.

Consider the capacities that Tom, an engineer, must have to do his job effectively: He must be observant, careful, and precise, but he must also be able to analyze facts and create solutions to problems. He must be able to translate his ideas both visually and verbally to anyone he works with, regardless of *their* strengths. If Tom does not function well in one of these skill areas, he will not be as successful as he could be, no matter how well he "does his job."

Other Factors and Resources

Are your learning skills as effective as they can possibly be? Of course, there is more to effective learning than knowing your learning style. There are personality characteristics that can determine whether you succeed in distance learning, or in any undertaking. We all know of those people who overcame tremendous odds to attain their goals. They conquered obstacles despite all indications to the contrary, proving that you don't have to be a "perfect candidate" to triumph. You can learn to conquer the obstacles in your path, as well.

As you well know, success has as much to do with personality as it does with skills. It may come as no surprise, then, to hear that the concepts of learning styles are rooted in the idea of psychological type, a measure of personality preferences. For this reason, a small section on personality assessment has been included in the examination of learning style theory.

Learning style and personality preference instruments are available on-line so that you can determine your own preferences and styles. Please note that all assessment instruments are open to interpretation, so avoid the temptation to label yourself. Because these are *self-assessments,* your results will depend greatly on your honesty with yourself. Because they are on-line, there is a high degree of privacy. The only one who will see your specific results is you. You can find links to on-line assessments at the Online Resources page, but you may first want to read through the section on common learning style and preference theories to acquaint yourself with the vocabulary of learning styles.

 You should be aware that some of the self-assessments available on-line have not been tested for reliability or consistency. Use them only as an indication of your likely preferences.

LEARNING THEORIES

There are a number of theories about how we learn, and several of the major theories are described here. People often think of a theory as something fixed and unchanging, but quite the opposite is true. A theory is merely an interpretation based on sets of observations or other information. They can change as new information becomes available and as ideas and interpretations are examined and reexamined. Of the theories presented in this chapter, none is better than another. They are simply different. Some are more comprehensive than others and seek to incorporate a wider range of application. Many will seem quite similar. Some will sound quite plausible to you, whereas others may sound far-fetched. Which ones will you find most relevant to your own experiences?

As is the case in the business world, different concepts and practices in education go in and out of fashion. The most popular current theories and the applications they prescribe are presented here first. These currently popular theories also happen to be the most pertinent to learners like yourself as you continue your educational journey. Other, older learning theories were developed only with educators in mind and are more removed from the learner. However, they warrant investigation here so that you will be better able to recognize their application should you experience them.

You may notice that many of the theories seem to say the same things in different ways. This is because each theory is a different way of approaching the complex mechanism called learning. This is by no means an exhaustive examination of learning theories. These very brief descriptions are only an overview. They are offered to help you become accustomed to the vocabulary of learning theories, so that the terms will be familiar when you come upon them in the literature you will review before choosing a course or school. Those interested in further information and research on learning styles may begin at the *Learning Theories* link in the Online Resources. The annotated bibliography at the end of this text also provides lists of helpful references for better understanding this complex subject.

Learning Styles

The research on learning styles is, to a large extent, an alliance between developmental and clinical psychology. It examines both the way people grow and mature and the ways their brains work to determine their reactions to the world around them. Two different ways of perceiving and processing are identified. Learners can be stronger either in *concrete* or *abstract* perception. Concrete learners absorb information by interacting directly with it; doing, feeling, acting, and the like. Abstract perceivers, on the other hand, are more likely to prefer analysis, watching, and thinking about a subject. Processing, or the way new learning is incorporated and used, can be stronger either in an *active* or *reflective* mode. (Active and reflective are referred to in some theoretical frameworks as *random* and *sequential,* respectively.) Active learners try their new learning out by using it immediately; reflective learners tend to make sense of new learning by relating it to what they already know. Learning styles classifications, and their characteristics, are described as:

> Concrete Reflective/Sequential: These learners ask *Why?* and want explanations of how material relates to their experience.
> Abstract Reflective/Sequential: These learners ask *What?* and want information organized logically.
> Abstract Active/Random: These learners ask *How?* and want to work on well defined tasks that allow safe experimentation.
> Concrete Active/Random: These learners ask *What if?* and like to apply material to solve real problems.

Do you find yourself asking one of the questions in italics more often than the others? Listen to yourself and see if you can tell which style is most comfortable for you. Because traditional schooling tends to stress abstract perceiving and

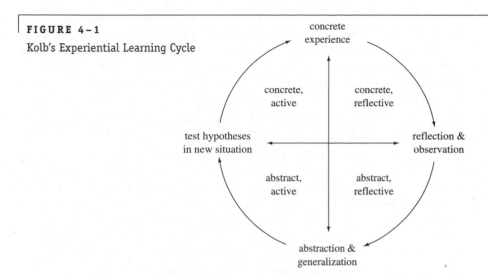

FIGURE 4–1

Kolb's Experiential Learning Cycle

reflective thinking, those who are not as strong in these style areas often experience frustration.

One of the leading learning theorists, David Kolb, suggested that adults learn in a cycle of four steps, shown in Figure 4–1. Concrete experience (1), leads to reflective observation (2) on that experience, followed by the development of a theory or hypothesis (3), which is then tested by active experimentation (4) that leads to further concrete experiences.

As a simple example, you have realized that the presence of clouds is a possible indication of rain (concrete experience) and that you can get wet when it rains. Because you do not like to get wet, you watch for awhile and develop the theory (reflection and observation) that it is more likely to rain when it is cloudy in the morning. So, even when the weatherman says you will not need one, when it is cloudy in the morning, you take your umbrella (test your hypothesis). If what you have "learned" is reinforced, it is more likely that you will repeat the behavior. If what you have learned to expect does not happen in subsequent experiences, in this case, if the weatherman is proven right, you may question your assumptions, and perhaps alter them. Thus, you are in a constant state of acting and adjusting, whether you know it or not. All of this thinking and deciding happens in a split second and is well below your threshold of conscious awareness, but is a very small example of the way that personal styles develop.

Much of what is identified as learning style theory is based in the classification of psychological types, the leading instrument of which is the *Myers-Briggs Type Indicator* (MBTI). The MBTI assesses personality preferences according to scales derived from psychologist Carl Jung's theory of psychological types. There are four pairs of preferences, which combine to yield 16 different personality types. Thus, you could be either:

an *introvert* (focus on inner world and ideas) or an *extravert* (focus on people and trying new things);

a *sensor* (practical, detail oriented, and factual) or an *intuitor* (imaginative, concept oriented, and open to possibilities);

a *thinker* (logic based, skeptical) or a *feeler* (make decisions based on instinct, consider others' feelings);

a *judger* (seeking closure and following agendas) or a *perceiver* (flexible and resisting closure until all data is available).

You probably have a pretty good idea of which traits you already possess. If you would like to find out how your traits may influence your learning and your interactions with others, check the Kiersey Temperament Sorter II, which indicates your learning style based on your MBTI score. You may follow the link from the Online Resources Web site, where other information on learning theories can be found, as well.

Multiple Intelligences

Currently, one of the most-discussed theories of how people differ in the way they learn is Howard Gardner's theory of Multiple Intelligences, which is actually a compilation of a number of theories. In his earlier writings, Gardner discussed seven **modalities,** or ways of processing, that people use to take in and make use of information. These are referred to as **preferences.** Multiple Intelligences outlines strengths in ways of perceiving and processing information, called *intelligences.* For many years, seven different preferred ways of learning were thought to encompass all possible intelligences, but Gardner has recently added an eighth and ninth modality.

Dr. Gardner defines intelligence as "the ability to find and solve problems and create products of value in one's own culture." He defines the nine intelligence modalities as sets of skills that we all have in varying degrees. In most people, some sets are developed to a higher degree than others, and some people possess particular talents in one or more of the areas. The modalities, identifying skills, preferences, and learning strengths are:

- Verbal/Linguistic: The ability to use words and language. Likes to read, write, and tell stories. Learns best by saying, hearing, and seeing words.
- Logical/Mathematical: The ability to use logical reasoning, numbers, and pattern recognition. Likes to experiment, figure things out, work with numbers, ask questions, and explore patterns and relationships. Learns best by categorizing, classifying, and working with abstract patterns/relationships.
- Visual/Spatial: Ability to visualize objects and dimensions. Likes to draw, build, design and create things, daydream, look at pictures/slides, watch movies, and play with machines. Learns best by visualizing, dreaming, and working with colors and/or pictures.
- Musical/Rhythmic: Ability to recognize tonal patterns, sense beats. Likes to sing, hum tunes, listen to music, play an instrument, and respond to music. Learns best by rhythm, melody, and music.
- Bodily/Kinesthetic: Ability to know one's own body, move with control and grace. Likes to move around, touch and talk, and use body language. Learns best by touching, moving, interacting with space, and processing knowledge through interacting with it physically.
- Interpersonal: Ability to communicate and form relationships. Likes to have lots of friends, talk to people, and join groups. Learns best by sharing, comparing, relating, cooperating, and interviewing.
- Intrapersonal: Ability to internalize, be aware of self, reflect. Likes to work alone and pursue own interests. Learns best by working alone on individualized projects, self-paced instruction, and needs to have own space.
- Naturalist: Interacts well with and regards highly the natural world and has an affinity for recognizing, classifying, and understanding the natural world. Likes sorting and seeing interdependencies, values and is attuned to environment. Learns best by observing and interacting with the world.

• Existential/Spiritual: Capacity for insight, alternative consciousness; ability to relate abstract concepts to practice. Likes philosophical and moral issues and discussion, seeing the 'big picture', questions about life and death. Learns best when value of the learning is clear or can be discussed in depth.

Brain-based Learning and Right-brain vs. Left-brain Thinking

Both Brain-based Learning and Right-brain vs. Left-brain (RBLB) Thinking are based on the structure and functions of the brain. Brain-based learning posits that everyone does learn, but that traditional teaching methods inhibit optimal learning because they ignore or punish natural learning impulses. Brain-based theorists believe that we have the capacity to perform several activities at once, that meaning comes to us through finding patterns, and that we have two types of memory: spatial and rote. In addition, proponents of brain-based learning state that learning engages the entire body. By that, they mean that emotions are critical to learning, which can be enhanced by challenge and inhibited by stressors. Moreover, each brain is unique. Brain-based learning experiences include immersion, as is used in many foreign language classrooms.

Right-brain vs. Left-brain Thinking suggests that different sides of the brain literally control two different ways of thinking. Who has not heard someone described as "right brained?" You may even have used it to describe yourself! Investigation into brain function has revealed that the two hemispheres of the brain are sources of different kinds of thinking. Further, we each tend to prefer one way of thinking over the other, although some people are adept at thinking "with both sides of the brain." Left-hemisphere thinking tends to be logical, sequential, rational, analytical, and objective, whereas the right hemisphere has been found to be the source of random, intuitive, holistic, subjective thinking. Traditional education has focussed on left-brained thinking modes, while minimizing right-brained activities, like the arts and creative pursuits.

An instrument that has been used to determine what section of the brain is dominating an individual's thought processes is the **Herrmann Brain Dominance Instrument (HBDI),** which classifies in terms of people's preferences for thinking based on how the brain functions physically. There are four modes or quadrants in this classification scheme (think of a pie cut into quarters) consisting of two sections each in the cerebrum and limbic system:

Quadrant A (left brain, cerebral). Logical, analytical, quantitative, factual, critical;

Quadrant B (left brain, limbic). Sequential, organized, planned, detailed, structured;

Quadrant C (right brain, limbic). Emotional, interpersonal, sensory, kinesthetic, symbolic;

Quadrant D (right brain, cerebral). Visual, holistic, innovative.

 If your children are experiencing difficulties in school, perhaps they are not being taught in a way they prefer to process information. Stressing the same activities does not help, it just frustrates everyone.

Can you estimate which quadrants you use most— and least—often? Awareness of the kind of thinking you are most comfortable with can help you to design your study processes more effectively. Such awareness can also help to provide clues if you are exploring career options, helping you to choose an occupation that requires the kind of thinking you are best at and most comfortable with.

Constructivism

Constructivism is the educational philosophy currently dominating scholarly discourse and practice. Proponents of constructivism believe that we *construct* meaning and understanding based on our own, individual experiences in the world. Each person is the author of her own rules or "mental models" that guide the ways that she makes sense of her experiences.

Constructivists believe that learning is, first and foremost, a search for meaning. Making sense of information requires understanding of both the relationships between the separate pieces of information and the concepts connecting each piece and the larger whole. The process of learning, therefore, focuses on primary concepts, not isolated facts. Assessment also plays a vital part in constructivist learning model, becoming part of the learning process. Instead of utilizing standardized measurements, constructivist educators use personalized evaluation, often in the form of projects. This ensures that students participate in their learning fully and receive direct information on its quality.

Constructivism is inherently interdisciplinary and inclusive, which simply means that those educators who are guided by this philosophy draw learning materials from many different topic areas and mold it to correspond with students' prior knowledge. Educators focus on making connections between experience and new information, facilitating understanding through dialogue and open-ended questioning. Instructors encourage students to analyze, interpret, and predict information, and tailor learning to work from student's understanding toward a synthesis.

Program literature that includes phrases such as "values your understanding," and "a learner-centered philosophy," generally indicates a constructivist attitude toward education.

Communities of Practice

Many distance learning institutions strongly stress the importance of a learning community, which can be a powerful component in learning support. However, this is somewhat different from the Communities of Practice (CoP) theory, which grew out of the Institute for Research on Learning, itself an outgrowth of the Xerox Corporation. In Communities of Practice, learners and mentors share values, beliefs, and social relations. This active, integrated approach to learning assumes that all learning comes from solving problems and working together in social groups. Membership in the community and learning processes are intertwined. Each member's identity, as well as his relationship to the group, changes as learning changes. Here, knowledge comes from and leads to practice; by doing, learning occurs—for everyone.

Programs that stress Community of Practice concepts offer real-world opportunities to learners, like apprenticeships, service learning opportunities, and internships.

Behaviorism

A theory governing both human and animal learning, behaviorism focuses only on observed behavior. No attention is given to underlying mental processes. Behaviorists define learning as no more than an acquisition of new behavior.

Nearly everyone is aware of the experiments done by Pavlov to condition dogs to salivate at the sound of a bell. This **classical conditioning** took advantage of dogs' natural response to food (salivation) to condition them to expect food when a bell rang. **Operant conditioning,** on the other hand, rewards or punishes particular behaviors in an effort to reinforce or decrease the targeted behavior. Although behaviorism has many critics because it completely disregards the mind, it is still often used by teachers and parents—often quite successfully—to mold behavior.

Piaget's Development Theory

Although he specialized in child development, Piaget's theory influenced many other psychologists in the examination of human development across the life span, including Erikson and Maslow. Piaget believed that children develop cognitive structures, or **mental maps,** for understanding and interacting within their environments. He maintained that as children grew, their mental sophistication grew, as well. He developed models of mental functioning that correspond to stages of development.

Piaget's ideas have been examined and expanded to apply to stages of adult development and have been integrated into student support programs and coursework. Such programs seek to connect with learners from an appropriate point in their own development and help them to progress effectively through learning experiences. With appropriate support, learners can adjust to new challenges and integrate knowledge successfully.

Observational Learning

Also called social learning theory, observational theory states that an observer's behavior changes after viewing a model's behavior. There are several principles guiding observational learning theory, which involves four processes: attention, retention, production, and motivation. Obviously, the learner must pay attention to learn, but this seemingly simple process depends greatly on how the model, or teacher, is viewed and what the learner expects. After the information has been modeled, the learner must be able to remember the information and reproduce the behavior. In order to produce the behavior desired, the learner must be motivated to do so. Obviously, many factors can interfere with the learning situation. If the model is not effective, or expectations are frustrated, the learning process will be hampered. If the learner cannot remember or is unable or unwilling to perform the steps shown, the desired outcome will not be met.

You might think that a theory termed "observational" would have little place in distance learning, yet many institutions foster peer collaborative learning. This is a highly social learning method, in that you learn from each other. Imagine a group project in which each participant has responsibility for researching and presenting a different aspect of the topic. In this case, the way that you view your classmates' level of understanding, credibility, and preparation, as well as their perceptions of you, can impact directly on the learning experiences of all participants.

These are just a few of the many learning theories that help define how teachers teach and what institutions expect. Are you confused yet? Relax, it is all written down and you can come back to it later, if you wish. Right now, though, why not take a few minutes to find out what kind of learner you are? Try any—or all—of the assessments by following the web links on the Online Resources Web site at <www.delmar.com>. Click on 'Self-Assessments' to see how you "score". You might also want to enlist a friend, relative, or coworker to do the assessments together and learn more about each other! If you prefer, you can always wait until later to try the on-line assessments, and continue reading about the different teaching strategies that educators use. You have probably experienced several of them.

You can make a note of the scores to the different tests here, for future reference:

_____

_____

STRATEGIES EFFECTIVE TEACHERS USE

Now that you have read about learning theories, you may be able to identify which of the strategies examined in this section are influenced by different theories. Theories form the framework, or ideology, to explain why teachers may introduce a particular activity or approach. Strategies are the methods used to transmit the knowledge or understanding. Of course, many instructors use a variety of techniques to engage as many types of learners as possible.

You may still be wondering _why_ it is important to understand how people learn best. Learning theories help educators and instructional designers understand how people learn. By understanding the different ways that people learn, they can design ways for more people to learn better. In order to make learning effective for the greatest number, different teaching strategies are used to transmit material in ways that different kinds of people can understand it. If you find a program in which instructors use teaching methods that integrate well with your learning styles, you can enhance your learning, cut study time, and increase your interaction with classmates. That is effective learning!

Often, the material a student is expected to learn, usually referred to as **learning outcomes** or **learning objectives,** will determine the technology and strategies used to teach a course. Obviously, an art course will have a strong visual component, but how might it—and other topics—be taught on-line? How will the learner experience and contribute to the material? The answers to those questions run the gamut from highly involved and structured to passive and open teaching methods. In addition, program technology ranges from the height of technical wizardry with all the bells and whistles to technology geared toward the lowest bandwidth so learning can be accessed even by students who have slow dial-up connections and modems. Much is dependent on what level of access and ability institutions expect of their learners. (Technical requirements are reviewed in Chapter 5.) Knowing the orientations and strategies used by your chosen learning provider _before_ you start will help you to have a successful learning experience.

The convergence of distance learning and educational technology will continue to produce ever-richer ways of delivering educational materials. For now, though, the traditional written lecture is still the most common. After all, this is the method that most teachers were exposed to when they were in school. Many

Read the school's mission statement to help understand the ideas that drive the institution. The mission statement will provide clues to the kind of learning experience you can expect.

distance institutions, realizing the challenges such a format poses, enhance the lecture model with activities that encourage collaboration and reflection. We can only imagine what enhancements educational technology will allow in the future. Still, these basic teaching methods will likely remain a part of the way learning is transmitted for some time to come. Which strategies outlined below do you think will work best for you?

Lecture and Explanation

Most of your past school experience probably took the form of a "lecture and explanation" teaching strategy. Here, the instructor stood at the front of the class and talked while you took notes and, occasionally, asked a question. If you were lucky, you were interested and the teacher was both knowledgeable and excited, and the excitement was contagious. If not, you were dozing in your seat.

Although this may not seem to be a good strategy for on-line learning, you would be surprised at the number of professors who have simply transferred their lecture notes to the computer screen. After all, this is the method they are used to, so it must work, right? Not necessarily. Reliance on a lecture and explanation strategy means that courses are oriented more toward introverts. Lectures are presented statically, and the emphasis is on individual assignments rather than active class involvement and cooperative learning. From a Multiple Intelligences perspective, this teaching style favors strong verbal/linguistic learners, who read and comprehend well. Not helpful if you are a highly kinetic learner with a visual disability!

There are many ways to fortify learning presented statically. Printed text can be combined with **streaming audio,** a technology that allows you to hear audio files as they are downloading, so you can begin to listen without waiting for the entire file to get to your PC and then open. Even with the use of audio technology, though, a dull lecture is a dull lecture, and it can be downright boring unless elements are added to engage the students.

The main benefit of the traditional way of presenting information on-line in a text format is that you can save it and reread it as often as necessary. As noted before, this is currently the dominant way of presenting the basic course materials, with interaction conducted with e-mail and discussion boards. These are included in educational software, also referred to as **courseware.** Courseware is a kind of computer application, or platform, that provides a consistent look and feel for the entire class. It often includes areas where participants can post personal information, view schedules and assignments, post comments, and store material related to the course for easy access. Some courseware includes links to libraries, advisors, and other student services. Examples of commercial courseware platforms include Blackboard, and WebCT.

Training and Coaching

Another popular strategy in on-line learning is the training and coaching strategy. A step-by-step process that builds on previous learning, this method can include self-tests, reviews, and electronic "pats on the back." It is the kind of instructional style you will often see in self-mastery programs and off-the-shelf packages, like CD-ROM training programs. You may have tried this technique to learn material so you could pass a certification exam or use a software program. With these, you read the lesson, take a test, and move on to the next lesson, or repeat the subjects you missed until you can satisfactorily answer the test questions. CD-ROM training applications, and their server-based cousins, computer-based training (CBT), have one clear advantage over Internet-delivered learning: no waiting for download. Here, all of the information is encoded on the CD, so media-rich presentations can be made available at a mouse-click. Many corporations utilize CBT for in-house training accessible from an employee's desktop. Certainly, this is an area that will only grow as training requirements increase.

A training and coaching strategy using CD-ROMs is especially good for learning skills that require memorization. They presuppose that you will pass the test and go out and immediately use what you have learned. If you do not, you will quickly forget it! They can be very useful if you are good with detail and like to learn things in a sequence. However, you must be disciplined enough to continue to the end on your own. To excel with this method, you *must* be self-motivated, a problem for many of us. In addition, these packages usually do not give you an opportunity to interact and discuss material with other learners, which many educators believe is really the way adults learn best.

Inquiry and Discovery

An inquiry and discovery technique provides more interaction than do CD-ROMs developed to utilize training and coaching strategies. In fact, it is central to the learning process. Here, learners interact with a teacher/facilitator, who challenges them to think beyond what they already know and to make new connections. The primary relationship is between the learner and the teacher, so this style is often found in those programs that utilize one-on-one tutorials. This is a good style for those who learn best by doing and discovering things on their own with a guide to support and challenge them. It is often typified by laboratory work, like Internet library searches and scenarios, which allow learners to try things out in a safe environment. This strategy employs a great deal of writing and critiquing between learner and teacher. This learner-mentor relationship can become very close and remain strong for many years.

Some institutions and software companies have developed discovery learning modules, which can be used to guide investigations. Although they can be very effective, discovery learning modules are not yet widely used. However, their use is increasing as both learners and teachers see how effective this form of instruction can be, and as interest increases.

Groups and Teams

In a groups and teams strategy, learners interact to construct knowledge together. This way of learning on-line may be the most labor intensive for both learners and teachers, because planning for and interacting effectively in an on-line group environment is time consuming for everyone. However, the skills learned in classes structured for group experiences teach skills that are in great demand in the marketplace: Collaborative problem solving, shared decision making, interpersonal communications skills, and a tolerance for and understanding of others' points of view. Here, everyone is considered equal and the teacher often learns as much as the students do. The discussions have the potential of being incredibly rich and diverse. This method works best when the classes are small, as it can be difficult to keep larger classes organized.

The collaborative orientation to adult learning is increasing as on-line learning becomes more commonplace, and not only because it meets 'emerging market needs.' On-line learners are demanding a learning experience that puts them in intellectual contact with others, where they can form bonds that are strong and nurturing. Many of the schools that stress "creating a learning community" in their mission statements provide this kind of learning experience.

The collaborative teaching strategy of groups and teams is likely to flourish as schools turn to enterprise learning packages (which utilize integrated software to allow seamless interaction, information management, assessment, and reporting). In addition to the real learning benefits of this process, it mirrors modernizing companies, which are moving to institute a collaborative team management style and integrate training functions within the practice of doing business. Learners educated in this way will become highly sought after because they have already developed the skills needed to be successful in a modern business climate.

Experience and Reflection

Learners studying human service subjects such as social work and psychology can benefit from a strategy called experience and reflection. This is a strategy in which learners are urged to think about, and reflect on, their experiences and to draw conclusions and meaning from them. That makes it a useful strategy, as well, for those who undertake the process that translates life learning into college credit. Understanding is enhanced through the discussion of ideas, readings, and reactions with other learners. Here, the focus on learning is both individual and on the interaction between learners, who serve to validate and solidify each others' insights. The facilitator usually plays a subordinate role, making sure that discussions stay on track and everyone has the opportunity to interact.

Perhaps you have been involved in a discussion group in which others described their own experiences and, by expressing them to others, gained insights about their own lives. It may seem strange to consider interaction with others as the basis for learning in an on-line environment, but it is a strategy that we all use as part of our development as human beings. We often ask others about their experiences before undertaking something new. In fact, there is at least one Web site that is solely devoted to exchanging information about others' practical experiences with all sorts of things ranging from travel destinations to infant strollers. The need to 'find out' before committing to making a change or a purchase is strong in many of us. It may be the primary reason you are reading this book!

To Sum Up. . .

In this chapter, we have briefly touched the surface of a wide variety of ideas and points. We discussed the reasons why *how* you learn can have a dramatic impact on *what* you learn. You may have discovered more about yourself than you ever knew!

We examined, if only briefly, major learning theories and the concrete teaching strategies that arose from them. We discovered that theories are based on observations, which can be drastically different depending upon the observer's point of view. We also found out that theories can be fluid and interpreted in a variety of ways. Perhaps you now understand why the teachers you had made the instructional choices they did, even if you did not at the time.

Armed with this knowledge, your next educational decisions can be rationally informed. You can request learning experiences that give you the greatest return on your educational investment. Even though you already have a great deal of information to make an informed decision, more information is available. By using the Online Resources Web site, you can access advice and links related to these topics. Check out the Web site at <www.delmar.com.>.

Notes to Yourself

Now that you know how you learn best, and some of the different ways that information in on-line courses can be delivered, you should know what educators of adults—on-line and off—expect of their students. That will be covered in Chapter 5. Before you turn the page, though, take a moment to record here any notes you would like to remember for later. Which theories seem most interesting and real to you? Which strategies would you like to experience in your next class? What would your perfect class experience be? Record it here now, and return later to see if your future ideas remain the same!

_____

_____

_____

_____

_____

_____

CHAPTER 5

Of Course You Are Self-reliant. . . . Right?

Many adult learners think of themselves as consumers of education, in which they are purchasing a service called 'education'. They want the service to be prompt and have straightforward policies and clear expectations stated in advance. They expect the same kind of customer service they receive from any other merchant they deal with. New and returning adult students may not be aware that there are other orientations to learning that can guide curricular and institutional goals. Sometimes, there is a dissonance of expectations between learners and learning providers. Knowing this in advance, and knowing what to ask, can avoid frustration, save time, and enhance the learning experience significantly.

Most adults return to school, whether in a traditional classroom setting or in an on-line environment, expecting to learn a subject and gain important credentials. They bring with them experiences, a lifestyle, and relationships. These, in part, determine their very choice to return to school. Along with the knowledge they already have, adults also bring expectations to the classroom, expectations about the ways they should be treated, how others should interact with them, and what work they should be expected to do.

Few adult learners think in advance about how their education will change them. They do not expect their relationships or the way that they experience them to change. Yet it is well known that learning can induce a change in the way you perceive yourself and the people around you. Far from being a bad thing, though, this is often stated as one of the most rewarding results of returning to school. Even if you think that you will "just be sitting in front of the computer," remember that technology is merely a delivery medium for knowledge, knowledge that can have a profound impact on the way you view yourself. On-line learning has the flexibility to fit your own schedule, but it is still learning. How will your study affect you? What do you hope to change? Thinking about these questions is part of the learning process, a process that is your responsibility to direct.

"You cannot teach a man anything; you can only help him find it within himself."

—*Galileo*

55

WHAT IT MEANS TO BE SELF-RELIANT

If you have already taken classes at night, you might have found that most adult educators are learner-centered teachers. This means that they work collaboratively with students to integrate new knowledge with existing experience. They do not simply lecture at you, they actively work at finding ways to help you understand and successfully integrate the new information into what you already know. The best teachers help you to develop lifelong learning goals that can be pursued independently. In other words, adult educators expect their students to be self-reliant.

But what does it mean to be a self-reliant learner? Many people assume that self-reliance is simply the ability to take care of oneself, complete assignments effectively, and move through the system efficiently. But it is much more than that. Self-reliance means:

- the ability to take responsibility for learning,
- knowing how to set goals and standards,
- knowing how to approach and do library research,
- having initiative,
- having the ability to manage time, and
- having the ability and willingness to evaluate yourself and others critically.

You would not have gotten this far in life without being able to do many of these things competently already, but you will get *much* more for your effort if you learn to do them even more effectively. The good news is that almost anyone can learn these things—it is often just a matter of putting your mind to it. Adopting an attitude of personal responsibility for your own learning is the first step. Beyond that, knowing what to expect and developing a plan to meet those expectations will help you achieve your goals.

Many students who have been out of the classroom for years forget what school was like. Most of us remember being told what to do and when to do it. We may remember school as a place where we memorized facts so we could get a good grade on a test. Once the test was over, we forgot what we had crammed to learn, because much of what we learned had little relationship to the rest of our lives. But much of education—especially for adults—has changed dramatically, as you now know.

There is one important thing about school that you *may* remember. When you were a kid, school was your job, and it was a job where you were usually told what to do (and what NOT to do!), and when and how to do it. Now, you are often the one telling others what is expected. Now you have other responsibilities, people that depend on you, and deadlines that must be met. Now you may have children of your own to raise, aging parents to care for, and activities to coordinate. In addition, you have to consider your own emotional and spiritual needs. All this, *plus* the requirement or desire to fit education into your life. Life, as you well know, is certainly more complicated than when you were a youngster.

As your life has changed, so must your expectations of school. If you approach school now with expectations formed in childhood, confusion and irritation will result. It is this clash of expectations and the opposing pull of responsibilities that can lead to failure. In fact, it is just this clash, and not the inability to complete academic requirements, that causes thousands of adult learners to drop out every year. Consider Sandy's situation:

Sandy had been working hard for many years. Her associate degree in finance had gotten her an entry-level job at a major bank nearly 20 years ago. Smart and willing to take risks, Sandy had progressed through the ranks to her present position as a vice president. She decided that the time had finally come to complete her bachelor's degree. She considered the options available. She decided that choosing to do her degree on-line would let her maintain her career responsibilities and fit better into her busy schedule. So, with the support of her company and her family, she began taking courses on-line through State College.

The first course went well; she could bring real-world experience to her understanding of the concepts and provide examples for others. It was difficult with a full-time job, but she managed to find time to study by cutting back on her community activities. She was happy to be able to complete assignments to her own perfectionist standards. She even made a few new friends through her on-line class discussions. It was great to know that she could handle it.

Her next on-line course was an elective she had always wanted to take: child psychology. Having raised four children, she thought this would be a snap! The first inkling that things might not go as she expected came during the orientation, when the instructor asked everyone to write a paragraph explaining what they hoped to learn in this class. "Is *he* not supposed to tell *us*?" she thought. She read through some of the responses before posting something that answered the question—sort of. Feeling a strange disquiet that was unfamiliar to her, she read the weekly assignment, wondering if anyone else was having trouble understanding it.

The following week, the instructor asked everyone to write a response to the reading assignment and include a short explanation of their project. "*Project?!*" Sandy thought, panic stricken. It should illustrate one of the principles or theories outlined in the course textbook, the posting said. "How can I illustrate something I do not understand?" Sandy wondered.

Not one to give in when the going got tough, Sandy doubled her efforts. She hated to look dumb, so she vowed to figure it out for herself, instead of asking the questions that were crowding her mind. She continued reading—sometimes going over a chapter two and three times—and answered questions as best she could. No matter how hard she worked, though, the material just seemed to slip away from her and became harder and harder to understand and concentrate on. Each week brought more confusing information and more panic as she began falling behind. She began to doubt her ability to understand at all, and even wondered whether she had learned anything from being a mother. Had she even been a *good* mother?

Just as these doubts and fears assailed her, a crisis at work cut into Sandy's available study time. She was upset that she could not seem to devote the time to studying that she should, but this was a crisis! She spent less and less time on confusing schoolwork, devoting her energies to her job. At least she felt comfortable that she could deal effectively with her work-related responsibilities. Eventually, dispirited and disappointed, she concluded that she was not cut out for college and she stopped even logging on to the class Web site.

What did Sandy do wrong?

What would you have done differently?

LEARNING HOW TO LEARN

Sandy fell into several of the common traps that plague returning students. As soon as many returning learners enter a classroom, they fall into a subordinate role, forgetting to behave like the confident, competent people they are at home or in the workplace. Because they have no other experience to compare it with, they expect school to be the same as it was when they were children. They expect to be told what to do and helped along to find the "right" answer. As they may have in earlier educational experience, they may try to figure out what the teacher wants, and give it to them, whether it means anything to them or not.

Adults returning to school may have read that adult-centered colleges expect "self-reliance" of their students, though this is usually not defined clearly or, often, well supported. So, even when they consciously understand that expectations are different than when they were children, learners often do not realize that education itself is different than they remember.

If you are successful in your job and life, it is easy to assume that you have all of the skills necessary for educational success. After all, you are doing fine. How are you to know that the transition from the school as you remember to the learning experiences of today can be such a difficult one? How do you know if you are a self-reliant learner? Or if you are not? What can you do to be sure that you will have what it takes to be as successful in learning as you are in life? How can *you* become a self-reliant learner?

As noted earlier, self-reliance is a complex combination of abilities and attitudes: Responsibility for learning, setting goals and standards, doing research, taking initiative, the ability to manage time, and evaluating oneself and others critically. These are the core competencies of self-reliant learners. But being self-reliant is as much about acquiring an attitude as it is about mastering a set of abilities. The good news is that abilities can be learned, practiced, and mastered. The first step toward becoming a successful on-line learner is to develop a successful attitude. It can be done, and it will very likely impact other parts of your life, as well.

Let us look at each core competency in greater detail:

Taking responsibility for your learning means that *you* make a conscious commitment to the learning task. This includes, among other things:

- making the time necessary to study and following through with your schedule,
- understanding your weaknesses and taking action to strengthen them,
- asking for help or clarification when you need it,
- learning to say no to things that interfere with your goal,
- getting and staying motivated,
- finding ways to meet needs that you cannot meet by yourself, and
- fostering an idea of yourself as an active seeker, not a passive receiver, of knowledge.

If the emerging picture is of a person who knows what he wants and figures out how to get it, you are getting the idea. To help you *become* that person is one of the primary purposes of this guide.

Setting goals and standards and *managing your time* may be very familiar to you if you have ever managed a project. Even a small project can have clearly stated goals: what is required, when it is due, what are the resources and limitations, who and what else needs to be involved, how much is already available, and so on. You do not need more than a pocket calendar to map out a plan to keep your coursework under control and on schedule.

To help plan your personal learning journey, you can use the Time and Activity Analysis Worksheet from Chapter 3. Then, in Section IV, "Get It Done," further tips are provided for keeping your learning tasks under your control. One of the tools included is a Time and Task Adjustments Worksheet. This worksheet

Remember that it took a long time to get where you are now. Go easy on yourself!

will help you to delegate, change, or delete those responsibilities that currently take up so much of your time. Both worksheets are designed to be used together to help you identify and organize your time and your life. Copies of all worksheets can be downloaded from the Online Resources Web site, and are included in the appendix, as well.

Knowing how to approach and do library research is expected of those who undertake any college learning. It is absolutely required beyond the bachelor's degree. Being able to do research is also an important life skill. The ability to find accurate and timely information and to discriminate between truth and falsehood in what you have found can make a tremendous difference in your work and home life. Research skills and support for academic success are covered in greater detail in Chapter 14.

Having initiative means that you accept the responsibility for your own learning without being prompted to do so by anyone else. Other behaviors that show initiative include:

- asking questions instead of waiting for someone else to;
- seeking information beyond the minimum requirements of the class;
- offering help before it is asked for;
- taking the first step willingly.

Initiative has become synonymous with "taking risks," but these risks are not life threatening. In fact, they can be life enhancing! What they do threaten is your idea of yourself. Remember that you have decided to undertake this learning journey to change *something*, so you should *expect* to experience some change yourself. Even if you do not think of yourself as a person who easily embraces change, learning new things and interacting with others cannot help but have an effect on you. Some of the changes you can expect learning to bring will be discussed in Chapter 16.

The *ability and willingness to evaluate yourself and others critically* is a key competency for academic success. The techniques related to making judgments about what is correct and logical are similar to those used in evaluating research. You probably do not need to be told that the ability to evaluate others—and yourself—fairly and tactfully is a skill that can be useful in any area of your life. To make fair evaluations, you must recognize that we all have biases and learn to put aside those bias and personal feelings.

It is actually easier to overcome some of your reactions—particularly the visual ones—when engaging in on-line courses, because all you "see" is what your classmates and teacher have chosen to write. If you are perceived as a fair and helpful colleague, your fellow learners will be encouraged to return your treatment similarly. Being willing to admit your own inadequacies and share your own triumphs will help set an open tone that encourages communication. This is just one of the on-line support-building skills that will be covered in greater detail later, as well.

The library is now more than a place to go for story time. Technology has changed it, too. Take the time to reacquaint yourself with it.

ARE YOU A SELF-RELIANT LEARNER?

As you can see, self-reliance can mean different things to different people. Now that you know how the educational community defines self-reliance, how do you rate yourself? Look back over the components, and note areas that you will want to remember to enhance your future success. For example, if you tend to give up when you can not find what you are looking for, you may remind yourself to ask for help instead of letting stressful frustration build up. Keeping in mind that no one is perfect, what are some of the areas in which you feel you could benefit from improvement? You might want to refer back to the On-line Learning Self-Assessment in Chapter 3 for ideas, as well.

To help you evaluate yourself, here again are the attributes of a self-reliant learner:

- the ability to take responsibility for learning,
- knowing how to set goals and standards,
- knowing how to approach and do library research,
- having initiative,
- the ability to manage time, and
- the ability and willingness to evaluate yourself and others critically.

Which attributes are you especially competent in? Which could use a little reinforcement? How can you help yourself to become the most effective learner you can be? Writing here those areas you know you need to focus on is the first step in becoming that powerful learner that you can be:

_____

_____

_____

Much of the literature about adult learning and self-reliance arises out of research in developmental and educational psychology. Links are provided from the Online Resources site, should you wish to learn more about this subject. In addition, you can check the annotated bibliography or conduct an on-line search. Tips for on-line searching are included in the Chapter 6, "The Technical Connection—Requirements and Skills for Distance Learning" as well as additional links from the Online Resources Web site. First, though, let us hear the stories of three very different learners who had one thing in common: The need to enhance their educational accomplishments.

LEARNER PROFILES

Distance learners can come from any walk of life and be searching for vastly different learning opportunities. One person may need professional certification to advance in her career, and another may be interested in delving more deeply into a cherished hobby. Yet another will turn to the Internet to find others with whom he can network to learn, share, and grow.

Greg, Ellen, and Brad come to on-line learning with different needs, abilities, and expectations. Each has different reasons for choosing the paths they have. One of them may seem to be telling *your* story, too. Let us meet them now. They will join us again throughout the book to let us know how they are doing, in their own words.

Learner Profile

Greg: Master Mechanic and More

This whole distance learning thing came as somewhat of a surprise to me, but maybe I am different from other people. I do not know. Anyway, I am one of those "middle managers" you hear about, going to work every day and getting things done, at least that was the way I saw it. I joined the company after serving a hitch in the military, which was the only way I was ever going to get out of the town I grew up in. The service was okay, once you knew what the rules were. I guess that is the same anywhere. I learned a few things about how to take care of machines and I really liked knowing they were purring along out there because I had done a good job. I was really proud of the fact that not one of the machines I was responsible for ever broke down in the field. Ever.

Anyway, when my term was up, I decided to try life out in the "real world", as they called it. There was no way I was going back to life in a small town, especially the one I grew up in. I had seen enough of the world while I was in the service to know it would be a mistake. So, I took the first job that was offered to me that was in a good-sized town. It was a facilities position, and in a lot of ways it was really similar to what I had done in the military—maintaining equipment so it would run the way it was supposed to. I met someone at work and pretty soon we were talking about getting married. Another thing that happened like it was supposed to, I guess, only I really lucked out. My wife, Sharon, is a nurse and also served a hitch in the military, so we had a lot in common, except she had more schooling than I did, but that did not matter to us. So we got married, found a small house outside the city that was convenient to my wife's job, and got used to having a life together. It was not long before our son, Donnie, was born.

About the same time, I was offered a promotion at work. It was a good pay increase and more responsibility, and it would let Sharon work part-time and spend more time with Donnie, so I took it. It was a management position, and I all of a sudden had to supervise people I had worked along side of. It worked out pretty well, though, because we all had respect for each other. We all knew each other and could enjoy working together, and it was an opportunity for me to help other people and tighten up the operation at the same time. Sure, there were some problems, but we all managed to work things out and make the department work better and better. Things were going along just fine when we got the word that our company was going to merge with a much larger competitor.

When my new boss called me into his office, I thought that I was going to be laid off. I probably should have been worrying about the mortgage, but the only thing I could think of was that my son's birthday was coming up and he was wanting a bike in the worst way. I kept thinking about that bike in the store window and wondering if I was going to be able to afford it after today.

Well, what happened was not what I expected at all. My new boss—he is an alright guy, I guess—told me that everyone was impressed with the work I had been doing and that they did not want to disrupt things too much, so they wanted me to stay on, and that, in fact, a promotion might be in my future. But the company had a policy that managers had to have a college degree. Their benefit program would pay for it, he said, but I would have to do well and get at least a few classes under my belt before we could have any further discussions about promotions. He gave me a brochure about the educational benefits and said I should talk to this lady in human resources about what came next, but that I should think about it, talk to my family, and decide if I wanted to pursue it or not. I guess I looked shocked or something, because he just handed me the brochure and said, "Why not think about it for awhile."

Well, I did not know what to think. First, I got all this praise about doing a good job and then he told me I was not good enough for something better. At first, I was really mad. I do not remember what I did the rest of the day, but by the time I got home that night I was steamed. Sharon could tell the minute I walked in the door. She just handed me a beer and sat down to listen. What a saint. I just went on and on about how the suits wanted to change the rules and it was not fair and what the heck did I need a college degree for. I had just about run out of steam when Donnie came trailing in and climbed up in my lap. He did not say a word, but I thought about that bike and shut up.

Later, Sharon and I talked about it. If I did not take this opportunity (that is what she called it—I was not so sure), would I get passed over for advancement in the future? I had done just fine in high school and had really liked most of my classes, but college was never an option talked about in our house; you either went to work in the mill or joined the military. Growing up, everyone I knew that had gone to college had seemed to be going somewhere, like they had their life ahead of them. One kid had gotten a scholarship to an engineering school and I remember thinking how lucky he was, even though I did not have too good of an idea what engineers did. Some of the people in town had made fun of the college kids, but you could tell that they were jealous, too. I had always wondered what it was like, whether it really made a difference, like some of my teachers had told me.

The more Sharon and I talked about it, the more questions I had. I realized I had more questions than answers, and I was going to need some answers before we would be able to make a decision. It was clear, at least, that it was something we would all have to decide on, because it would mean changes at home, as well as at work.

The next day, I made an appointment with Mrs. Carter in human resources, wondering what I was getting into. Well, I kept the appointment, even though I had my doubts. Again, things worked out different from what I expected. Instead of like being in the principal's office, she allowed as how it must make me feel angry to get this kind of news, and that I was not the only one that had gotten the same message. The company's policy, she said, was to support its employees' efforts in self-improvement, because the people that ran the company believed that the more educated their employees were, the better they were able to do their jobs and keep the company healthy. She went on to give me details about what the company could do for me if I chose to take advantage of the educational benefit, and what would probably happen if I chose not to. I would not be fired, but would probably be passed over for promotions. But that was entirely up to me. She let that sink in for a bit, and then I asked what to expect if I took advantage of the program.

She told me about some of the options: there was a community college where I could start, if I wanted to, and some other employees who were doing the same thing and had even started a lunchtime study group. I was surprised to hear that some of the people in my own department were in college, guys I never would have thought of as college types. I was even more surprised when she told me that I would probably be able to get some college credit for my military experience.

Then she told me about an on-line degree program that some other employees were trying out. Nobody went to class, they just used the computers to do work, send it in to the school, and interact with other members of the class. Some of the people in the class lived as far away as Brazil. That was the part that really got me. Best of all, she said, if we did not have an Internet connection at home, we could use the computers right there at work, and not have to go to class at night or any other particular time. She gave me the catalog, and I took it home to talk to Sharon about.

I still had lots of questions, but the possibilities were starting to get me excited. I saw that there were programs that could lead to degrees in things I had never even heard of before! Maybe Sharon was right, and this was my opportunity to do something with my life, even if it was unexpected. Maybe I could even become an engineer. As I was leaving the parking lot, I realized I was smiling.

Learner Profile

Ellen: Looking at the Future for Her Family

From the first time I heard about distance learning, I knew I would have to try it. After trying to fit regular classes into my life without success, I knew that, for me, there had to be another way. Oh, I tried night school, but it did not work out. As a single mom with two kids in elementary school and a full-time job, there was no way that I could afford childcare and education, even if I wanted to spend any more time away from my kids than I already had to. I did worry about whether I had the stamina and motivation to keep up with the work, but all I had to do was look at my kids, and the feeling that I had to improve all of our lives got stronger.

Luckily, I did have some college under my belt. Back in what felt like the dark ages, I completed an associate degree in business at the community college near where I grew up. It was hard, because I also had a part-time job and had to help take care of my dad, who was a diabetic. But I did okay and kept my head above water by being very organized. I got a decent job with a local insurance company and started to put some money away, finally. Joey, one of the salesmen at the company, asked me out, and we just clicked. The next few months were a roller coaster of emotions, as my dad declined and then passed away and Joey's and my bond got stronger. When we found out I was pregnant, getting married just seemed the right thing to do.

After the twins were born, there never seemed to be enough time or money for everything. We started fighting a lot and, well, it is the same story lots of people tell, right? We were pretty good about keeping the kids first and kept the name calling to a minimum. I was lucky to have my mom close by, and she asked me and the kids to move back in with her. It was not the ideal situation, as any adult who has lived with their parent knows, but it certainly helped me get back on my feet again, and mom loved having Mark and Missy around. Having her to rely on made it easier for me to get a full-time job again.

With an associate degree and some experience, it was not too long before I had a decent administrative job at the local hospital. A few years went by pretty quickly, but not so quickly that I did not notice that younger people with more recent education were starting to move ahead of me. By then, I had also learned a lot about healthcare management just by observing what was going on around me. But when I asked about applying for some of the jobs that were becoming available, the human resources representative told me that most of the people they were hiring had college degrees and, though I had the right experience, I really needed more education, especially in management. Did I know that the hospital had an educational benefit?

Maybe I should have been mad, but I saw right away what she meant. The two-year degree I had completed had been mostly about accounting and there was a lot more to business than numbers, I can tell you. I really wanted to—needed to—learn how to supervise people and plan on a larger scale than just for my immediate area. With the hospital paying for classes (as long as I passed), I thought I could not go wrong. At the suggestion of Sherrie, the HR person, I signed up for a night class in healthcare administration that started the following week.

It was a bit of a commute, so I could not get home after work and my mom had to feed and bathe the kids, but that was okay with her, because it was only one night a week. Of course, I was late for the first class, between traffic and not being able to find a parking space, but I finally made it and settled in to learn something.

The first thing I learned was that the book, which my employer's benefit would not cover, was going to cost over a hundred dollars. The budget in my head started churning, as I calculated these additional costs. As the professor explained what would be expected of us in the course, I realized that I would need more than one night a week to study and prepare assignments. Oh, boy, I wondered, how would I explain to my kids that we would have to give up more of the little time we had together? Just how long was this going to take, I wondered further, realizing that I had not really thought through what I was doing, and what I was hoping to get out of either this class or a degree. Even more homework, I realized. Maybe I had been too impulsive, (yet again!) and bitten off more than I could chew.

As the professor talked about what he said was going on in healthcare, I also realized with a shock that he did not seem to have any real-world understanding of the industry. I kept that to myself, though, figuring that there must be other things I could learn about management theory and stuff I had no idea about yet. But when it came time for a break, I could tell from what some of my classmates were saying that others felt the same way. The next day, I decided to be impulsive again—or at least take some time to evaluate before spending any more time or money—and dropped the course. I really had to figure out what I needed to do and what my options were before I committed to something that could take longer to complete than my marriage had lasted.

I started by doing some research at the library. While Mark and Missy searched for information for a class project on Peru, I reviewed the reference material on college degrees and jobs in healthcare management. Although there were a few good programs mentioned in the guides, all of them were too far away. That is when I noticed a book about getting a degree without going to class. Intrigued, I began to learn about programs that allow students to complete coursework at a distance, without ever going to class or finding a parking space. Excited, I used the library's Internet connection to request further information from a few of the schools mentioned.

It seemed to take forever, but when the information arrived, I read through all of it. It seemed as though it would be something I could do, even though I was not quite sure how it was done. The next step was to clear the coursework with my employer, if I wanted that benefit. I had been in healthcare too long not to know the importance of prior approvals!

Sherrie looked a little concerned, but when she looked up the policy, it only said that coursework had to be taken at a regionally accredited institution. "Just be sure of that," she told me, "and we will reimburse your tuition costs after you prove you have passed." I was not quite sure what accreditation meant, but made a note to check each college. There were still other costs, I already knew, like books and an Internet connection. At least I already had a computer, and would not have to pay for commuting costs or childcare. Just to be sure that I was on the right track, I asked for job descriptions fitting the kinds of jobs I would be qualifying for, and decided to discuss my plans with my own supervisor, Joan.

"So you want my job, huh?" Joan joked when I outlined my plan. She gave me some tips, told me about some of her own college experiences, and said that she was glad to know I was taking this step to improve my situation. "Let me know how it is going. I have been thinking about distance education for a master's degree." As she shared a hilarious experience on the pitfalls of night school, I began to feel a warm glow and the certainty that I could accomplish this goal, because I had the support of others and a desire to move ahead. It felt good.

Learner Profile

Brad: Trying to Get Ahead

I guess I was luckier than some of my coworkers, because I had the opportunity to complete a bachelor's degree right after high school. It was actually pretty easy, too, once I had figured out that no one was going to stand over me to make sure I got things done. That, and that it was really hard to sit through class when I had a raging hangover. For me, college was as much about growing up as it was about getting an education.

So anyway, I did well enough. Even though I really did not know what I wanted to do, I knew I wanted to make a good living. My dad kept telling me that I should take a year or two off before I went to college—that some real-world experience would help me make a decision—but I did not want to get left behind when all my friends went off to school. You know, at that age it was all about your friends, anyway, not what your parents wanted. They were supportive, though, even if they could not afford a lot.

I went to a state school because in high school sports were more important to me than grades, so I did not qualify for a scholarship at a private school. But my grades got much better once I straightened up. And I really liked being in college, surrounded by other people who were as clueless as I was, and having fun anyway. I played some intramural sports, but when it came to choosing a career path, I knew I did not have what it takes to make it as a professional. Most of the courses I took were fine, but I liked working with computers best, so that is what I majored in. I thought that would be a good way to get a decent job. When I think about how uninformed my planning process was then, I have to laugh. Well, I did say we were all clueless, did I not?

My school had an internship program, so I got to work in a large computer company, which was a great introduction to what work was really like. Other than lifeguarding in the summers, I had no work experience at all, because all of my nonschool hours had been taken up with sports. Boy, was that a wake-up call. But I found that I really liked accomplishing things, especially the feeling I got when the program I had written worked flawlessly. I guess they liked me, too, because I was offered a position in the IS department before school ended. So there I was, on graduation day, with the traditional graduation car, a new job, and my life ahead of me. It was hard to think that life could get any better.

After about six months on the job, I began to really notice little problems here and there. I may be a jock but, hey, I am not stupid. I saw that the same problems kept coming up over and over again, and that no one seemed interested in fixing them. Like the workarounds that had evolved to provide accounting with end-of-month reports. I could see that there were much easier ways of querying the database, but no one seemed to care. When I brought it up, I just got these disgusted looks. When I mentioned that I could try writing a program to make the process more efficient, my supervisor said , "You do not understand how complex the system is," but what I heard was "Do not make waves." It was frustrating.

But I kept on with my work. It really was not bad; the people I worked with were pleasant, the work was not especially difficult, and the commute was easy. Even with all the positives, though, I began to feel that I could do more. And, it seemed, every day I saw more evidence that confirmed my growing suspicion that I was allowing myself to get behind in a fast-moving industry. I decided that it was time to think about going back to school.

I recognized that if I wanted to make things happen, instead of just taking orders, I would have to get a management position. And in the computer industry, that meant MBA. So I started looking around at the programs in my area and found that most of the classes were in the evening. Big problem, because if there was going to be a problem in IS, Murphy's Law kicks in and the worst problems happen at the worst possible times. I just could not count on having a solid schedule. It did not take a rocket scientist to figure out that if I was working all day, spending evenings in class, and some problem came up at night, it would not be long before either the job or the schoolwork would suffer. I was not sure what to do.

Then, one morning while I was riding in to work, I saw an ad for a distance MBA and thought, "Perfect!" No set class times would let me work when it was convenient to me, and because I was comfortable with technology, anything that came up would be easy to fix. Or at least I hoped so, I thought, remembering how simple some of the worst problems had seemed—at first. Filing that thought away, I decided to find out about available on-line MBA programs.

As soon as I had a free moment, I ran an Internet search for on-line MBA programs. Boy, was that a mistake! I expected a handful of programs to turn up, but I got at least a hundred! It was really confusing, and the more I read, the more confused I got. Maybe I was being dumb, but I had just thought I could fill out an application and some other paperwork and get going. And here most of the schools wanted an entrance exam, the GMAT. I hate taking tests to prove that I know something. I have always been one of those people who does things pretty much on his own, but it was starting to look like I was going to need some help with this. Maybe this is not as easy as I thought it would be.

Rather than get depressed over it, I went to the gym, where it is easier for me to think. While I was there, I ran into Karen, a friend who I remembered had been talking about on-line grad school awhile back. I asked her how it was going, and asked if it was hard. She laughed, "You know, deciding where to go and getting in was the hardest part," she said, then leaned toward me, and got serious. "Actually, Brad, I feel like I am learning more, because it is, like, always there. The on-line classes are not bad, but they are not as easy as I thought they would be. But the hardest part is finding time to get all the work done!"

She went on to tell me about how she had just finished a group project with people who lived on the other side of the country. "I really have to stay on top of everything because people post messages at all hours. I find myself thinking about it a lot, too, and feel like I am sneaking at work when I check to see what messages have been added since the last time I looked." It sounded a little strange to me, but she seemed really happy about it.

Karen told me about a few books she took out of the library, and that there was one especially for helping prepare for the GMAT. It looked like I was going to have to take the test if I wanted to go any further, unless I could find a school that did not require it!

To Sum Up. . .

We will hear more from Greg, Ellen, and Brad later and throughout the text, charting their own learning journeys. Before we move on though, let us review what you have learned about yourself so far in relation to distance learning.

In this chapter, you discovered just what teachers mean when they say they want their students to be self-reliant. All of the attributes of a self-reliant learner were examined, so you know whether you are ready to be successful right now. If not, you have an idea which specific attributes you will need to pay particular attention to.

You will also have found that much of the literature about adult learning and self-reliance is the result of research in developmental and educational psychology. If this subject is interesting to you, you may wish to review some of the additional resources provided from the Online Resources site. You can access that site by pointing your browser to <www.delmar.com>.

Notes to Yourself

Did you recognize many of the self-reliance skills in the stories of Greg, Ellen, and Brad? Which one of the three is closest to the kind of person you are? Can you predict how they will do in their educational explorations?

We will hear more from them later. Right now, you may want to make notes here on other topics you may want to follow up on, or anything else you may want to remember about your learning journey:

_____

_____

_____

CHAPTER 6

The Technical Connection—Requirements and Skills for Distance Learning

"Any sufficiently advanced technology is indistinguishable from magic."

—*Arthur C. Clarke*

Obviously, if you want to utilize a computer and the Internet to engage in educational activities, a basic technical requirement will apply to allow you to access information and participate in on-line activities. So, one of the first things you will need to do is be sure that the equipment you have is equal to the task. To determine this, you must ask yourself two questions:

- Can I connect to the Internet at a reasonable speed? and
- Do I have the ability to work with the software once I am connected?

The World Wide Web has had an impact on the way we communicate, do business, and obtain information. It has had a profound influence on the practice of education. But, in order for you to actually participate in on-line learning, there are additional requirements.

BASIC TECHNICAL REQUIREMENTS

Every educational provider will list the minimum technical requirements for participation in courses on their Web site. This will include requirements for computers and connection speeds. This is usually a clearly marked link from the home page, and may look like this:

- Computer : IBM compatible 486/33 (Pentium preferred) with Windows 5.1 operating system or higher (Windows 95 or 98 preferred), or Macintosh 7.1 operating system or higher; 16 MB of RAM; and 20 MB of free hard-drive space or higher
- Disk drive—one 3.5 inch
- Modem—28.8 bps or above

- Web browser that handles frames, tables, and Javascript. (Netscape 3.0, Internet Explorer 4.0 or above)
- Internet and World Wide Web access through an Internet service provider (ISP)

In addition, it is very helpful to have a printer, so that you can download and print assignments and make hard copies of papers for revision away from your desk. Otherwise, you will have to put whatever materials you want to print onto a floppy disk, take it to work or a copier store, and pay the per-page fee. Also, your e-mail program should allow attachments, for when you want to submit word-processed documents. All of the most popular current e-mail programs do, but if you are connecting from work or using a free e-mail service, you will want to check to be sure that you can utilize this time-saving option.

In most cases, unless your computer is five or more years old, you will have more than enough speed and memory to take care of any on-line learning tasks. Any improvements to the minimum requirements will speed connections and generally make life easier. There are ways to check these things, of course.

GETTING THE TECHNOLOGY YOU NEED

If your computer and/or ISP do not meet these minimum requirements, or if you do not own a computer, there are several things you can do. If you do not own one

Using an old computer can be risky. If your equipment does not meet the suggested minimums to undertake a school's program, download times will be lengthy and frustrating, and you may not be able to utilize all features of the on-line class.

If you are not sure that your system meets stated minimums, you can check your owner's manual (if you can find it). Otherwise, for PCs running the Windows operating system, here is how you can check speeds and specifics:

1. Click on the 'Start' menu and choose 'Control Panel'.
2. To check system and speed, choose 'System'. A window will open, showing the operating system installed (for example, Windows 98), processor (for example, Pentium®) and RAM (random access memory).
3. To check modem speed, choose 'Modem' from the Control Panel window. A window will show the kind of modem being used. Click 'Properties' to see the maximum speed of the modem.

and are not sure about whether you really want a computer at home, you can still try on-line learning.

Most public libraries now provide free access to the Internet, as well as computer use for word processing and other tasks. Of course, on-line use may be subject to time limitations, so that others can be assured of availability. You may have to take breaks from connecting so that others may use the equipment. The library offers ample space to study quietly and many of the print resources you may need. Help is usually available, as well. Check this option if a good library is convenient to you.

Another option to consider would not require frequent travel to a library. You may be able to connect to on-line classes from work, if your employer allows. Be sure to clear the use of company resources before undertaking your study. You may find that you can be a leader for others who are considering distance learning, too.

If you were just waiting for a reason to purchase a computer, or to upgrade the one you currently own, you probably already know that computer technology is becoming more and more inexpensive. Systems that possess far beyond the minimum capacities described above are available for less than a thousand dollars, and the cost is dropping almost daily. If you do decide to purchase a new computer, you will be better off to purchase the best machine you can afford. This may not be the fastest, or the most gadget laden, but the one that best meets the needs of the person or people who will be using it. If you are not sure how to make the decision about which model and what features to purchase, you can pick up one of the many guides that walk you through the forest of acronyms and numbers. Or, you can opt for a seminar at the local community college, where a knowledgeable person is available when you have questions. Do not rely only on the advice of salespeople, who can receive commissions based on the brands they sell. And do not listen just to cousin Joe the programmer or your teenager, either. They will have different requirements than you will. Just as if you were researching the purchase of a car, look for the features you need, do your homework, and your result will be a satisfactory one.

Choosing Internet Services

Just as you may need to research and then purchase a new computer, you may need to subscribe to an Internet service so that you can connect to your virtual classroom. These are available in a wide variety of formats, from free services to ones costing more than $20 per month. Review what the providers offer. Free Internet service does come with a price. Because advertisers essentially pay for the service you receive, you can be inundated with advertisements that can make your educational work extremely tedious.

Be aware of 'bundling,' which can seem to be a savings, but is usually quite costly in the long run. An example of bundling is the sale of a computer at a 'discount' if you also purchase an Internet service agreement. Although this can appear to be a good deal, the service offered is almost always more costly per month than others that are easily available elsewhere. Such deals can also require a long-term, iron-clad contract. Therefore, any savings you may have realized at time of purchase will quickly be eaten up in service fees later.

Focus, instead, on what you *need* in a service provider, and then look at price. It is probably wise to consider only those services that provide unlimited connection time. Internet connection service is not always sold on a monthly subscription basis. You may be able to save money by purchasing an annual plan. Again, be sure to choose a plan that works for you. If you are limited to a set number of hours per month, be aware of the overrun fees. On-line classes can require a great deal of connection time for you to satisfactorily complete all message reading, posting, and research requirements. You do not want to be worrying about how many minutes you have used. Similarly, as all ISPs will tell you, your dial-up connection, the phone number that your computer's modem uses to access the Internet, may not be a local one. If it is not, those phone bills will add up very quickly! To save money, be sure that your dial-up access number is a local one, or any savings you realize for service will be eaten up in connection charges.

E-mail services are generally included in Internet provider services. So, your e-mail address will largely be determined by the service provider you choose. This is not a change of address you will want to make too often, if you can help it. Be sure to factor in the amount of time it will require to let everyone know of a change in your e-mail address. If you are the kind of person who changes phone companies or credit cards frequently to get the best deals, however, you might be likely to change ISPs often, as well. If so, you may wish to think ahead and secure an e-mail forwarding service, also called a redirect service. These allow you to maintain one e-mail address and reroute messages whenever your service changes. You can even use this service to forward messages to another mail account when you are on the road. One of the oldest e-mail redirect services is Bigfoot, but there are many others out there.

Be sure to base your decision on the features you think you and your family will need and use for some time into the future. Is it likely that your children will use the Internet for homework? Will you use it to plan vacations, check local traffic, or access your team's scores? Will you be prone to avoid lines and aggravation by shopping on-line? Do you have a large extended family that can use e-mail to keep in touch? Do you want to have a family Web page, where you can display pictures and cite accomplishments (including your on-line learning triumphs)? Even if you do not know the answers to all of these questions now, you can choose an ISP that can grow with you.

In addition to print resources, there are many sites on the Internet that furnish comparisons of providers, computers, and anything else you may want to shop for. These are called recommendation services. One example of such a recommendation service on the Internet is C-Net <www.cnet.com> for recommendations in print, a popular example to consult is *Consumer Reports* magazine. Be sure to pay attention to any customer service issues, too. An ISP that provides on-line training manuals and no customer service line waits is much easier to deal with than one that does not. It is not all about price!

Speeding Tickets

On the highway, there is a limit to the speed you may drive. On the Internet, the higher the speed, the better. But there are several issues that may *prevent* you from speeding. You should be aware that the speed with which you connect and

Keep connection costs down by:

- using an unlimited-minute connection plan,
- choosing an ISP with a local dial-up number,
- looking for the features you need, now and later, and doing your research!

manipulate information across the Internet will be limited to the lowest speed on the system. This is similar to the adage about the chain being no stronger than its weakest link. For example, you may access your dial-up connection with a 56K modem, but if your Internet service provider uses 28.8K connections, that is the maximum speed at which information can pass between you and the rest of the world.

The speed of the system can also be affected by the number of people using it at any one time, so it is helpful—and less stressful—to be aware of your ISP's busiest times. For example, I can always tell when the teenagers in my local calling area get home from school in the afternoon, because traffic on my home dial-up connection becomes very slow as the kids begin to interact and do research for their own homework!

You can connect at much higher speeds with a cable modem, although this may not be available in your area. Additional hardware—a cable modem, ethernet card, and access to the cable line—is required. If you hope to connect using a cable modem instead of a dial-up connection, you should know that there are lowest-speed rules in effect here, as well. The number of users on the cable system at a time will have an effect on transmission times, although the difference may seem negligible if you are used to a dial-up modem connection. Availability and costs will also vary widely from one area to another, with services generally beginning in range of $40 per month.

As you can see, having a fast connection or a zippy computer may not translate into quick downloads. And, as you probably already realized, getting ready technologically to undertake on-line learning can require almost as much forethought and study as preparing mentally and academically. Still, thousands of people do it every day, and you can too.

So far, we have discussed accessing the Internet and learning opportunities primarily from your home, using the Internet. This is not the only technology for delivering educational material, however. Educational and training options at your workplace may be provided through the company **intranet.** Here, instead of utilizing the World Wide Web to reach learning materials across distances, training is stored on and accessed from private servers owned or leased by your company.

Because learners are connecting to an internal network, connection speeds are usually far quicker. The material housed on an intranet is not accessible to the general public, unless a line has been made available for that purpose. This makes it safe from hacker attacks. Intranets can be configured to include a wide range of media that may be difficult to access with a home dial-up connection, such as full-motion video and high-resolution graphics.

Many companies place training materials on in-house servers to allow their employees 'just in time' access to company information. This information can be easily updated and changed as necessary by internal information technology or human resources personnel. In this way, employers can provide training and other necessary information on demand, saving time and steps. Does your company use its intranet to its fullest advantage?

GETTING READY TO SURF THE LEARNING WAVE

Although this text presumes that you have the basic skills required to navigate your way around the Internet, we can all benefit from learning more about this expanding universe. If you feel that your confidence would be increased by taking a classroom-based course at your local continuing education center, by all means, have fun! If a project is one of the requirements of such a class, you might even use your search for a learning program to kill two birds with one stone! However, were you aware that a number of excellent tutorials are available on-line for no more than the price of Internet access? (Remember that you will need to have Internet access to take courses on-line.) Tutorials are listed on the Online Resources Web site, and even include one site that provides an interactive skills test and free competency certificate. At the Online Resources site, you will also find links to tutorials to help you get the most out of e-mail, learn about e-commerce, design your own Web site, and become comfortable with all of the connectivity options the Internet and World Wide Web have to offer.

HOW SEARCHING THE 'NET WORKS

Actually doing research and searching the Internet for materials to help you complete course requirements is covered in depth in Chapter 14, where skills for on-line and library-based research are discussed. However, you will find that distance learning, or any educational pursuit, will follow more than one path. Paths will overlap and your learning will be *iterative*, in that you will find different ways to say things and build upon what has gone before.

Much of the information on the Internet is redundant, in that echoes of related material—or even exactly the same material—can be found in many places, with many distinct paths winding between and around them. You will find, then, that when you access any of the Internet tutorials listed in the Online Resources Web site, many of them will also include sections on how to search the Internet. You will find out quickly that there is so much to know that you can not know everything. It will be necessary for you to decide exactly how much information you really need to satisfactorily answer the questions you have.

You will also notice that, despite the overwhelming number of sites encompassing the Internet, several sites answer almost all the questions you might have about a specific topic. These will also be the ones that other sites will continually refer to. It will not take too long to come to the conclusion that you will need to structure your Internet searches to be effective. Luckily, this is not difficult to learn. Knowing how search tools work will help you to configure your on-line searches more effectively. So, what does happen?

Searches are transacted with the use of **search engines,** on-line tools that sift through literally millions of Web sites in seconds to find material that matches the criteria you have established. It is important to be clear and focused in your searches, so that you do not receive thousands of unrelated **hits.** (A hit is a single Web site given in response to your query.) However, you should be sure not to make your criteria so focused that you miss important material.

Another way not to miss important material is not to rely on just one search engine. After all, you would not expect to use just one tool to build a house, would you? Each tool has a specific job, and it is useful to know how each works. So, because different search engines work in different ways, it is a good idea to regularly try different ones.

The term "search engine" is often used generically to include all the ways that searches are conducted on the Web. But how listings are compiled varies from one tool to another. This can make a tremendous difference in the reliability of the material you receive. For example, the Yahoo® search engine is run by indexing. This means that people are employed to research Web sites and rank them with words that relate to their content. When you *post a query* (ask a question), a list of sites indexed under that word appears. Each site is a 'hit'. The search engine Google®, on the other hand, works automatically. When you post a query, the software returns a list of results that indicate the strength of the relationship between the sites shown based on how many people who entered your word also visited those sites. This is referred to as a "relevance indicator."

Search engines have three major elements: the spider or crawler, the index, and the search engine software. The spider visits a Web page and reads it, also following any links that are in it. Then it returns information to the index, which actually copies everything that the spider finds. Finally, the search engine software combs through all of the material in the index to find and rank matches to a posted query based on the logic that has been programmed into it.

Different search sites use different ways of searching. Some search all of the text in a page, some only parts, such as the header materials. Other search engines look just for titles in HTML code, the programming language that Internet browser software 'reads'. These titles are inserted into the site's programming to increase the likelihood of a hit. Programming not visible to your eye, but seen by the search engine you use, can be inserted in the title to help assure that the page is viewed by certain engines, even if the site is something completely unrelated to your search criteria. This is why you may receive pages devoted to 'Pamela Anderson', even if you asked for pages about 'Germany'.

There are all sorts of search criteria and different search engines that use them to find references to the word or phrase you enter in the request box. Every search engine site also includes tips for searching effectively on that site. This is a good area to investigate, as it will help make the most of your time on that site. Here are a few of the most popular search engines and their Web site addresses. You will find that each looks and acts just a little (or a lot) differently. Try each one, and remember to keep trying different search technology so that you do not miss important new information.

- Google™–<www.google.com>
- Metacrawler®–<www.metacrawler.com>
- Microsoft Network–<www.msn.com>
- InFind™–<www.infind.com>
- Ask Jeeves™–<askjeeves.com>

Which of the listed search engines do you like, and why? You may want to bookmark your favorite search sites for easy access. If you are not sure how to bookmark sites, this will be covered within the next few pages.

Another good source of information about search engines, including reviews, user tips, and update information can be found at Search Engine Watch <www.searchenginewatch.com>. This link, and other links to search engines and their usage, can also be found at the Online Resources Web site, where you can click directly there without entering the address in your browser's address window.

SEARCHING FOR LEARNING

Although the tutorials provide information and assistance so that you can be comfortable trying all aspects of navigation on the Internet, they are general and not specifically directed at you, the on-line learner. As there are differences between reading for pleasure and for learning, there are differences between searching for fun and searching directed at a learning objective. The latter type of searching requires a greater focus, more concentration, and better organization than the

Search terms can be interpreted in many ways. 'Adult' learning can also return 'adult' matter with sexual content. Be sure to phrase your search terms carefully!

former. This applies to the way you organize the information you find, as well. Review the following tips to help you make the most of your browser, whether searching or organizing what you have found.

The most important search tip is to *write down what you searched for*. This may seem a little too basic, but once you have found a great site, you do not want to lose it. Sure, you can bookmark a site, but how did you get there in the first place? Which combination of words and phrases did you use? With something like seven million Web pages being posted *every day*, how will you know if you have missed something new once that particular combination is forgotten? To help you remember, you might want to keep a special section in your notebook just for search criteria, engines used, and links followed. To make it easier, you can use the Search Reminder Worksheet (Figure 6–1), located in this section (and again in the appendix) to keep track of the searches you conduct. Copy the form as many times as you need to keep track of searches for classwork or other information-gathering exercises.

Try a Search

Why not take the time, right now, to try out a few searches and see what you come up with? This will be a good illustration of how search engines can differ, and will give you the opportunity to decide which ways you prefer your information organized. You can use the Search Reminder Worksheet, if you wish, but it is not necessary for this exercise. Follow this process:

1. First, log on to the Internet.
2. Choose a search engine to use from the list above.
3. Enter a word, phrase, or question (if you chose Ask Jeeves™).
4. Press 'Search', 'Go,' or 'Ask'.

You will receive a list of 'hits' based on the criteria you selected. Forget, for the time being, about whether the list you received was too long or short. Keep the list and continue, as follows:

1. Open a new browser window (File/New/New Window).
2. In the address bar, insert the URL of one of the other search engines.

To tile windows in any IBM-compatible PC,

1. Place your cursor in the blank space on the bar at the very bottom of your screen.
2. Right-click the mouse.
3. Choose 'Tile Windows Vertically' from the list of commands.
4. To resume a single screen, choose the 'maximize' icon in the upper left corner.

 Two excellent tutorials on Boolean logic and searches can be found on the Internet at:
<florin.syr.edu/webarch/searchpro/booleantutorial.html>, and
<www.albany.edu/library/internet/boolean.html>
These are also accessible from the Online Resources Web site.

FIGURE 6-1

Search Reminder Worksheet

Date _____   Subject/Course _____

Search criteria	Engine used	Useful results (URLs, X bookmarks)

3. Perform the EXACT search as you did in the first one.
4. Compare the lists. (To compare them simultaneously, tile the windows. See the box for directions on tiling windows.)

What happened? Were the results different? How were they different? Did your searches reveal what you were expecting? Were you too specific, or not specific enough? You probably can see from just this short illustration, that it is important to be precise. So, before just entering in a word or phrase, *think about exactly what information you are looking for.*

If, for example, you are interested in finding methods for training your dog to play baseball, searching just under 'dogs' will result in an overwhelming array of information, most of it unrelated to your search. Instead, you may need to enter your request in Boolean terms, that is, using AND, OR, NOT, and specific punctuation.

A search for information, using Boolean terms, on how to train your dog to play baseball may look like: "dogs" and (baseball). This could give you a good line on the method you want, but you might also get the page for the 'Diamond Dogs' baseball team. However, these criteria may be too focused to find the Web site that contains a really good method to teach your dog to play catch, a baseball fundamental. So, you might want to try search terms like: "dog" and (play). It may be better to make your search more encompassing, but still not overwhelming.

Learning to search effectively will take experimentation and practice, but do not be discouraged. Every search you do will teach you something. The cumulative learning will not only make you a better searcher on the Internet, it will also make you better equipped to organize the information that confronts you in the world beyond the Internet.

BOOKMARKS AND FAVORITES

If you do not know how to add a site to your list of favorites (Microsoft Explorer™) or bookmarks (Netscape Navigator™), the next steps will be impossible! So let us take a minute to go over how it is done. If you can, right now access the Internet and type in the site **URL** (uniform resource locator), the unique Web site address for the Online Resources Web site, <www.delmar.com>.

Look around a bit, if you like. The Online Resource site contains links to many other resources on the Web. Choose one to visit. When you find a site you would like to come back to later, choose one of the following *three* ways to add it to your computer's memory:

One way to retain a website in memory is:

1. When the site appears, click the Bookmark or Favorites icon.
2. Scroll to 'Add Bookmark' and select.
3. The site will now be added to the bottom of your bookmark list.

Or, another way is:

1. While the site is showing on your screen, *right-click* anywhere on the page.
2. Choose "Bookmark this Site" from the drop-down menu that appears.

Or, finally, try:

While on the page you want to save, select File/Save from the taskbar.

Any of these methods will add the site's URL to your bookmarks or favorites list. It is so easy that, pretty soon, you could be overrun with bookmarks. That is why it is important to know how to organize what you have saved.

Organize, Organize

You can organize your bookmarks or favorites (named depending on which browser you use) into folders. You probably do it already for your e-mail and the documents you produce, but many of us do not manage our bookmarks as rigorously as we do our other documents.

Of course, many people do not care to bookmark a large number of sites. But many people are not about to learn on-line, as you are. During the course of a study program, it is likely that you will search for and bookmark many more sites than you would under 'nonschool' conditions. This can create an information minefield, full of hidden knowledge that is not readily accessible. As a result, you waste time searching through and opening bookmarks to find the special one you 'just know is there somewhere'.

You can think about how you will organize your system before the folders are made, or reshuffle as needed. Whether you delineate by topic, class number, or some other organizing principle, make sure that the system you decide upon makes sense to you. In that way, you can easily find what you have stored.

Next, make a plan to periodically review your folders and add or delete as necessary. The easiest way may be to set aside a time every week to spend a few minutes organizing everything, including bookmarks. Most of us do this too infrequently but, like weeding the garden or following a fitness regimen, a few minutes of regularly scheduled information handling helps keep you in control and your study healthy. This will also make it less likely that you become overwhelmed with the sheer quantity of material you have identified as helpful. This regular exercise (pun intended) will also reduce your educational stress and help you to stick with your hectic schedule by eliminating unnecessary research time when you already have sufficient material to complete assignments.

Renaming Bookmarks/Favorites

You may have noticed that the titles of bookmarks do not always reflect the content of the site they refer to. When that is the case, you can rename them to make it easier for you to remember what they are without having to open them.

All browsers have the capacity to rename Web pages you have filed as bookmarks, although the way to do it is slightly different in each browser. This process will *not* change the URL, only the way it is named on your computer. In this way, you can change a hard-to-remember address like <www.umc.edu/~smith/help212.htm> to 'My favorite Internet tips'.

After clicking on the bookmark/favorite icon on your browser's task bar, you can change the name by choosing 'Edit Bookmark (or Favorites'). This will display a list of your saved URLs. (It is in this view that you can also make folders and

Regular bookmark reorganization will also help to avoid saving the same site multiple times.

move bookmarks from one to another using standard 'cut and paste' shortcuts, or choose to delete them.)

To change the name, follow these steps:

1. Highlight the bookmark by clicking on it.
2. *Right-click* and choose 'Properties' from the drop-down menu that appears.
3. An edit box will appear, in which you can change the name. It will already be highlighted for you.
4. Type your changes.
5. Add any notes you wish in the comments box (for example, 'Sue thinks this is the best recipe for pumpkin pie').
6. Click 'OK'.

The bookmark will now show the name you have given it. Was that not easy?

Other Ways to Find Saved Pages

Even the best intentions sometimes get left behind when there is too much to do. You may not remember the name of the Web site you saved, but you know you need it *now*. All is not lost. If you have an idea of at least one of the words in the bookmark, or other information, try the steps below:

1. Click the Bookmarks icon and choose 'Edit Bookmarks'.
2. Open the Edit menu and choose 'Find in Bookmarks'.
3. Type in the word(s) you are looking for.
4. Click checkboxes to narrow your search. ('Location' refers to words in the URL.)
5. Click OK.

You may also wish to reorganize the bookmarks momentarily in the 'View' menu, if you can not remember the name, but have an idea when you found it or last visited it.

1. Click the Bookmark icon, then 'Edit Bookmarks'.
2. Click 'View' and choose 'By Created'.
3. The list will be reorganized by date.
4. Click 'By Name' to return the list to its previous organization.

These steps will help keep you from having to search through everything in your folder to find just one item. Additional tips and user tricks can be found right in your browser's 'Help' file. Look there first for help specific to the software installed on your computer.

More Help Is Just a Click Away

Perhaps you already know a great deal about how to use the Internet; perhaps you just need help with, say, advanced search techniques. We do not devote a large

---

To manage your saved information:

- Write down what you searched for.
- Organize your bookmark/favorites into folders.
- Periodically review your folders and add or delete as necessary.
- Know what the titles of bookmark/favorites refer to.

section here to Internet navigation and Web search skills, because everyone's level of skill is different. If you need assistance on a specific skill or set of skills, choose the tutorials and tip sheets that correspond to your own needs from the large number available at the Online Resources Web site. You can find it at <www.delmar.com>.

To Sum Up. . . .

In this chapter, the technical requirements and processes for getting around on-line were reviewed, including the equipment you will need to participate in this growing educational delivery method. We discussed what you will need and what you need to be aware of in making equipment and service choices.

We spent some time in this chapter discussing how search tools work and how you can use them effectively. After that, we tried some of the popular search engines and noted how they can respond differently. We reviewed some of the ways to keep track of the vast resources on the Internet and pointed to other places where you can find help.

You may feel overwhelmed now, but with a little practice, searching and managing the vast array of information available to you will become as natural as breathing. Well, almost. At least there is always help available at the Online Resources Web site, <www.delmar.com>. Visit the site often for new ways to search for the information you need.

Notes to Yourself

Now that you have an idea of the kind of learner you are and can be, and the technical requirements for becoming an on-line distance learner, it is time to move on to the next section. There, you will find out what possibilities exist to help you meet your educational goals. You will also find resources to help you define the education that you want and then find the school that can give it to you. The questions that you have about distance learning will be addressed, as well as those questions you should ask that you may not yet know about. It is all straight ahead. And specific help is always available, day or night, at the Online Resources Web site, by accessing <www.delmar.com>.

You may want to create a bookmark/favorite file called "Success in On-Line Learning" for copying the sites you like best, or you may want to note them here:

_____

_____

_____

Know the Possibilities

This section provides information that will help you make informed choices among educational providers and programs. In this section, you will learn what to ask and where to look to find the facts you need to make a competent educational selection.

The chapters in this section are:

PREVIEW

In this section, you will learn what you need to consider before choosing a distance learning program that is right for you. Depending upon your situation at this moment, and the responsibilities you have to consider, you probably have many questions. Because there are many possible issues to consider, and many possible questions *you* may have, the information in this section takes the form of several sections of **Frequently-Asked Questions (FAQs).** The first group of questions is specific to on-line learning. The next group of FAQs deals with questions that first-time college students may have, and the final group pertains to issues and concerns for those returning to college after a break of a few or many years' duration.

Statistics compiled by the National Center for Education Statistics and the U.S. Department of Education indicate that most adults who consider distance learning are more interested in upgrading their skills to maintain currency in their present occupations than they are in seeking a degree. That may be *your* current goal, but you are not a statistic, and your goals and aspirations may not fit neatly into current statistical studies. Keep in mind that your situation may change, and questions you skip over now may be a higher priority later.

If you find that your question is not addressed in any of these sections, be sure to visit the Online Resources Web site, where you will be able to post your questions and view questions—and answers—posted by others. In addition, throughout this section you will find checklists that will help to make your search for a learning provider simple and organized by prompting you to ask and record the answers to questions that you *should* ask before you commit your time and money to a particular program.

The FAQ sections will be followed by sections exploring the important issue of accreditation and the financial aspects of completing a learning project, whether or not it leads to a degree. After looking at these credential and financial considerations, the text will outline the different methods for receiving credit for learning acquired outside of the classroom, an area of great interest for many adults who know that valuable learning can be a product of work or life experiences.

The final chapter in this section will present concrete tips for choosing an educational provider using the new information you have gained in the earlier parts of the section. Like other sections of this text, this section will be supplemented by Web-based information accessible from the Online Resources Web site, available at <www.delmar.com>.

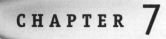

CHAPTER 7

Questions Distance Learners Should Ask

Anyone who considers something for the first time—especially something as relatively new as distance learning—is likely to have many questions. In fact, it would be cause for concern if you did not! Listed below are some of the most frequently-asked questions about distance learning. The Online Resources Web site also provides links to question and answer lists that are available on-line. These are produced by and often specific to individual institutions.

Who uses on-line learning?

All kinds of people access on-line learning, from college students who want to "beef up" their basic skills to business executives who need to gain training or credentials. People can choose to learn new skills, such as a programming language, or an entire degree. There are non-credit and credit-bearing educational opportunities available on-line for all ages and abilities, from grade school through postgraduate degrees. More is available literally every day.

Why should I consider on-line learning?

Anyone who cannot commit to a regular schedule may consider a course or an entire program on-line. You might also choose distance learning if you need to meet degree prerequisites, want to accelerate degree completion, or complete courses not available locally. You might choose distance learning if you travel extensively for business or are stationed overseas during a military assignment. You might choose distance learning to gain personal enrichment and satisfaction or to prepare for a second career.

"The person who knows "how" will always have a job. The person who knows "why" will always be his boss."

—Diane Ravitch

What kind of personal characteristics will influence my success?

In Chapter 3, you will have determined whether you are likely to be a good candidate for distance learning. To reiterate, people who have been successful in the past have at least some of the following characteristics:

- academic and emotional maturity,
- specific goals,
- the ability to work unsupervised,
- the capacity for self-starting, self-understanding and self-motivation,
- persistence,
- patience,
- self-confidence,
- reading and writing ability,
- contacts who can help with content problems, and
- an academic support system (at home or at work).

See the On-line Learning Self-Assessment form in Chapter 3 (an extra copy can be found in the appendix) to help you identify the areas you should consider before you enroll in any classes. This self-assessment exercise will help you avoid frustrating and time-wasting experiences by giving you a way to evaluate yourself before you commit to a course of study.

What degrees can I pursue?

You can complete a high school diploma or any of the college degrees, from an associate's (the conventional two-year) through a bachelor's (four-year), master's, or doctorate either entirely on-line or with short **residency.** Residency refers to one or several time periods when you must meet with your program group at a central location. Although you do most of your work at home, these short required meetings are designed to add depth and face-to-face interaction to your study. It is important to take residency requirements into account when choosing an educational provider. See the next question and answer section for more information about degrees.

Do I have to be pursuing a degree?

Not at all. If you are not interested in a degree, you may choose to complete one of the increasing numbers of training or certification programs available. Each program is different, and you should examine them closely to be sure that they meet your needs and goals. The Online Resources site provides links to sites that can help you find a program that matches all of your criteria.

Can I find a good distance learning provider only by looking on the Internet?

It is a good place to start, but should not be your only information source. The Internet is still unregulated, so anyone with a Web site can claim to be a university! To complicate matters, the .edu (education) domain extension on Web and e-mail addresses is not presently regulated either. To protect yourself from unscrupulous operators, carefully check all information you see. Be sure, as well, to read the section about accreditation and diploma mills later in this chapter.

Are classes impersonal?

That is a common misconception. Most learners find that once interaction with other group members begins, an on-line learning environment can be very rich and very personal. Participants often establish on-line friendships that outlast the individual class. Learners find that they are more fully drawn into the subject matter of the class because of the discussions they get involved in.

"I haven't had any trouble with learning [on-line] and I can always find help on-line, either through e-mail, chat, or other messaging systems. . . . There are so many ways to learn now. E-mail is easy and quick. Phones work, but you can save money by typing. And that's part of the reason I like on-line."

— "Diamond Lightfoot"
e-mail

How does all this work? I am not that experienced with computers!

You do not have to be too experienced with technology, or even care about it very much. As a matter of fact, it sometimes helps if you have less experience! You do usually need to have access to a properly equipped computer and the Internet. (These costs can often be included in financial aid for education, too.) Any educational provider you are considering will have information on technical requirements. See Chapter 6 for more information on technical requirements and choices.

You do not have to be a great typist, either, although it does help to be familiar with the keyboard. Even slow typists can do fine, though. This is because you can generally prepare a posting or response **off-line** (when you are not connected to your Internet service provider's network) in your word processing program. Then, you can copy and paste it into the course program. This gives you lots of time to read over and revise what you want to say.

Learner Profile, Continued

Greg chooses a path

Well, the first class went well. I decided to take a course in something I had always been interested in, instead of something more work related, so I signed up for a history class. At first, I was afraid that it would just be a lot of dry reading, but the way the class was organized was really interesting. But maybe I should back up.

Some of the information Mrs. Carter gave me included stuff from the local community college, like she said. I figured that it would be good to know my way around the campus and the library, so that even if I did not take most of my classes there, I would know where to go if I needed help. Turns out that was a good idea, but I will get to that later.

Anyway, I noticed that there was this "interactive video and Web-based course" on the Civil War. It seemed kind of funny to me to use all this technology to talk about the past, but I figured "What the heck?" After talking with the advisor and reading what he had given me, I knew I would have to have some liberal arts courses, including history, to complete my degree. So I signed up. One of the people where I worked signed up, too, so we decided to work together.

The first class was held in the campus technology center, which looked like an auditorium with a big screen. At the front of the class, the teacher had all these gizmos and a computer that projected stuff on the screen. I kept hearing voices that seemed to be coming from the computer, and looking around, I could not see where they were coming from. Then it hit me. There were students somewhere else, listening and watching along with us! It was weird, but I got used to it quickly. The teacher said we would meet there in that room only four times, and the rest of our work would be done outside of class and on the computer. He handed out a bunch of information, including directions and passwords for signing on from home. The course outline was really detailed. You could tell he had put a lot of work into it. Then, we watched a short video about the political events leading up to the Civil War. It turned out to be something that had been developed by PBS, so it was really detailed and interesting. But it certainly was not all we had to do! Before we left class, the teacher's assistant went over how to connect and what to do if we had problems, and we went home to work on assignments.

The next few weeks were really great. I had a few small problems signing on from home, but got those worked out. It turned out to be a good idea that I was going to the campus, because the reading part was really hard for me. It seemed like I would read it over and over and it just would not sink in. So I went to the learning center, and after talking with one of the counselors there, we both figured that maybe I was one of those people who learned better when I was moving around. She suggested that I tape my books and then listen to the tapes when I was walking around the shop or exercising. That turned out to do the trick. Who knew?

It also helped to have someone at work to talk to about the class, but Jack's interests were not the same as mine, so we did not end up working together too much. Still, it was good to have someone else that knew what was going on, and we could ride together to school after work on the days there was class on campus.

Everyone in the class—even the ones that were at the remote sites, as they called them—was part of an e-mail list, and we all had to participate. It was part of our grade. There was also a class Web site, where assignments and Internet links were posted by the teacher. For most of the class, we had to read the book and answer the questions posted on the Web site. I really liked reading what other people got from the homework, because it made me think about it in different ways. We were also required to comment on some of what our classmates wrote. That got a little hairy at one point, when someone wanted everyone else to agree with him. You know the type.

But the best part of the class for me turned out to be the project. We had to choose someone from the time of the Civil War and write a paper as though we were them, talking. The teacher said it might be easier to pick someone you felt you could relate to, whatever that meant. At first, I was going to pick one of the generals, but I did not feel right about that. So I started digging around on the Web. I read all these Web pages that people had worked on about their ancestors who had been in the Civil War, and decided to write my paper as though I were a regular soldier. I do not think I have ever worked so hard in my life! It was great. There was so much information, it was hard to stop. And I ended up with an 'A' in the course!

I think sometimes that Sharon wonders whether she created a monster, but I have to admit that I enjoy it as much as she said I would. I can not wait for the next class to start, and that is only a piece of the good news. The advisor at the school said that my military experience can be translated into as much as 24 credits at the state college that they have a transfer agreement with. So all that grunting and sweating will be worth even more. I am talking to the state college transfer advisor next week about that. Right now, though, I have got to get to work!

Then what? How do I 'go to class'?

Early computerized distance learning relied primarily on e-mail, but most institutions now use one of a number of integrated, browser-based courseware packages that include areas for the teacher or class leader to post questions, comments, discussion topics, contact information, and requirements. This means that the "classroom" looks like a Web page, and is "attended" by accessing a Web site address. There are usually small pictures (icons) that represent the different course areas, including class schedule, discussion area, personal information, and the like. Most on-line educational institutions have a section on their Web page that gives you a preview of what their courseware is like, sort of a "try it before you buy it."

I am hopeless with new technology. What kind of help do they give you?

Once you have chosen your course and registered for it, the institution you choose should provide an in-depth tutorial or orientation to familiarize you with the way the courseware operates. (Be sure to ask about the availability and length of tutorials and orientations when you are doing your research.) Remember, they want you to be successful, so they try to make sure that everyone understands the processes needed to complete the work. One way many schools ensure your familiarity with the technology is to *require* the completion of an orientation before you are allowed to enter the class space.

Even if you are technically savvy, because changes occur quickly in educational technology, it is wise to complete the on-line orientation before any problems pop up. Each class and institution differs, so specific instructions will vary. However, be sure to always **bookmark** your course Web site in your Web browser so you can get back to it easily.

How are the courses structured?

Many U.S. institutions still adhere to the traditional classroom structure, in which a group "meets" together for a specific length of time. This is not true of all providers, though, so you should check the schedule to see that you can fit it into your own. Some programs consist of courses in which the learners can be different for each new topic; some institutions put together a 'cohort group' of students who progress through all classes in the program together.

If you are not interested in learning with a group, you may choose to complete coursework in a one-on-one tutorial system, sometimes referred to as a mentorship. This is a model that most European on-line institutions use, primarily for graduate-level study. The primary benefit to this one-on-one structure is that you can proceed at your own pace and are not tied to other learners' or an institution's schedule. If you are highly motivated and have clear goals, this can be the quickest way to complete a degree.

How often do I have to visit the course site?

Because of its anytime, anywhere (asynchronous) nature, learners can access (visit) the course site at all hours of the day and night, whenever is convenient for them. It is not like going to class once a week! To avoid getting bogged down reading and responding to many messages at one time, it is strongly suggested that you check in at least every other day.

Some on-line packages include an option of having responses to your own postings e-mailed to you, so you will know when—and what—a classmate has responded. That way, you can think about your reply before you connect, and before you actually type and send it.

Isn't on-line coursework easier than 'regular class'?

As you may have figured out by now, the answer to that question is often an emphatic "No!" Still, many people continue to have the conception that convenience equals ease.

The majority of distance learning participants report that they find on-line classes more difficult, and much more rewarding, than traditional classes they have taken in the past. Learners are more aware of the amount of thought they give to topics and to the discussions that arise from them. They also report that a greater amount of self-discipline and planning is required.

How can I be fairly evaluated without the teacher seeing me?

Almost any form of assessment or evaluation is possible with on-line classes. Objective measurements such as traditional quizzes or tests with multiple choice

"Everything is twice as expensive, twice as hard, and takes twice as long as you think. If you're going to dabble, do it with one course, not an entire program, so if you decide it's not for you, you haven't created an immense loss."

— *Rich Douglas, e-mail*

questions or problems are used by some schools. It is even possible to take timed on-line standardized tests, which are the norm with skill-based courses. On-line testing can actually be more effective than paper and pencil tests, because it is possible to create *adaptive* tests. Here, the testing program chooses more and more complex questions based on the test taker's prior responses, so you are not forced to consider questions that waste time and are beneath your skill level.

Many on-line programs use assignments, projects, and work-related tasks that involve critical thinking, creativity, problem solving, and group discussion/interaction, which are thought to be more appropriate for adults than the more simple objective measures. Asking about the evaluation methods should be part of your research before deciding on a particular school.

How do they know I am not cheating?

This subject always comes up, and is more appropriate to the objective tests, because projects that are unique to an individual are difficult to copy, and are easier to validate from previously completed assignments. Yet, this is an issue that is seriously considered by most institutions. To minimize the possibility of cheating, tests are sometimes given in a local setting such as a regional library or study center, where they can be supervised. Ask about how tests are administered and where you might have to travel to take them as you consider your options.

What is plagiarism, and how does it apply on-line?

Plagiarism is another form of cheating often discussed in academic programs. Plagiarism is the use of another's work represented as your own. Even smart people sometimes resort to plagiarism. With the wide variety of information available with just the click of a mouse, it is easy to find material that can simply be cut and pasted into another document. But doing this without giving credit is unethical and illegal. At most educational institutions, which encourage academic honesty, proof of plagiarism can lead to dismissal. Plagiarism and how to avoid it are covered in depth in Chapter 14.

Historically, it has been difficult to detect plagiarism, but once again technology is changing the way instructors review papers. Screening software has been developed to help teachers detect and avoid plagiarism in student writing. You can try it free yourself on-line, to see if you have inadvertently copied someone else's work. The Web site address for this software is listed among the links on the Online Resources site.

Can I transfer on-line coursework into or out of other degree programs?

That depends on several things, including accreditation status of the credit you wish to transfer and your school's policies. Each school has different policies. Some schools will accept any coursework passed with a grade of C or better; some will accept only courses that are like the ones taught at that school or in the program you want. Information on transfer policies should be available in the school's catalog. The best advice is to check with both the registrar's office (who makes the general transfer decisions) and the dean of the department (say, business if you want to study accounting) you are applying to. Most schools will offer an unofficial transfer evaluation to help you make your decision. Read the section called "Accreditation and Diploma Mills" later in this chapter to understand this issue further.

Can I get credit for life experience on-line?

It is possible, but depends on many factors. Some schools, like Excelsior College (formerly Regent's College) and Thomas Edison State College (NJ), do offer programs that can include credit based on an evaluation of your experiential learning. However, you should be aware that you must almost always be seeking a degree, not just a certificate, to participate in these programs. Further, you will find that experiential learning can be applied only to certain degrees. The vast majority of these are bachelor's degree programs.

You should also be aware that these evaluations are based on academic criteria. Your learning, though important, may not be easily converted to college credit. The issues and processes surrounding **assessment of prior learning,** as it is called, are covered in depth later in Chapter 9, "Credit Where Credit is Due." You should know that you can receive credit only for documented learning that is equivalent to college-level knowledge. No evaluations are automatic, and they can require *at the very least* taking an examination to prove your mastery. Other ways of proving your understanding are discussed in Chapter 9. The Online Resources site includes links to further resources, as well.

What about financial aid?

Face it, education can be expensive. Because adult students usually study part-time, they cannot take advantage of some of the traditional financial aid resources available to full-time students. There are, however, a number of possibilities that are only available to "grown-ups" that are discussed in Chapter 10, "Financing Your Learning Journey."

OTHER QUESTIONS YOU MAY WANT TO ASK

There are many things you might want to know about an institution and the way it manages distance learning before you decide to study there. In addition to the questions listed above and in the section on accreditation and diploma mills, consider the issues addressed by the questions listed below. Before you even set "virtual" foot in class, consider your personal learning needs. How well educational institutions might meet them is your primary research task. How well institutions fit into your lifelong learning goals will determine whether or not you will succeed.

You can use the School Decision Checklist form included later in this section to prompt you when you undertake your educational exploration. Further, many

---

Advice from one who has been there:

"Adults contemplating a distance learning course of study should carefully examine their reasons for pursuing their education this way as opposed to traditional, classroom-based instruction. Some may have reasons that are solid; others may be fooling themselves.

Solid reasons include:

- The course of study I want is not available via the classroom.
- I want/need the flexibility of scheduling my own study time.
- I want to proceed at my own faster/slower pace.
- I want to move quickly through subjects I already know about.
- It is less expensive.
- I want to be able to work while studying.
- I want to incorporate my work into my studies (and vice versa).
- The credential/certificate/degree will meet my present and future needs.

—Rich Douglas, Ph.D.

of the questions listed below apply regardless of whether the program you are considering is delivered on-line or in the classroom. Some of the questions you might consider asking prospective schools include:

How are courses structured? Is there a time limit to completing each course?

The organization of traditional degree programs is based on the **semester** system, in which classes are offered during two major units. Each unit is fifteen weeks long, beginning in the fall and spring, respectively. There are often one or more supplemental, concentrated summer sessions available, as well. Among the primary reasons for the persistence of this model are issues of physical space available to teach classes in. Distance learning has removed this space barrier and allowed institutions to offer any grouping or organization of coursework, from semester-based, highly structured offerings to loosely organized, self-paced opportunities and everything in between.

Perhaps you know that you will need the structure of an organized class; perhaps you would prefer to work at your own pace. Now that you have a better idea of the requirements of distance learning, you can make your choice based on your understanding of your own needs and characteristics. If you choose to enroll in a program that is concentrated, for example, in which courses are intense and completed within five to eight weeks, be sure that this structure fits within your own schedule and abilities.

Is there a time limit to completing the entire program?

Both traditional and nontraditional (i.e., distance or off-campus) degree programs will often limit the time one has to complete all requirements. This is done to maximize financial aid efficiency and to discourage "foot dragging." It is always good to know what that time limit is, even if you plan never to exceed it.

Can I take time off if I need to?

Taking time away from an educational program can have serious ramifications. Any break should not be allowed to extend into months and years, a particularly tempting possibility when classes and classmates are 'virtual'. Keeping goals in sight helps to achieve them. Still, sometimes life events make it necessary to turn attention toward something more urgent than education. In those cases, it is important to know how to negotiate the options.

Some schools will allow you to take time away from the coursework only in extreme circumstances, and with proof of need. This is mostly to encourage learners to continue to completion unless there is an overwhelming reason not to. If you take time off without approval, you may have to reapply, including resubmitting an application essay, transcripts, and reference letters. What a pain!

If you must reapply, you would enter under the rules stated in the catalog in force at the time of reapplication. This does not, of course, apply to all schools. Institutions that work exclusively with adult students know that sometimes there are circumstances that require your complete attention and can make it easy to take a break from school. It only takes a moment to notify the appropriate people, but asking at the time that you are considering enrolling may make a difference in your choice. Think of it as a courtesy to those who are helping you attain your goals.

What are the program requirements? Do they meet my needs?

Ask about all requirements, including thesis writing, residencies, and any other work required to prove competency. Ask yourself if these requirements are within your abilities and desires. Do these requirements seem reasonable to you in light of your ambitions? Be aware, as well, of any special requirements based on the subject studied. For example, if you are learning about mainframe computers, will access to a mainframe be required?

Will the body that licenses my profession (if this applies) accept the coursework?

It is your responsibility to check with any professional associations to ascertain whether the learning you are considering will be applicable to your career goals. For your protection, be sure to get any documentation of approvals in writing.

Who teaches the classes? What credentials do they have?

The institutional items reviewed in the accreditation process include screening of academic credentials. This is important, because these are the people to whom you will be entrusting your education. Like you, the accrediting bodies want to be sure that the people who are teaching are qualified to do so. They look at the number of instructors who hold advanced degrees and whether they correspond to the topics they are teaching. One questionable area to be aware of is whether a large number of teachers or administrators hold degrees from the very school you are considering. There should be a balance of credentials throughout the organization.

How long has the program/institution been in existence?

To protect yourself from "fly-by-night" pseudoinstitutions, you should be aware of how long the college has been offering degrees, as well as how long they have had accreditation, if this is important to your goals. If the institution is well established and is offering a new program, ask how the new program was developed. At this point, you may be directed to a dean or program chair. This is an appropriate redirection, as the dean or chair, and not an admissions counselor, will have academic responsibility for the accountability of the program. Knowing the criteria that guided the development of a new program will help you assess whether this is a good choice for you.

How many students have graduated and how have they done?

Be wary of the answer to this question. Although admissions representatives may not have exact figures, they should be forthcoming with a round number. You should be easily able to find out how many other learners have graduated, and in what subject areas degrees were awarded. Most schools, unfortunately, are not required to maintain employment statistics on their graduates. If statistics are offered, ask how they are derived, for example, are surveys mailed so that only people who return them are counted?

How many students are presently enrolled?

This is a straightforward question and should be answered almost without hesitation. You might also be interested in asking how many of those students are returning learners, as this will help give you an idea of how well the institution meets the needs of its learners to the *learners'* satisfaction.

Can I talk to current or former students?

Many schools, both traditional and non, enlist the ambassadorial services of their successful alumni to help prospective students decide to attend the school. It is a good idea to talk to one or more of the people in this role, to obtain a learner's view of the institution. Be sure to ask about library services, as well as the class experience and any other issues that are important to you.

Is class size limited? If so, to how many?

Large classes are difficult to manage if the course requirements include reacting to others' writings or participating in a regular on-line **chat** (same-time connectivity for communication purposes). They can also be an indication of the amount of time instructors spend responding to each learner. If you desire a deep learning opportunity, class size is an important consideration.

What happens when there are more who want to enroll than there are spaces?

You will not want to get shut out of classes because there is only one section available, or have a class you really need cancelled if there are too few enrolled. How will the institution work with you if they have to change the academic schedule?

What are the prerequisites for admission?

Does the school require recommendations? If so, who should they be from? Do you have to take any tests, like the GRE? Are you interested in a program that requires writing or art samples? Can application fees be waived? What is the time frame recommended; in other words, how long does the application process generally take?

What documentation is required (i.e., transcripts, letters of recommendation, test scores)?

Be sure you have enough time to have transcripts of any previous coursework sent. Also, give those who are writing recommendation letters plenty of advance notice, as well as any guidelines provided.

Do you give grades or are classes pass/fail? Can I get a grade if my employer requires one for reimbursement?

This is usually an arrangement you make with each instructor at the beginning of class, but ask to be sure.

How much does each course or program cost?

Be wary if you are quoted a per-degree cost only, as this is a common tactic of diploma mills. For institutions whose work is done on a self-paced basis, costs may be quoted by the semester or year. Ask, as well, if there is a minimum number of semesters of enrollment required regardless of how quickly you complete, as is the case with some graduate schools. This will give you a clearer idea of how much your total education will cost.

What is the average cost of books and materials?

Although this will vary, an average estimate should be available.

What are the residency requirements?

If the institution requires that some time be spent in face-to-face meetings with faculty and other students, these should be spelled out before you apply. These are often viewed as essential components of the learning experience, where you can test newly acquired knowledge in a safe atmosphere, form peer relationships, and participate in intensive tutorial sessions. The length and content of any residencies can vary greatly from one program to another, and you should be sure that they will fit within your schedule and lifestyle before you apply.

What are the costs associated with residencies, if applicable?

The costs of residencies at most schools will include only the on-site meetings and will not include travel, meals, or lodging. Others will include some or all of these items. Ask to be sure.

Are there other fees (graduation, dissertation recording, etc.)?

There are inevitably fees beyond the basic tuition, beginning with an application fee. Information provided should include a list and a clear explanation of all fees.

What kind of financial help is available?

One of the real benefits to attending an accredited institution is the availability of federal financial aid. Many accredited institutions that offer distance learning also have "brick and mortar" identities, and their students are eligible for federal financial aid or state loan programs regardless of where they physically take courses. Some of these extend their on-campus scholarship opportunities to distance learners.

If you are considering a graduate degree (master's or above), ask if the institution participates in that time-honored practice of employing research assistants. Like work-study at the undergraduate level (although that is a federally funded program), some schools will reduce or waive tuition in exchange for work that benefits the institution or its students. This can also be a 'foot in the door' if you are considering entering the field. Ask about these opportunities and the time needed to meet the requirements.

There are many financing possibilities, from loans to grants. Be sure to ask about both need-based (criteria based on income) and merit-based (criteria based on achievement) opportunities. See Chapter 10 for further information on financing your learning journey.

What learning support is in place (libraries, writing centers, etc.)?

The availability of adequate library and student services is a primary concern among distance learning professionals. Access to these essential services can make the difference between a smooth, enriching experience and a major hassle. If you know you will need help with writing papers or preparing presentations, know what your options are. Even if your research and writing skills are exemplary, access to a good—preferably university-level library—is crucial. This is especially true if you are interested in a graduate degree, where scholarly research is expected.

Will I have an assigned advisor?

An advisor can help immeasurably in the successful completion of your program by helping you make decisions on the kinds of learning experiences to pursue, as an interpreter of guidelines and regulations and a source of industry information. The advisor-learner relationship can also be a source of mutual distress, so be sure to ask if changing advisors once you are enrolled is possible.

Is there a clear explanation of who I go to if I have problems?

The most customer-friendly institutions provide this information as part of their admissions materials, because they know that even little problems, if ignored, can escalate. Although this can apply to both academic and technical issues, the existence of a 24/7 technical support line may be most important to you.

Is there a 'real' graduation, where I can march down the aisle?
An achievement should be celebrated with an appropriate milestone event. If this is something that is important to you, be sure to ask if it is available.

Is there any employment search assistance or career development advice available?
Although it should not be your only source of employment leads, an educational institution often provides a wide range of employment services, ranging from links to job sites to industry partnerships. A source for internships in your new area can be a key stage in the transition to employment in that field, particularly if your new learning is a drastic career shift.

WHAT *YOU* WANT TO KNOW

Do you have additional questions that have not been addressed here? Perhaps you are interested in a school that will combine classroom with distance options. Or, you may be interested in research opportunities to both increase your understanding and ease the financial pressure of school. Maybe you have other concerns or ideas, like options for incorporating your work into your learning or opportunities to showcase your research at conferences. Perhaps there is a particular mentor you are interested in working with. What matters to *you?*

Write your questions and concerns here, so you will be sure to include them when you are doing your research. Be sure to add your special interests to the School Decision Checklist supplied in Chapter 11, "Choosing an Educational Provider". And do not forget to check the on-line learning FAQs available at the Online Resources Web site, at <www.delmar.com> for further ideas.

_____

_____

_____

_____

_____

_____

ACCREDITATION AND DIPLOMA MILLS

The rapid proliferation of distance learning options makes it hard to know just which are legitimate and which are not. These are prime operating conditions for unscrupulous operators, who promise easy degrees with "no books, studying, or exams" for a "small fee." These **diploma mills,** as they are called, take your money and send you a certificate ("suitable for framing!") that is worth about as much as the paper it is printed on. You could save your fee and print a similar certificate yourself!

As you probably have discerned by now, diploma mills are very different from the hundreds of legitimate providers of distance learning. Not all of these legitimate providers have achieved, or even desire, regional accreditation, which is the generally accepted benchmark of academic legitimacy. The reasons for this are as complex as the accreditation process itself.

Why Accreditation Is Important

Accreditation is an important issue to consider as you choose a learning provider if you wish to have a public record of your learning that will be widely accepted by employers, professional associations, and other colleges and universities. Chances are, if you completed some college courses back when you were younger, accreditation was hardly mentioned. The fact that it has become one of the questions used to determine the worth of a program is emblematic of the upheaval currently occurring in higher education. Accreditation has been an important issue for higher education institutions for years, but recent developments in technology, lifelong learning and training demands, increased sophistication of learners, and ever-increasing competition among educational providers have provided a fertile arena for deception and confusion.

The key to choosing between programs is knowing and understanding your own needs, one of those self-reliant skills we discussed earlier. If you are interested in learning more about computers, for instance, you would not choose a school because your friend the English major liked it or your grandmother went there. You must ask yourself, "Do my personal, academic, financial, and career goals require an accredited degree?" Seek your own answer. Talk to people who are doing the work you want to do. Also, talk to colleagues, potential employers and, most importantly, the licensing or certifying personnel in your topic area. Take advantage of all available sources of information, but do not be swayed by opinions or prejudices. Ask for documentation. The accrediting bodies themselves are very good sources of reliable information.

The reasons that accreditation may be important to *you* are related directly to what you plan to accomplish by undertaking any learning program. Are you fulfilling licensure requirements? Do you have to meet the guidelines of any professional societies? Will you be progressing on to further education? These decisions will be easier to make if you understand what is meant by accreditation.

What Accreditation Means

The conferring of accreditation on an institution indicates that a rigorous, independent evaluation of educational programs at that institution has been conducted. The evaluation has established that the learning offered is of a uniform and sound quality. Evaluation criteria can be very different depending on the type of accreditation considered.

In the United States, schools may be state accredited, regionally accredited, professionally accredited, or have achieved a combination of these. Professional accreditation indicates that a program is approved by a professional body, for example, the National League for Nursing (*NLN*) for nursing degrees or the American Bar Association (*ABA*) for law schools. Professional accreditation may not be a requirement of your occupation, but you should determine whether it is before spending any money on additional learning that may later prove worthless.

The most widely recognized form of accreditation for degree-granting colleges and universities in the United States is *regional* accreditation, and this is generally the kind of accreditation implied when accreditation is an issue. There are six regional, nongovernmental accrediting agencies in the United States that exist to validate effective and ethical institutional practices and assure academic quality.

Attaining and maintaining accreditation is often essential to institutional continuation. It indicates to the outside world that the institution can be trusted

Include the hiring managers in the field you are interested in when seeking advice on the course of study and accreditation status you need to be considered as an employment candidate.

to be academically sound and likely to remain so. This means that it can apply for and receive federal funding, participate in scholastic athletics, attract desirable faculty and students, and meet all the criteria that the accrediting body requires. Requirements include such things as keeping adequate records, fostering faculty development, providing adequate student services, and meeting the statements put forth in the institutional mission. Regional accreditation is, despite what most people believe, a voluntary and nongovernmental process and is not the only arbiter of quality.

Accreditation is a long and expensive process, which can take several years for an institution to complete. It includes an internal review and comprehensive report, a team review by peers from similar institutions, and a great deal of information gathering. Planning mechanisms and problem-solving processes are examined for appropriateness to the healthy continuation of the institution. All aspects of the institution are studied, from administration to academics. Review teams may recommend changes before granting full accreditation, or they may grant provisional accreditation pending further study. Institutions granted full accreditation are reviewed every 10 years for continued adherence to criteria.

The six regional accreditation boards are viewed by one another as being equal in the depth of their reviews. This allows students, teachers, and administrators to regard all accredited institutions in this country as fundamentally equal, no matter where they are located. This means that, as a student, you can:

- transfer courses from one accredited institution to another,
- know your degrees and credits will be recognized as valid anywhere in the country,
- be assured that your transcript and other student records will remain available, and
- be eligible for more kinds of student aid.

Outside of the United States, schools are run and/or licensed by national governments. They do not utilize the same accreditation bodies as are consulted by U. S.-based schools. If you, as a distance learner, are considering a school that is based outside of the 50 states, you may be wondering whether your credential will be professionally recognized.

To ascertain whether an international school is recognized as worthwhile, the text to consult is the *International Handbook of Universities,* published by UNESCO. This publication lists, in English, over 6000 international university-level institutions in 174 countries. It is an invaluable resource for anyone who wishes to study abroad, or at a distance institution based abroad. Each listing has been rigorously examined and entries include enough information to completely compare size, program offerings, library facilities, tuition prices, faculty, and many more items. Because this is an expensive text, you may want to check nearby college libraries or bookstores first. Further information on this and other resources is included in the Selected Bibliography at the conclusion of this book.

Other Types of Accreditation

When you ask about accreditation, be sure to add "regional" to the question, because there *are* other types of accreditation. Certain programs that prepare teachers, for example, can be state accredited, and not be regionally accredited. This can make it difficult for teachers licensed in a particular state to easily obtain teaching credentials in another state. Technical schools and training programs, which may provide wonderful programs and be well regarded by industry and state agencies, are rarely eligible for regional accreditation because of their specialized focus or concentration on skills over theory. State accreditation, which assures program viability and continuity, may be all you need to meet your goals. Again, your own goals should drive your decision.

It is possible to get a good education at a nonaccredited school. Lack of institutional accreditation at a regional level sometimes leads to the inference that the institution in question is a diploma mill. There are many differences between quality nonaccredited programs and diploma mills. There are also many reasons why schools that provide quality coursework would choose not to seek accreditation. As noted earlier, accreditation is an expensive process. Often, these colleges teach subjects that may not be readily found at a "traditional" university, such as holistic animal health, for example. Their teaching methods may be different from the traditional ones, or the school may be young and gaining credibility. If the subject or method is one that is important to you, do not let a lack of regional accreditation stop you. Just be aware of the ramifications of any program you choose.

Similarly, if the learning you seek is provided by a corporation, certifying group, or non-profit organization, make sure that the certification or training provided matches goal requirements. Be aware that this learning will be unlikely to transfer toward fulfillment of academic requirements at a regionally accredited, degree-granting institution. For example, the designation of Microsoft Certified Engineer (MSCE) is a highly desirable certification in the computer industry, but this certification alone will not be recognized as equivalent to college credit by a traditional institution. This is largely because such certifications are usually too specific to be applicable across a wide range of course requirements, and not because of any lack of their inherent value.

Besides the regional accreditation bodies, other nationally recognized accreditation bodies exist. One of the best known of these is the Distance Education and Training Council (*DETC*), an agency for colleges that provide education through distance learning. The DETC reviews *only* that coursework provided by an institution through distance means. It does not review at all many of the other areas reviewed in the regional accreditation process. Because of the differences in accreditation criteria, many regionally accredited institutions will not yet accept coursework in transfer from colleges whose *only* credentials are supplied by the DETC.

It is expected by many in higher education that differences in accreditation policies and standards will be normalized in the future. Obviously, the development and deployment of distance learning has repercussions across the educational landscape that will continue for years. Recently, the six regional accreditation organizations published criteria for best practices in distance education. This is a first step toward a set of policies that can be understood and followed by institutions and students alike.

Despite the fact that MCSE certification may not transfer into a degree program directly, you may very well be able to include it as documentation toward receiving credit for experiential learning. See Chapter 9 for more on this topic.

Spotting and Avoiding Diploma Mills

Some of your friends and family may think they know about on-line learning, and mistakenly assume that any degree available over the Internet must come from a diploma mill. Yet there are hundreds of on-line learning degrees available that are completely legal and accredited and are earned, not bought. As we have already discussed, many on-line learning programs require more work and study from their students than traditional programs do. There are also times, as we have seen above, when nonaccredited learning may be appropriate for you. This is clearly the case with training programs and continuing professional education. If you are aware of what to ask and what to look for, those organizations that provide valuable, highly sought training opportunities will not be hard to find. But how do you recognize 'diploma mills', so you *can* avoid them?

Diploma mills exist because they exploit people's lack of knowledge and confusion about accreditation. They may advertise that they are "fully accredited," when the agency doing the accreditation is as bogus as the school offering the degree. A diploma mill is just another name for a scam. It is a fraud that operates primarily to make money by issuing credentials without any thought to ensuring that an education actually takes place. Diploma mill operators literally crank out, or "mill" a paper diploma to anyone who pays the requested "tuition."

Unfortunately, there are many who have taken this questionable route to certification. Because they usually require no coursework, testing, or proof of understanding, diploma mills may sound like a quick, easy way to gain a credential. But like many quick and easy schemes, a diploma mill is too good to be true, and usually illegal, to boot. If a learning provider—like any offer—sounds too good to be true, it probably is.

It is your responsibility to check out potential learning providers carefully. Some of the signs that you may be looking at a diploma mill include:

- The name sounds similar to a well-known college or university.
- There are spelling or grammatical errors on the Web site or in written materials.
- There is frequent mention of cost of attendance, but not admission requirements.
- Accreditation, if mentioned, is provided by an 'agency' at a similar address.
- Degree completion requirements, beyond cost, are hard to find or are vague.
- Costs are often quoted by degree, instead of by credit or course.
- Offers of special deals (a second degree for half price, for example) are mentioned.
- A diploma is prominently displayed in the advertising.
- The promotional materials state things such as, "No classes to attend, no books to buy."

If you are confused by the claims of any institution you are considering, check the official independent guide to such matters, The American Council on Education's *Accredited Institutions of Postsecondary Education*. This annual official guide can be found in any college library or in the registrar's office at any accredited college. In addition, the Council on Higher Education Accreditation (CHEA) lists the legitimate accrediting agencies in the United States and their contact information at its Web site, <www.chea.org>. Or, peruse one of the many published guides prepared by legitimate publishing houses, a list of which is available at the Online Resources site.

Learner Profile, Continued

Brad becomes an executive

Executive MBA, that is. I found this really neat accredited MBA program that did not require the GMATs. It is also incredibly hard. One of the reasons it is hard is that it crams an entire program into nine months. Yup, I am going to give birth to a degree. Yeah, I know that sounds crass, but it sure feels like it! One weekend a month, everyone meets on campus for these incredibly intense sessions, and the rest of the time we are firing e-mails all over the place, doing Internet and company research, and trying to find time to do everything. I feel bad for the guys—and women, excuse me—who have families. I do not know when they find time. One of the guys told me that he also coaches his son's Little League team. I could not believe it. When does he sleep, I wanted to know. He said, although he was smiling at the time, that he has learned to do without much sleep.

We all have this special software package that is what they call scenario based. This way, we learn the basic information from the book or taped lectures, then we apply what we have learned by explaining what we would do under certain situations, or scenarios. The software even tells us when we go wrong and gives suggestions for being a better manager. On the weekends that we are on campus, we all get together and discuss the assignments we have done and come to some kind of agreement over what are the best ways to deal with the situation, and why. Then, we do a variety of exercises that include group problem solving with case studies, and team building or leadership activities. I have done a lot of those before at work, but at work we never discussed what they meant and why they were useful. I was not the only one who said they had felt cheated by the 'benefits' they got back at the office, but that is another story.

The weekends really start on Friday, and on both nights we all have dinner together and have a chance to get to know each other and have a couple of laughs. It really helps us to make the transition from work to school, and the social time is great for easing up after all that intense work. I am pretty lucky, I guess, because I live within a few hours' drive of the university. Along the way, I will usually swing by the airport and pick up one or two of my classmates, who are usually flying in from some business meeting. Some of them are so used to travelling, anyway, that taking a plane to go to school does not seem like a big deal.

And some of these guys—yes, and women—what powerhouses they are! Sometimes I feel tongue-tied just sitting in the same room with them, almost privileged to be part of the group. What stories they tell. Every time I feel like I can not go on, I remember some of those stories. Stupid bosses, dumb practices, people getting hurt, and customers suffering. It is enough to make you sick. But then, I have my own stories to tell, too, even if I am younger than most of them. Well, a few of them. And we are all using everything we know, together, to get this big project done.

By the end of the weekend, our brains are so tired that it is a real downer to think that the next day it is back to work in the 'real world'. I usually drive home on autopilot, with things I should have said going through my head. Now and then, I get a brain wave and the light bulb goes on. Good thing I carry a microcassette recorder everywhere with me now!

I certainly need it to remember everything I have got to do. I keep telling myself 'it is only nine months', and before I know it, it will be over. And I can sleep.

It's funny, too, with all this stuff going on in my head, the stuff that used to bother me at work does not faze me anymore. I still see better ways to do things, but I am more interested in the big picture now, so the little problems do not seem so important. Strange, huh? The other thing that is really strange to me is how much I like learning this stuff. When I did my undergrad degree, it just seemed like something you had to get past. I do not remember it really seeming so important to me. This MBA material, though, is more like something you *go* through. It all seems so much more relevant to me now that I have been out in the world and can apply it to things I have done. Maybe my dad was right. I bet he would laugh now if I told him that. He had better be there when I graduate!

Questions You Should Ask about Accreditation

To protect yourself and your future, you should direct questions about accreditation to all institutions you are considering attending. These questions are included with all others you should ask about in the School Decision Checklist located in Chapter 11, "Choosing an Educational Provider." These questions specific to accreditation are explained in detail below so that you can understand your reasons for asking them and the answers you receive. Be sure to ask:

Are you accredited? If so, by whom?
Be sure that the agency mentioned is a recognized agency. If you are uncertain, check with CHEA.

Does this institution meet my career goals?
Be sure that the accreditation and the institution in general provide the learning you want and need for your desired career path. Be particularly aware of any special requirements placed by agencies that govern licensing. If you are unsure of these requirements, contact the agency directly to determine them.

Does this institution meet my personal goals?
There are other reasons for learning besides career pursuits. If accreditation is not as important to you as, say, the opportunity to study with a particular mentor, there are other criteria to consider. Review the mission statement and educational philosophy to see whether the institution's values mirror your own. Talk to other students, both current and graduated. Test your expectations against their reality. Your own learning will be more enjoyable and meaningful if your teachers and peers share your passions.

To Sum Up....

In this chapter, we reviewed the questions that prospective distance learners want the answers to, as well as the questions they did not know they should ask. We looked at the various meanings and importance of accreditation, both in the United States and internationally. We refuted the popular misconceptions that paint distance learning as less rigorous than that offered by traditional, brick-and-mortar educational institutions, but we did look at the proliferation of supposed educational opportunities called "diploma mills." With the information in this chapter, you will now have the tools to tell the difference between legitimate institutions and illegal scams. The chapter concluded with questions to ask both yourself and the institutions you are considering to help you meet your educational goals.

The Online Resources Web site, located on-line at <www.delmar.com>, provides links to lists of questions provided by educational institutions, as well as links to accrediting agencies and other resources. You will also find downloadable forms to help you keep track of your researches and the answers to your questions.

In the next chapter, we will examine the concerns held by adults who are undertaking college-level learning for the first time, as well as those who are returning after years out of the classroom. We will also review the college application process, which could be the hardest part of going to school as an adult! But with this guidance and the help of professionals at your chosen schools, the research and application processes will be easily mastered.

Notes to Yourself

Accreditation can be confusing and overwhelming. Why not take a moment to note here any other questions or items that are important to you, so you remember to seek those answers, too:

_____

_____

_____

_____

_____

_____

_____

CHAPTER 8

Never Been to College? Questions for First-timers

"The important thing is not to stop questioning."

—*Albert Einstein*

The questions listed below may have puzzled you for years. If all of your questions are not answered here, ask your question on-line at the Online Resources Web site. Also, be sure to check the Glossary of Selected On-line Learning Terms to increase your educational and technological understanding. You can look through the glossary in the back of this text or search the glossary database on-line at the Online Resources Web site.

ABOUT DEGREES AND REQUIREMENTS

How many credits do I get for each class I pass?

Most colleges and universities grant three credits for each successfully completed class. There are always exceptions to this rule, of course. For example, many colleges in the state of Minnesota based coursework on a four-credit per class model, which is equivalent to other schools' three-credit class. The number of

Please note that the questions listed here refer primarily to credit- and degree-granting institutions, and are generally applicable to both on-campus and distance learning efforts. Rules governing noncredit training providers may be very different. If you are undertaking education to prepare for a specific career goal, be sure to ask about specific licensing and credential requirements.

credits is based on the number of hours spent in a traditional classroom, and is referred to as **contact hours,** or the number of hours of contact a student has with the professor in a classroom. Classes that include laboratory time will earn more credits. To maintain credit consistency, courses completed by distance means are usually assumed to be similar in length, content, and level to their classroom-based counterparts. This is true even though many studies have shown that more time is spent "in contact" with peers and teachers in the on-line environment.

How many credits do I need to complete to earn a degree?

This can vary from institution to institution and program to program, and is decided based on a number of criteria, but the averages are:

- associate degree: 57–65 credits
- bachelor's degree: 120–124 credits (total, including associate degree credits, if applicable)
- master's: 36–60 after the bachelor
- doctorate: 45–90, or more

Can I get credit for my experience?

This question, a common interest and complex issue, is covered in Chapter 9, "Credit Where Credit Is Due." The many ways of receiving college credit for knowledge gained outside of the classroom are explained in great detail, including tips for maximizing your credit potential.

What are the different types of degrees?

The **associate degree (AA)** is also referred to as a "two-year degree," because that is the length of time that it takes full-time students to complete it. The AA, which stands for *Associate of Arts* is a general degree, which comprises the first, general courses of the bachelor's degree and lends itself to transfer. Examples of AA degree titles include "Liberal Studies," "English," and "Business."

The associate degree can also be a technical or specialist degree, in which case it is referred to as an AAS (Associate of Arts and Sciences). This is often designed to career certification specifications and can be the basic certification required for entry into a particular field. Examples of AAS degree titles include "Occupational Therapy Assistant," "Veterinary Assistant," and "Telecommunications Specialist."

The **bachelor's degree,** whether a Bachelor of Arts (BA) or Bachelor of Sciences (BS), is also referred to as a "four-year" or **undergraduate** degree. It is also known as a **baccalaureate** degree. When people say, "I'm getting my degree," this is the one they are usually referring to.

You do not have to complete an associate degree to begin a bachelor's. However, many people find it more convenient and economical to complete "the first two years" at a local community college before transferring to a four-year school. If you already have completed several college courses or an entire associate degree, you should know how your prior coursework can help you earn the degree you seek now. Using courses completed in the past toward current certification is referred to as **transfer.** Transfer-specific questions are covered under the heading, "If You Are Returning to College."

The bachelor's degree provides a sound footing in a wide range of general courses, such as history, communications, and literature, as well as a concentrated group of **major** courses (explained later in this chapter). The major is what will be listed on your **transcript** so, for example, it may state that you have earned a bachelor of science (degree) in engineering (major).

The Master of Arts or Master of Science degree is a **graduate** degree, or is undertaken after a bachelor's degree is completed. In completing this degree, you have the opportunity to focus more closely on the topic—or an aspect of it—that you majored in while completing your bachelor's degree. Requirements for graduation usually include a long study or project, called a master's **thesis.**

There are many professional occupations for which a specialized master's degree is required before you can be considered for certain professional jobs or take the appropriate licensing exam. These include the Master of Social Work (MSW) and the Master of Science in Nursing (MSN), which have other licensing requirements, as well, like a certain numbers of hours of supervised experience by a licensed practitioner and competency examinations.

Perhaps you are interested in another graduate degree path that is unlike the clinical professional degrees noted above. You might choose to follow your bachelor's degree with an MBA. The Master of Business Administration (MBA) degree is, as its name suggests, a business-focussed degree for management professionals. It is aimed at providing the skills and understanding essential to successful business managers in any field. For example, you may have a bachelor's degree in engineering and chose to go on for an MBA. This would prepare you for executive positions in the engineering field. Or, your bachelor's degree might be in mathematics, in which case your MBA study could be focussed on the statistical or economic sides of business pursuits. MBA programs can vary widely in their structure and expectations. Be sure to choose one that matches your goals.

The Doctor of Philosophy (PhD) or Doctor of Education (EdD) degree is conferred on those who complete requirements beyond the master's degree. Most commonly, doctoral students do research in a very focussed area and must prepare a book-length document called a **dissertation,** which explains the research and its findings.

The length of time required to complete a doctorate can vary greatly, depending on the scope of the research, institutional policies, and the motivation of the student. Because of these variables, a doctorate can be completed in as little as two years, or can take 10 years or more. Institutions that offer doctoral programs at a distance also vary greatly in their approaches to completion, interaction, and approach to scholarship. Here, again, it is important to know what you hope to achieve by undertaking this focussed study and to ask the questions necessary to be sure you are choosing the right program to meet your goals.

The bachelor-through-doctorate progression is sometimes referred to as an academic degree model, because it is the study course that aspiring academic professionals undertake. One of the exceptions to this bachelor-through-doctorate model is the preparation of professionals in the fine and performing arts, where a Master of Fine Arts is the highest degree available. Examples of these areas include "Acting" and "Writing." Of course, there are other degrees available that do not follow the traditional academic model.

You might chose to follow a different path after your bachelor's degree and complete a *Juris Doctor,* better known as a law degree. The same person who chose to follow his undergraduate engineering degree with an MBA could opt for legal study, instead. This could prepare him to become a lawyer for an engineering firm. Many people also choose to add the JD after completing master's degrees, particularly if they are interested in influencing policy by becoming politically active in a particular area of the law. The possibilities are endless!

How am I going to pay for this?
For information and ideas on how to complete your degree without going broke, visit Chapter 10, "Financing Your Learning Journey."

Type of degree	Time to complete	Where completed
Associate of Arts (AA) Associate of Arts and Sciences (AAS)	2 years full-time 3–6 years part-time	community college or technical school
Bachelor of Arts Bachelor of Science	4 years full-time up to 10 years part-time	college or university
Master of Arts Master of Science	averages three years —as little as 18 months	graduate school of a college or university
Master of Business Administration (MBA)	averages three to five years—as little as 18 months	graduate business school
Doctor of Philosophy (PhD) Doctorate in Education (EdD)	2–10 years, or more	graduate school or university
Juris Doctor (JD)	1–2 years full-time	law school

FIGURE 8–1

Academic Degree Progression

About the Vocabulary

The school catalog says I need to take a certain number of core courses and a certain number of major courses. Can you explain what that means?

Your degree plan is something like your diet; to be most effective, it must be balanced. A balanced degree plan includes selections of courses from a **core** (also called "general education requirements") or classes that everyone must take. In addition, course selections are made from the major and, if there is room, **elective** selections.

The core includes topics that the school has decided are important for students to know to be "well rounded". They are usually basic courses that serve as a foundation for more advanced work and, in fact, can be referred to as "foundation" courses. Usually included are courses that teach mastery of academic skills, like college-level writing, thinking, and research. Each school can differ in how it approaches learning that it deems important. Clues for this will be found in the school's mission statement. For example, a school with a strong activism tradition may require students to study social change or undertake volunteer activities.

Core courses can be specific and required by all, such as Freshman Composition. Or, they can be competency-based, in which students choose a selection from a menu of options designed to fulfill a required understanding, such as Cultural Awareness. At some institutions, the approach can be a combination of each model, where students complete certain required courses and then choose supplemental requirements from a list of options. Yes, it can be quite confusing, which is why academic advisors can play an important role in academic success.

Major courses usually have less flexibility, because they have been determined by the faculty or accrediting associations as embodying the concepts and practices one needs to know to be successful in a chosen field. Major courses usually constitute one-third to one-half of all courses in the degree plan.

Accrediting associations, not to be confused with regional accreditation bodies, are national organizations that establish educational needs for a specific area, certify certain schools to provide approved courses, and license the graduates. For example, the National League for Nursing (NLN) dictates the kinds of educational experiences that nursing students must undergo to become licensed healthcare professionals. Institutional requirements for NLN approval include the credentials of the teachers, class sizes, number of hours of clinical experience, and subjects studied, among others. Colleges that wish to graduate nurses who can be professionally licensed will conform with these guidelines.

Students may choose to pursue a double major, which means simply that they complete all of the major courses in two different areas, for example, computer science and mathematics. Students can also choose to complete a **minor,** or concentration, in a subject complementary to their major. This is often done by those who wish to teach a specific subject in a middle or high school. The minor is simply a group of courses from a specific area that total fewer in number than those needed to qualify for a major.

The third category of courses that are included in the typical bachelor's degree is elective courses. These are classes one takes that fulfill neither a core nor a major requirement, but can nevertheless be used to earn credit toward the degree. They are called electives because you get to choose, or elect, them. The number of elective (E) courses you can choose is determined by subtracting the total required core (C) and major (M) courses from the total number of credits required for graduation (G). So the equation to determine the number of electives available to you is $G - (C + M) = E$. Some students will have more elective options than others; some students may have no room in their degree programs for electives. It all depends on what path you choose.

To see an illustration of a sample degree plan and schedule, see Chapter 9, "Credit Where Credit Is Due", where the plan to attain a degree includes credit for experience. The sample incorporates both transfer and experiential learning into a complete bachelor's degree plan, so that you can see how experience and classroom learning completed in the past can be combined to approach a present goal.

How is what is studied in a master's degree different from a bachelor's degree?

The bachelor's provides a basic understanding in a broad range of topics, and a bit of depth in one or two. The master's degree allows you to delve more deeply into an area within a major that you are particularly interested in. It requires a level of scholarly research and discourse that is generally not expected of undergraduates. The majority of the courses included in a master's study are of specializations within a broad area, but are included in a comprehensive program that prepares a graduate to participate competently in the area as a whole. Consequently, courses within this degree generally include consideration of ethical, historical, and legal problems specific to the topic.

 If this is a new undertaking, it is all right to be a little confused by all of this. It will become clearer as you become more accustomed to the 'lingo'.

For example, you and a friend could complete bachelor's degrees with business as your common major. The major courses studied would include accounting courses, as well as courses in management, marketing, information systems, and several other business-related areas. Later, both of you might decide to continue for an MBA, but one of you could choose to focus in human resource management, and the other in accounting, or any of a score of possible business avenues, depending on your individual interests, aptitudes, and career plans.

Why is accreditation important?

For a comprehensive answer to this question, please see the heading in Chapter 7 called "Accreditation and Diploma Mills."

About the Process

Why do I have to write an essay as part of my application? What should it say?

If you are nervous about writing your essay, it might help to know that your nervousness is normal. Lots of people have said that they were more nervous about and had more trouble with the application essay than any of their class papers! Of course, you want to make a good impression; if you did not worry a little bit about it, you would be unusual.

The essay helps the people that consider your application to decide if you are likely to do well and benefit from going to that school, and can also help to explain a less-than-stellar academic past. You do not have to worry about whether you are being creative enough or sound "smart" enough. The essay is a snapshot of the kind of person you are, how you think, and what is important to you. It should also show how you express yourself, and in some cases, how you view a particular question. Here are some guidelines that have worked for others and may work for you:

Give yourself plenty of time and be aware of the application deadline. (The deadline means when all required paperwork must be in the admissions office, not postmarked or sent.) When you get ready to write, make some notes about what you would like the people at the school to know about you. If the directions are specific, be specific. Once you have figured out basically what you want to say, write a letter as though you were talking to someone you are interested in, who wants to get to know you better.

When you get to the end of what you want to say, review your writing, making sure that you have explained your ideas well. Be especially careful to check for spelling and grammar errors. Because it is often difficult to catch your own mistakes, make sure you have someone—a good writer—look over your essay. Finally, copy your final draft into the space provided on the form and send it off!

 Do not put off writing the essay! Get the worst part out of the way first!

It seems like so much work. Why should I even apply?

It *is* work, but it is work worth doing if you have goals, right? There are several good reasons for applying, as opposed to just taking courses. First, you cannot be considered for a degree program without doing it. Applying is the first step in becoming an "official" student, also referred to as **enrolled** or **matriculated** into a degree program. As an official student, you are often eligible for benefits that are not available if you just take a class here and there.

The most important benefit for most people is the availability of financial aid. Most lending programs require that you be enrolled on at least a part-time basis to be eligible. A part-time student is usually defined as one taking six credits or two courses per semester. Second, you receive the benefit of an advisor, usually a faculty member in your field, who can answer questions and help you to plan your education to meet your career goals.

By enrolling in a degree program, you protect yourself in the event that requirements change, because your accepted application becomes a contract between you and the institution. That way, if anything changes, you are subject to the rules that existed at the time you matriculated.

Not applying can also have drawbacks. At a large number of schools, you may be limited to a set number of courses before you *must* apply. Similarly, many schools impose a limit on transfer courses and may treat courses you took before applying as transfer courses, *even if they are exactly the same courses you would take as a degree-seeking student.* The lessons here are: Assume nothing. Always ask. You can use the *School Decision Checklist,* located in Chapter 11, "Choosing an Educational Provider," as well as in the appendix. This form will help to guide your researches and prompt you to ask the questions that will elicit the answers you need to save time, money, and frustration.

Application Essay Guidelines

- Know the deadline.
- Give yourself plenty of time.
- Draft, draft, draft.
- Review and revise.
- Complete the form.
- Check that all materials are enclosed.
- Send it!

 If you have the intention of earning a degree at all, you should certainly consider applying sooner rather than later.

IF YOU ARE RETURNING TO COLLEGE

Many people have completed several college courses without attaining a degree, sometimes at more than one institution. In fact, the average adult takes courses at three different institutions before completing a bachelor's degree. There are many reasons for this phenomenon.

Many who began college as teenagers were unable or unwilling to continue for one reason or another. Some did not do as well as they had hoped. Some ran out of money; some faced pressures that did not allow time or energy for school. Some were simply not ready to be away from home, and some were just not prepared to have to work hard. If any of these scenarios apply to you, you are *definitely* not alone. Many very smart people feel that not having completed college is something they should apologize for. But past college experience, no matter how long ago it was completed, can often help you attain current educational goals more quickly than you may realize.

Using Past Work to Meet Present Goals

As long as you completed the coursework with a passing grade, the time spent in class eons ago can help you attain the degree you want now. As you will find from reading the answers to the questions that follow, you *could* think of any past college experience as "found money." You may have almost forgotten about it, but it can save time and money now.

As you probably know by now, this "old" credit is referred to by the school you hope to attend as "transfer" credit, which is similar to transferring money from one bank to another. In that case, both banks agree on the face value of the money, and agree to credit it to your new account. (Unlike money, though, your "old" credit also remains at your former educational institution, ready to be used if you return to study there, or even go somewhere else.) Hopefully, the "old" credit fulfills requirements at your new institution, as well. This will be determined by a combination of the institution's policies and your goals. It is entirely possible that your career goals have changed so much that previous schooling will make little or no impact on your present course of study. We all change, after all.

At the baccalaureate level, anyone who seeks to transfer credit is referred to as a transfer student, no matter how old the transfer courses are. Sometimes, institutional policies are different for transfer students than they are for first-time students, and it is wise to read the catalog closely.

Actually, it is *always* a good idea to read the catalog thoroughly because the catalog that is in force when you are admitted contains the rules that apply to *you*. It is, in effect, your contract with the school. If rules change in subsequent catalogs, the changes will not affect you, as long as you are enrolled. Of course, if you choose to stop and then return at a later date, you may have to deal with any changes that took place in your absence. The possibility that things might change too much has kept more than one person plugging away even when they felt like giving up, believe me! You can get through those difficult moments

 Do not throw anything away, especially your catalog!

that inevitably arise by making sure you know what your responsibilities are and taking into account the possible consequences of any actions before you take them.

All of the questions listed here are regularly heard by academic advisors and cover those concerns most important to adult learners. If you do not see your question listed here, go to the Online Resources Web site at <www.delmar.com> and see whether someone else has already asked it, or add it to the list.

Transfer Q&A

It has been years since I went to school. Do they keep records that long?

All educational institutions are required by law to maintain a safe repository for academic records, including transcripts. They may be in the basement or on microfiche, but they are there.

What is a transcript, and why is it important?

A transcript is an official record of your educational experiences, sort of like a birth certificate is an official record of your identity at birth. It documents the accumulation of education completed in the past (though it does not guarantee you still remember what you learned!).

The school wants an official transcript. How do I know if mine is official?

When a signed transcript goes directly from the registrar's office in one institution to the same office of another institution in a sealed envelope, it is considered official. You may have exactly the same information on an unofficial or "student" copy. It is the signed and sealed transmission from one to the other that is important.

You may request official transcripts in sealed envelopes be sent to you—they remain official *as long as you do not open them.* That way, they can be given by hand to the registrar, or enclosed with your application. It is believed that transcript transmission will eventually be able to be conducted electronically from one secure mainframe to another, but that is still not a widespread practice.

How do I get my transcript?

You will need to contact your former school(s) *in writing* with a request. The cost to send a transcript varies, but it is usually $5–10. Be sure to allow plenty of time (at least six to eight weeks before the application deadline at the school you hope to attend) for this process. If it is convenient, you can also go in person directly to the registrar's office of your former school. Identification will be required, so do not send someone else to do this for you.

The school I went to has closed. Help!

Contact your state's Department of Education. They will be able to tell you where your records are being kept. Alternatively, the registrar at the school you have chosen should also be able to tell you whom to contact, as this information is printed in an annual guide published by The American Association of Collegiate Registrars and Admissions Officers (*AACRAO*) and sent to all member institutions.

Before I got serious, my grades were really bad. Is sending a transcript worth it?

Most colleges require that you include previous coursework as part of the admissions process. The good news is that you start with a clean slate at a new school; your old grades do not follow you, only the credit for the courses you passed. That way, you still have the chance to be a straight-A student! If you are still hesitant, remember that even if only one class will transfer to fulfill a requirement, that will bring you one class closer to graduation.

How do I know which, if any, of my old courses will be accepted toward the degree I want?

Each institution sets its own policies with regard to transfer courses. Some accept any courses taken at a regionally accredited college in which you earned a 'C' or better; some will take only courses completed within a specified time frame. At many schools, the department that governs the chosen major also sets the transfer policy. This means that if you want to get a degree in, say, computer engineering, the professors in the computer department may have decided that any course that is more than five years old is too outdated to be counted. These policies can make a real difference in how close you already are to graduation. Colleges' policies differ; it is your responsibility to check!

The admissions representative should be able to provide you with a *tentative* credit evaluation before you begin the application process. Though not a guarantee, because only the registrar can make an official evaluation, this is usually very close and will give you informed options.

If you want to, you can also review your own transcript to anticipate how past classroom work will transfer. This is a process that can have several positive effects. Just being aware of each institution's policies relative to transfer will also help you decide between otherwise similar programs. In addition, if you are considering utilizing the learning you have acquired through experience to earn credits toward your degree, having an idea where those credits can apply will very likely be part of the credit-earning process. At the very least, this self-review gives you the benefit of retracing your class experiences and anticipating possible areas of confusion before they occur.

Just how are transcripts evaluated?

The registrar compares the courses on 'incoming' transcripts to those taught at that institution. The registrar is looking for coursework that is similar in *content, nature, and scope*. That is, they should cover similar material, with a similar point of view, with similar depth and breadth to topics taught at that school. From there, the registrar looks at which courses will fulfill core requirements (that every student has to have to graduate) and major requirements (that every student who studies that particular topic has to complete). Every effort will be made to match requirements to past learning in a way that is most beneficial to you.

When will I get the official evaluation?

This will be completed during the admissions process. You must fill out an application and enclose or have sent all necessary materials, including transcripts, recommendation letters (if required), application statement and fee, and any other material requested by the institution. Your application must be complete before it will be sent from the admissions office to the registrar for official evaluation.

During the time that the evaluation is being processed, the rest of your application package will be processed, and you will probably be notified of acceptance or any conditions before you receive the official transcript evaluation.

What will the transcript evaluation tell me?

Most evaluations will tell you what was accepted and where those credits will be placed in your degree plan. In addition, it will tell you what was not accepted and why.

A transcript evaluation is not written in stone. The Registrar will re-evaluate if there is compelling evidence to do so.

Can I do anything to maximize my credit transfer?

Absolutely. The more information you can provide to the registrar, the better. The registrar does not have first-hand knowledge of every school or course in the country, so there is always a possibility that some transfer credit will be initially denied, even if it seems to you to possess all the necessary criteria. This can be particularly true if you are considering transfer into a school that is in a different geographical area from where you took your last coursework.

Remember that all the registrar has to work with is a transcript; your courses could have unusual titles that are hard to identify. A good strategy to adopt if you are considering transferring in old courses for credit toward a current degree is to include a copy of the catalog pages that describe the courses you took way back when. If you had the foresight to keep that material in a box somewhere, good for you! If not, contact your old school and ask for copies of the appropriate catalog pages from when you attended the school. Do not worry about their not having them; they *must* keep copies of this information just for such instances. The course descriptions usually can provide the registrar with enough additional information, like academic level and range of subject studied, to help the decision go in your favor.

A transcript evaluation is not written in stone. The Registrar will reevaluate if there is compelling evidence to do so (like course descriptions and syllabi). Pleading is, unfortunately, not evidence. Please note that there is usually a time limit on appeals, too. Read the fine print to be sure of your reasons for requesting reevaluation.

If you are dealing with a campus-based institution, do not just show up, schedule an appointment with the registrar to be assured of having your case heard. The best time to schedule an appointment with the registrar is after you get your official evaluation and before you have indicated that you will actually accept the school's offer of enrollment, though this may be considerably more relaxed for on-line institutions. In dealing with distance institutions, expect to make a number of phone calls and send several e-mails. Although you might not need to, this is not an unreasonable expectation. Because distance institutions are subject to the same rules as campus-based institutions, you will receive all changes in writing. Keep correspondence organized.

The Application Process

Perhaps you are not sure whether you want to pursue a degree at a particular school yet. You are rarely required to go through the application process before you can attend. Quite the opposite. Usually, you will be encouraged to try courses before you make the commitment to apply. After all, the application process means work both for you and the admissions committee (all of the people who look at your application, which can include people from the admissions office, the department in which you want to major, and sometimes others). In addition, a course or two taken at a school you are considering for a degree will give both you and the institution an idea of what kind of student you are.

The application process is, according to many learners, the most daunting part of college attendance, so if you feel overwhelmed, you are not alone. Remember that if you do not know something, *you have to ask*. For a capsule view of the process, see box.

If you decide to apply and are accepted as a student, you will receive a packet of information. This will include a current catalog, registration information, and many other pieces of paper. *Do not throw any of this away!* As noted earlier, your catalog is your contract with the school. By accepting admission, you have agreed to abide by the rules and regulations printed. It is your responsibility to read the catalog and to ask about anything you do not understand.

Similarly, the school is bound by this contract to exchange your tuition dollars for learning and, if you maintain a good academic record and meet all class requirements, to confer a degree upon you. If anything changes in your program, you are protected by the rules in the catalog you are admitted under *as long as you are enrolled*. So begin—or resume—your college education on the right foot by organizing the material you receive.

The final piece of the application process puzzle is the assignment of an advisor. It is with this assignment that you officially make the transition from 'applicant' to 'enrolled student'. Together, you and your advisor will construct your course of study and review other requirements. In a distance situation, this will take the form of e-mails between you. Be sure to archive those e-mails and keep them in an electronic folder for future reference.

For awhile, it may seem that you receive more communications every day, as you become a citizen of the educational community. But remember: You are on your way to a degree!

> *It is your responsibility to read the catalog and to ask about anything you do not understand.*

The College Application and Admissions Process

1. Decide on a school.
2. Review the application deadlines.
3. Arrange to take any necessary entrance exams (like the GRE).
4. Obtain and complete the application.
5. Apply for financial aid/ Complete FAFSA/Confirm reimbursement process.
6. Have a good writer check your essay.
7. Ask references to write letters, if necessary.
8. Have official transcript(s) sent, if applicable.
9. Make sure your application is complete and send it, well before the deadline.
10. Wait.

You will receive a card, telephone call, or e-mail (or a combination of these) from your chosen school when all of the paperwork has been received in the admissions office, usually within a month. While your application is being evaluated, you will also receive information from the financial aid office and a report based on your **Free Application for Federal Student Aid** (referred to as the **FAFSA**), on which most institutions base aid awards. If you are using an employee benefit, such as a tuition reimbursement plan, you will generally not need to apply for aid. See Chapter 10, "Financing Your Learning Journey" for more information.

11. Receive a letter offering you admission.
12. Contact the school to let them know whether you will accept admission.
13. Thank the people who wrote letters for you.
14. Receive and *closely review* admissions materials, including your transcript evaluation. Follow up as necessary.
15. Follow the directions to register for your first class(es) as an official college student.
16. Write down and ask any questions you have as soon as they arise.
17. Work hard and enjoy yourself!

To Sum Up. . . . .

In this chapter, we examined those things both first-time and returning students should know about the college-level learning experience, whether they choose distance or traditional delivery. We looked at the special considerations that learners who have transfer coursework can take into account to maximize it toward attaining their educational goals. Finally, we looked at the college application process and the importance of knowing the rules and the deadlines before undertaking the application step.

In the next chapter, we will examine the many different ways that adults can translate the learning they have acquired outside of the classroom into college credit. It can be more complicated—and rewarding—than you might think! As always, look to the Online Resources Web site at <www.delmar.com> for additional information.

Notes to Yourself

Where are *you* in the educational journey? First-timer or old hand? Do you have other questions that have not been addressed here? Are there particular things you have read here that you want to be sure to remind yourself about when the time comes to fill out that application? Write them down here for future reference:

_____

_____

_____

_____

_____

CHAPTER 9

Credit Where Credit Is Due— The Experiential Learning Process

You may have heard about the possibility of receiving college credit for what you have learned outside of the classroom. As more institutions turn their attention toward adult learners, more emphasis is being placed on evaluating what adult students have learned through their life experiences. After all, not all learning takes place in the classroom! Work, community activities, hobbies, internships, reading, and other experiences can yield learning and understanding. **Prior learning assessment** (often referred to as **PLA**) is quickly becoming popular as a way to attract accomplished individuals, who add depth and quality to the educational experiences of all involved.

The assessment of prior learning is not a new idea; it began as early as 1900, when tests of aptitude and, later, achievement were developed by the newly formed College Entrance Examination Board (CEEB). As service people returned from World War II and began to take advantage of educational incentives offered through the GI Bill, the General Education Diploma (**GED**) examinations were developed. Then, in the 1960s and 1970s, programs for adults mushroomed, with some colleges created specifically for adults. PLA was often a part of these colleges' services to their adult learners.

Prior learning assessment credit has saved many adult learners both time and money. When you consider that most adults progress through required coursework at a rate of, at most, two three-credit courses a semester, the possibility of receiving "only" 12 credits saves more than a year toward a degree. With this in mind, you can see that the time needed to research your potential for receiving credit for your out-of-class learning can be time well spent. You may find that you are one of the many students who can save *years* by transforming learning into college credit.

Credits earned through PLA are generally less expensive to the learner than the tuition charges for "regular" coursework. This is because the process involves validation of the knowledge you already have, not mastery of new knowledge. Less

> *"In conventional education the [learner] is required to adjust himself to an established curriculum. . . . Too much of learning consists of vicarious substitution of someone else's experience and knowledge. Psychology teaches us that we learn what we do. . . . Experience is the adult learner's living textbook."*
>
> —Eduard C. Lindeman

time and fewer resources are needed by the institution than would be the case if you were participating in a group of courses.

The financial savings associated with completing a degree more quickly extend beyond the coursework to other areas of your life, as well. The less time you spend in class, the less childcare or eldercare you may need to arrange and pay for. There will be fewer textbooks to buy and more time available for leisure activities, not to mention the increased earning capacity that will become possible with accelerated degree completion. In addition, the ability to earn credit toward a degree with knowledge you already possess can be tremendously validating, confirming that what you know is worthwhile and respected.

Not all of your knowledge may be able to be credited toward earning a degree, however. Understanding what *kind* of knowledge is required in your situation is as important as taking advantage of the knowledge you have. Earning credit for what you have learned outside of a classroom depends on many things:

- that you are seeking a degree. Only in rare cases can your prior learning be applied toward certificate programs or other nondegree-based learning;
- the level and depth of your knowledge. To gain college credit, your learning must be college level;
- how well your knowledge applies to the degree you are seeking;
- the policies of the school you have chosen;
- how well you can prove your mastery to the satisfaction of an evaluator.

But just how do you go about proving that you have the knowledge that is equivalent to what is taught in a classroom? How does this magical transformation happen?

Credit for prior learning is usually achieved in one of four ways:

- standardized achievement tests
- team-evaluated training
- course challenges
- experiential portfolio evaluation

Each of these alternatives will be explained further. Keep in mind that different methods may be combined for maximum credit award, but each has its own strengths and specific rules. It can also seem as though every institution has different policies governing the amount and kind of credit you can receive through PLA. At one school, you will be able to translate your knowledge into credit only in your major; at another, it may be just the opposite!

A list of questions you should ask before undertaking any prior learning assessment methods is included at the end of this chapter. In Chapter 11, "Choosing an Educational Provider," you will find these questions included as part of the School Decision Checklist. The Checklist is provided to help you keep track of policies for each school you consider.

It is possible that you live near a campus that offers an advantageous PLA program. You may want to consider the savings in both time and money made possible by creating a hybrid program consisting of a number of on-campus classes, on-line coursework and PLA options.

CREDIT FROM STANDARDIZED TESTS

"Testing out" of a subject is often the easiest way of proving your knowledge. The most popular adult-oriented testing program is **CLEP** (College Level Examination Program), which is available to anyone who has a high school diploma or its equivalent. DANTES (Defense Activities for Nontraditional Educational Support) tests are similar, but are open only to people who are or have served in the U.S. military. Study guides are available to help you prepare for the exams. The guides include practice questions, suggestions for study, and sample tests. If you learn best with the interaction of others, you could consider forming a CLEP study group!

All of these assessment programs, which are administered by The College Board, consist of multiple choice examinations. They test learning equivalent to introductory college courses, such as U.S. History and College Algebra. To receive credit, you must answer a minimum number of questions correctly. The College Board makes recommendations on the score you must achieve to indicate mastery of a subject. However, this is a recommendation only. The exact amount of credit granted and where that credit is applied in your program is determined by the registrar at the college you chose to attend.

CLEP tests are scheduled at convenient times and places, usually at a community college or testing center convenient to you. As of this writing, each CLEP test costs only $44, plus a small administration fee. The College Board has announced that CLEP tests will be given only on computers beginning July, 2001. Current and former members of the military or armed services should contact their warrant officer to determine whether DANTES examinations are suitable for them. The CLEP Web site, accessible directly or from the Online Resources site, offers further information on the tests available, where they are offered, study guides, and a list of FAQs about the tests.

In addition to these national programs, Excelsior College (formerly Regents College) offers over 40 different standardized examinations to demonstrate college-level knowledge. These exams are accepted at nearly 1000 institutions in the United States and internationally, and are administered locally at Sylvan Learning Centers. If you are considering a CLEP test, it could be worthwhile to also research these examinations.

How Tests Are Reported

Credits awarded by examination are reported on a transcript and treated as transfer credit, just as if you took the course in a classroom at another school. As noted above, the registrar determines where that credit will be applied within your degree program. You may take the CLEP examination in College Algebra, for example. Depending upon the general transfer policies and the degree requirements, your passing score on the examination could be applied toward credit for a

If you have graduated from high school just within the last few years, you may still be able to receive college credit for AP (Advanced Placement) tests taken while in high school. If you think this might apply to you, check with the registrar at schools you are interested in.

general math course, to fulfill a specific course requirement, or as a general elective. As noted earlier, sometimes the recommended score is achieved but the institution chooses not to accept the recommendation. If this happens, it helps to be philosophical: at least you know where you stand and are aware of the expectations for success.

If you have taken college courses before, be sure that there is no perceived duplication between what you have already taken in a classroom and the knowledge you feel you can prove through examination. You will *not* receive credit twice for the same knowledge. (This is referred to as "double dipping.") For example, if you passed a course called "The Civil War and Reconstruction" years ago when you started college for the first time, you may not receive credit for the CLEP test in "History of the U.S. II: 1865 to the Present," even if you ace the test. Basically, it is the same material. As suggested in the section on transfer issues, study your transcripts closely and request an unofficial transcript evaluation. The college representative will be able to provide help and information specific to the institution.

TEAM-EVALUATED TRAINING

Team-evaluated training is performed and catalogued by the American Council of Education (ACE). Providers of training courses contract with ACE to evaluate and recommend college credit equivalencies for their sponsored instruction. Expert evaluators review course content in important instructional areas and make recommendations for college credit. These recommendations include the appropriate amounts of semester hours at the recommended levels that learners may receive. An example of a credit recommendation could be: "3 semester hours in accounting at the upper baccalaureate level."

These recommendations, as well as a brief description of the training and who administers it, are listed in the ACE *National Guide to Educational Credit for Training Programs*, a text that is distributed annually to registrars and college admissions officers. Through ACE, graduates of police academies, successful completers of banking and insurance courses and trade apprenticeships, and those who complete other workplace courses may receive college credit for their employer-sponsored learning. ACE also makes credit recommendations for certification examinations such as the Novell CNE and Microsoft MCSE through its Credit by Examination Program. These credit recommendations are published in the *Guide to Educational Credit by Examination, 5th edition.*

If you have served in the armed forces, you know that the military supports lifelong learning and educational growth through training, occupations, and coursework. Service members invest much of their time in military training courses and in their occupations, which can help them earn academic credit and achieve degrees from colleges or universities. ACE publishes the *Guide to the Evaluation of Educational Experiences in the Armed Services*, grouped by service arm, to help members of the armed forces to receive traditional college credit for military training reported on the Form DD–214. These texts are published biannually and distributed to U.S. colleges and universities. Recommendations are, of course, subject to an individual school's policies and your choice of major. Current or veteran members of the armed forces can obtain further information about receiving credit toward a degree from military training by contacting college admissions offices or by visiting the Military Programs page of ACE online at: <www.acenet.edu/calec/military/home.html>.

These ACE programs and texts are often included in the library of the PLA administrator or advisor. This is the person who will help you in determining the best way for you to receive the credit that you deserve for learning you have done outside of the traditional classroom.

COURSE CHALLENGES

Course challenges are usually developed and controlled by individual institutions and may include interviews, tests, or skill demonstrations. They are not available or published nationally as are standardized tests or ACE-sponsored credit recommendations. Course challenges may be quite common or not available at all, depending upon institutional policy. At many institutions, challenges require that students demonstrate competency by taking the final exam for the course. In other schools, you may be able to arrange an interview, during which a professor asks you to explain concepts and issues that students would have to know to receive a passing grade.

Competencies gained from specific training programs are not generally eligible for college credit, but they may allow you to bypass courses that you already know and substitute other, higher-level, courses. For example, because of the large number of people who are self-taught in computer programming and similar technical courses, demonstrating proficiency in C+ programming may gain you either credit or advancement to more advanced coursework, or both. To demonstrate proficiency, for example, a C+ programmer *might* be expected to write an effective program, find and correct the bugs in another, know the names and uses of common 'calls', explain a process or compilation, and be able to problem solve a complex hierarchy. Whatever the specific expectations are would be very similar to the objectives stated in the syllabus.

Some academic institutions may also have faculty evaluate the training programs offered at local companies whose employees constitute a large portion of the adult enrollment. By awarding "block credit" for specific technical or continuing education courses, institutions form partnerships with local employers, and everyone benefits. Your company may already have established a similar relationship with a local college or university. Be sure to include this area in your educational researches by contacting your human resources or training department.

EXPERIENTIAL PORTFOLIO EVALUATIONS

Aside from standardized tests, the most popular way of gaining credit for what you have learned in life is through the development of a **prior learning portfolio**, also referred to as an "experiential portfolio" or "portfolio assessment."

This process is the one most misunderstood by those who have not participated in it. It is also the most time-intensive assessment option, as well as the option that holds the greatest credit potential for those who are eligible. You should be aware that the explanation of portfolio evaluation given here is meant only to provide basic information about this complex and enriching process. There are other guides available—many listed at the Online Resources Web site—that deal *only* with this process, and you are encouraged to seek further guidance if portfolio evaluation sounds like a good option for you. To help you decide, self-assessment questions are listed later in this chapter.

The portfolio of prior learning is a personal document of the college-level learning (note that this is learning, *not* experience) that you have gained outside of the classroom. The distinction between "learning" and "experience" is a crucial component of portfolio evaluation. We all know people who have endured countless years of experience and have not seemed to learn anything! Portfolio evaluation is different from the opportunities discussed earlier. Unlike those, it is prepared *after* you have enrolled at a particular school, often at the same time that you are enrolled in 'regular' coursework.

If you are the type of person who has progressed "through the ranks" at work, who often takes a leadership role either at work or in the community, and who enjoys learning new things and taking on challenges, you may be a good candidate for portfolio development. Actually, many of these same qualities would be strong indicators that you could be a successful distance learner, too!

The experiential portfolio is developed by you, the learner, with assistance from a prior-learning specialist who is well versed in the academic and administrative policies of the school. Once the document is completed, it is evaluated by appropriate faculty, who determine whether the portfolio you have created should receive the credit you have requested because it is indicative of work that would be expected in a specific college course.

Your experiential portfolio is tied to your **degree plan**, which is, in effect, a personalized course of study that shows how you will meet the academic requirements of your chosen school, including major and elective courses. The degree plan is important because it becomes your personal road map for completing your coursework and achieving your degree, whether it is a plan that is already part of the college's offerings or self-designed. Depending on your chosen school's policies and your goals, it can serve as a personalized substitute for a program already approved by the faculty and listed in the course catalog.

The issues and complexities of prior learning assessment can, as you might expect, be interpreted differently at different institutions. To help these institutions maintain academic integrity throughout the process, The Council for Adult Experiential Learning (CAEL) serves as the oversight and policy organization for prior learning issues. CAEL has developed guidelines, training, and support for the portfolio development process. Although the specifics can vary from school to school, the portfolio document itself contains certain standard elements. As stated by CAEL, these are:

- identification and definition of specific prior learning for which college credit is being requested, including competency statements in each area of knowledge;
- an essay or narrative explaining how this prior learning relates to the student's projected degree program, from what experiences it was gained, and how it fits into the student's overall education and career plans;
- documentation that the student has actually acquired the learning claimed; and,
- a credit request listing exactly how much credit the student is requesting in each subject or area.

Identification of learning means that you must clearly name the course (or courses) you are seeking to claim as equivalent to your experience. This includes an explanation of what you have been expected to learn (referred to as **learning outcomes**) and evidence that the learning is college level. Usually, students find a course syllabus in the college's catalog or the catalog of another accredited insti-

 Doing your research ahead of time will help determine whether you can get the credit you deserve for the learning you have acquired in your lifetime.

tution that they feel equals the learning they have acquired through means other than traditional classroom learning. For example, your interest in and extensive reading about the Civil War may appear to have been equal to what is expected in an undergraduate history course about the Civil War. You feel this may be true because you have found a course on that topic offered at an accredited school. Or, after reading the course syllabus for "Personnel Management," you may feel that you have learned the same things through your work experiences that college students are required to know to successfully complete this course.

Once you have identified the college-level learning you feel you can articulate, most portfolio programs guide you in developing several narrative essays. The first is a biographical essay that puts your learning experiences from work and other past life events into context and articulates your plans for the future. The evaluators will look for ways that you hope to incorporate your prior knowledge into new learning, and what you hope to achieve by doing so. Subsequent essays are subject specific and explain how you have acquired this learning and how it relates to other coursework that you hope to include in your studies. In your subject essays, you must clearly state the amount of credit you are requesting and how it fits within your degree plan. For example, you may decide to request three credits in "Business Management" through portfolio evaluation, because that is the amount of credit that a student taking the classroom version would receive for successful completion of a course by the same title. Your degree plan, of course, should include "Business Management."

It is expected that the essay be supported by third-party documentation. This documentation provides proof that defends what you have written. In effect, it confirms that you are telling the truth. Depending on the subject you are seeking credit for, documentation can include:

- letters from supervisors and colleagues that attest to your abilities
- professional licenses
- certificates that prove workshop attendance or achievement
- transcripts from training or vocational courses
- newspaper articles about your accomplishments
- video/audio tapes of performances, speeches, presentations, etc.
- artistic materials
- annotated bibliographies of readings
- anything else that proves that you actually have the knowledge you claim to have

As noted earlier, much of the prior learning portfolio work is done while other classroom-based courses are in progress. So, it is important that you not take courses in which you may be able to gain credit through a portfolio process. Because the credit award is granted by faculty evaluation, nothing is certain until the evaluation is completed. You can see, then, why the process must be completed as early as possible in your degree pursuit. Early completion will allow enough time to adjust the degree plan, if necessary.

Because the process can be complex and confusing, and because credit policies differ at each institution, CAEL encourages colleges and universities to provide workshops to assist learners. In these workshops, students are guided in assembling the portfolio document to maximize their credit potential by helping them to understanding how they have learned what they know and how that learning will be objectively evaluated. The prior learning specialist will provide information and assistance to help you decide which courses or subjects to focus on, so you will not be left on your own to figure things out!

Is It Worth It?

Is the effort worth it? This is a question that you must answer for yourself. Most people approach the process of prior learning portfolio development with an attitude of saving money and time toward completing their degree. This is certainly an important factor, as portfolio evaluation can save *years* toward the completion of your degree, especially if you can take only one or two courses a semester. As you are deciding whether to undertake the experiential portfolio task, you should be sure that the process will help you reach your degree and career goals. In particular, check that licensing agencies that govern your field will recognize credit earned in this manner.

But the portfolio process can reap benefits far beyond the ability to speed up the degree process. Perhaps most importantly, it gives you the opportunity to examine your past at a time in your life when thoughtful choices can have a major impact on your future plans. You may have made similar choices when you were younger, but you will now have accumulated experiences about your own abilities, values, and aspirations that will aid planning in a way you were unable to do then. Preparing an experiential portfolio can help you to reexamine past 'mistakes' from an objective distance and reevaluate them critically. To secure needed documentation, you may have the opportunity to reestablish relationships you may have lost track of. In the process, you may review the priorities that guide your life. Other benefits often cited by those who have completed this process include:

- the opportunity to reflect on what you know and how you came to learn it
- the validation of your learning by established experts
- an understanding of your own learning habits and styles
- enhancement of your writing and thinking skills
- the respect of colleagues and evaluators
- increase in self-confidence and self-esteem

Experiential portfolio development is not always appropriate and it is not for everyone. Be sure to visit the Online Resources Web site for a list of Internet references to more information about the prior learning portfolio process to help you decide whether you are a good candidate for this powerful way of moving closer to graduation day!

 Check that licensing agencies that govern your field will recognize credit earned in this manner.

A Sample Degree Plan

To give you an idea of what a degree plan may look like, this sample details the plan for Sue S., who has decided to complete her bachelor's degree in business administration. Of course, each degree plan will be different, and you should use your chosen school's examples as your guide. The degree plan listed below happens to incorporate courses delivered by distance methods, but it could just as easily be made up of courses taken in a classroom or a combination of classroom and distance learning. Remember, distance education methods are merely a way to deliver learning; they are not subsequently different in what is taught.

Sue's story may be a lot like yours. She completed an associate's degree in accounting after high school because that seemed like a good way to make a decent living. She worked for a number of years in the accounting department of a media advertising firm. During that time, she taught herself many of the data functions and some software programming that allowed her to make her departmental tasks more efficient. Her willingness to take on tough tasks and her ability to interact well with others within the company allowed her to move into a supervisory role and gain an understanding of how the company as a whole worked.

Sue became interested in making a career shift into e-commerce management and is also considering developing her own business in the future. She has chosen her school based on the flexibility the program offers her to pursue those goals, and also on the fact that she has a very good chance of receiving credit through portfolio evaluation.

Starting slowly, Sue took a computer programming course in the summer to see whether she liked it and could fit homework into her life. After deciding that she could handle it, Sue applied and, with the help of her department advisor, figured out how her past and future could work together academically.

In the plan chart that follows below, the courses that she took at the community college while earning her associate's degree are shown as transfer courses, fulfilling course requirements in her bachelor's program. These are indicated with a "T". Credits she plans to attempt to gain through experiential portfolio are indicated by an "E". Other courses that she must take to both complete her degree and learn what she needs to meet her career goals are indicated by the date of the semester she has taken or will take them. For example, Sue began taking classes in the summer of 2000 (Su 2000) by taking "CS300—C++ Programming." Keep in mind that the semester-based academic calendar starts in September, so fall comes before spring. This is not true for all educational institutions.

Listed first are the school's liberal education requirements, those competencies that all students who pursue a degree are expected to demonstrate. These are followed by listings of courses that are part of her major requirements, with the list rounded out by elective courses, which Sue has used to add depth to her career plans.

Sue found it pretty easy to do one class on the abbreviated summer schedule, and she is anxious to complete her degree, so she has decided to take two courses a semester during the regular school year. She also plans to get right to work on compiling her experiential portfolio, and only take one class next summer so that she can complete it.

With this plan and the schedule of courses to take before her, Sue can expect to complete all of her degree requirements and graduate (assuming she receives all 18 of the experiential credits she will request) in June of 2003. The chart below shows how her courses and experience are integrated to achieve a bachelor's degree in business administration.

Student: S., Sue   S.S. #: 143–99–4453
Major: Business Administration   Advisor: Dr. H.

Liberal education requirements	*Course name*	*Credits*	*Fulfilled*
Communication (9 credits)			
ENG 101	Freshman English 1	3	T
ENG 102	Freshman English 2	3	T
COM 110	Public Speaking	3	E
Mathematics (3 cr.)			
MAT 102	College Algebra	3	T
Science (4 cr.)			
BIO 105	Human Anatomy/Lab	4	T
Historical Understanding (3 cr.)			
HIS 110	U.S. History to 1865	3	T
Language and Culture (6 cr.)			
FRE 101, 102	French 1 & 2	6	T
Technical Understanding (3 cr.)			
CIS 121	Intro. to Networking	3	E
Religious/Philosophical Understanding (3 cr.)			
PHI 141	Ethics	3	Sp. 2001
Wellness (1 credit or 1 class)			
PE 210	Tennis 1	1	T

Major Requirements:		
ACC101 Prin. of Accounting 1	4	T
ACC102 Prin. of Accounting 2	4	T
ACC201 Prin. of Accounting 3	4	T
ACC202 Prin. of Accounting 4	4	T
CIS250 Info. Systems	3	E
BUS100 Intro. to Business	3	T
BUS105 Marketing Principles	3	T
BUS204 Human Resources	3	T
BUS220 Public Relations	3	T
BUS235 Supervision	3	E
BUS320 Adv. Public Relations	3	Sp.2002
BUS340 Business Systems	3	Fa.2001
BUS400 Internship	3	E
BUS410 Sm. Bus. Mgmt.	3	Fa.2002
BUS420 Entrepreneurship	3	Sp.2002
BUS422 E-commerce	3	E
BUS440 Project	3	Sp.2003

Electives: Liberal education requirements	Credits	Fulfilled
ART140 B&W Photog.	3	T
CIS300 C++ Prog.	3	Su.2000
CIS310 Java Prog.	3	Fa.2000
CIS335 Sys. Analysis	3	Su.2002
CIS415 Expert Systems	3	Fa.2002
COM235 Media & Society	3	Su.2001
ENG215 Writing Poetry	3	T
MAT220 Prob.& Stats.	3	Sp.2001
PSY105 Psychology 1	3	T
PSY240 Consumer Psych.	3	Fa.2001
SOC240 Women in Culture	3	Fa.2000

Total Liberal Ed. credits:	32	
Total Major Credits:	55	
Total Elective credits:	33	
Total:	120	
Total Credits Required to Graduate:	120	

Everything listed above shows how Sue can combine her past education, her experience, and classes to meet degree requirements, but it can still be a little confusing. Sue's academic schedule for the few years ahead will look like this:

Summer, 2000—C++ Programming
Fall, 2000—Women in Culture and Java Programming
Spring, 2001—Probability and Statistics and Ethics
Summer, 2001—Media and Society and complete portfolio
Fall, 2001—Business Systems and Consumer Psychology
Spring, 2002—Advanced Public Relations and Entrepreneurship
Summer, 2002—Systems Analysis and room for another class, if needed
Fall, 2002—Small Business Management and Expert Systems
Spring, 2003—Project
June, 2003—Graduation!

Sue has allowed herself a little "wiggle room" in case her experiential portfolio credit award is not as great as she hopes. Still, with some conscientious planning, she will attain her bachelor's degree within three years of taking her first course. Then, she will be well on her way to effecting her goals of changing her career direction and preparing for self-employment, should she decide to take that step. In the interim, she will have gained technical skills and business process understanding that are currently in great demand.

SELF-ASSESSMENT QUESTIONS FOR PRIOR LEARNING CREDIT

Before you dive into any assessments or tests, you should first ask yourself a few questions and do your homework to begin to narrow the field of options. Remember that you are investing in yourself. It may seem like a lot of work, but taking the time to ask yourself these important questions can make the difference between a satisfying, enriching educational experience and years of frustration. You should ask yourself:

Am I interested in earning a degree?

The vast majority of assessed credit is earned by those seeking a bachelor's degree, although there are programs that will grant a limited amount of credit for associate degrees and certain graduate programs. With rare exceptions, most schools will not accept experiential learning credit toward completion of certificate programs. The Council for Adult Experiential Education (CAEL) compiles information on institutional policies with regard to assessed credit.

What are my time requirements?

If your primary interest is in simply completing a degree as quickly and efficiently as possible, keep an open mind. In other words, if you are willing to have a degree in 'General Studies' instead of 'Business Management', you may be able to save time and money. Of course, if your heart is set on that sheepskin saying 'Bachelor of Science in Marketing', then that is what you should go for. If you are uncertain whether it makes any difference what your degree is in, inquire at the human resources offices of your own company or of companies you are interested in joining. You may find that potential employers will be more interested in the courses you studied and the experience you gained than in what the degree is called.

If you already have at last 60 credits or an associate degree, a degree-completion program may meet your needs better than a traditional four-year program. These are degree programs that provide only the more specific last two years' worth of coursework in certain degrees, serving students who have attained the basics and are ready to move up. There are also a number of these programs available through distance means. If a degree-completion program works for you, be aware that lower-level PLA options may not be available.

Do I have the necessary financial resources?

Similarly, you should include the cost factor when considering prior learning assessment. All of the assessment options are *usually* less expensive than completing course work. However, financial aid or employer reimbursement may not pay for tests, assessment fees, or preparation texts (or time). Do not forget to consider the related costs of education mentioned earlier: textbooks, child or elder care, commuting, and the like.

Do I know my purpose for going to school?

This may seem like a no-brainer, but you would be surprised at how many adults just enroll in college with no idea of their academic destination. Knowing what you want and where you want to go will help you take the greatest advantage of any prior learning you have achieved.

 Determine what your requirements are *before* you contact institutions that look as though they may meet your needs. This will help you to keep focussed on what you need and help to reduce confusion.

What other factors do I need to consider?

Do you know what education you need to achieve your career goals? Make sure that you do. Are you interested in a career, like nursing or accountancy, that has professional licensing requirements? Be sure to check with the accrediting agency that governs licensing to determine the best course of action for you. Are you hoping to receive credit for experience that is not relevant to the degree you are seeking? If you are completing this degree to facilitate a drastic career change, you may not be able to make the best use of your past learning, however credit-worthy it may be. Write these and your other questions down before you contact specific institutions.

ASSESSMENT QUESTIONS FOR EDUCATIONAL PROVIDERS

As noted earlier, institutions have different policies about how credit you earn through assessment can be applied toward your degree. With policies varying greatly from one school to another, it is always wise to check policies with the schools you are considering before committing to a degree program. Once you have answered the questions related to your own goals and educational desires, you can narrow the field of possibilities by checking college guides, like the appropriate *Petersen's Guide,* or *Bear's Guide to Earning Degrees Nontraditionally.* Each guide publishes with slightly different criteria, so you may need to check several to find answers to all of your questions. Luckily, you can often find college guides for convenient use at you local library, high school guidance office, or bookstore.

You can also retain the services of an academic planning company. These companies provide a service to learners like you—for a fee. They will review your resume and transcripts and do all the research for you. The range of services included can be extensive, encompassing everything from transcript review to financial aid acquisition. You will still need to provide the service firms with lots of information, so expect to spend some time thinking and making lists before your interview.

Whether you do the research yourself or pay someone to do it for you, be sure to ask about the possibilities for gaining credit from your prior learning. These policies should be clearly stated in the school's catalog, though sometimes you have to be a mind reader to figure out where to find that information. Colleges, as you know, are primarily in the business of providing learning, not validating it. Where in the catalog you find information on PLA, as well as the language used

If you are not sure what the licensure requirements may be in your chosen field, inquire with the agency that accredits the field or ask someone who is already working in the career you are interested in entering. You can also check the Occupational Outlook Quarterly (OOQ), a publication of the U.S. Dept. of Labor, for predictions on employability of your chosen field. The OOQ is available on-line at <stats.bls.gov/opub/ooq/ooqhome.htm>.

to describe it, can be strong indicators of how important the program is to the institution. Remember, the catalog is your contract with the institution.

The School Decision Checklist at the end of Chapter 11 incorporates most of the following questions, for your convenience. Explanations following each question will provide clues as to why you may want to ask these questions, and help you include other concerns of specific importance to you in your search for an educational provider. A copy of the School Decision Checklist is also included in the appendix and can be downloaded from the Online Resources Web site at <www.delmar.com>.

Questions you will want to ask of possible educational providers include:

Do you accept any forms of prior learning assessment and if so, what kinds?

Many schools will accept passing scores in standardized tests in the same way that they accept transfer credits. No grades will be included in your record, just the notation that you have earned credit elsewhere. Many schools, however, will not accept portfolios of prior learning from other institutions. This is often related to the differences in rules from one institution's PLA program to another's. You may be required to participate in their own portfolio program, if they have one, or you may simply be asked to submit a previously successful portfolio for review. If you have already prepared a portfolio elsewhere, ask about the possibility and process at the school for reviewing it.

Do you have a program for portfolio assessment of prior learning or other specific assessment program?

If so, ask for the name of the advisor for the program. Policies and procedures vary from one institution to another, and it is always best to speak directly with the administrator or faculty member responsible for the program. Admissions representatives, despite the encyclopedic knowledge they may seem to have, are not expected to know the details of every program.

Is there a limit to the amount of credit I may receive through assessment?

For many institutions, there is a limit on the amount of credit you may transfer into your degree program from previous sources. All credit—coursework, experiential learning, test results, and so on—may be lumped together and called 'transfer credit', regardless of how it was gained. For example, School A may accept no more than a total of 60 credits in transfer, those credits being a combination of college courses you took years ago and tests you passed after years of working. School B, on the other hand, may accept as much as 60 credits in classroom-based course credit *and* CLEP credit, as long as you complete at least 30 credits there with a C+ average. The possible differences in policies from one institution to another are quite extensive.

Are there any time restrictions to my ability to include assessment in my transcript?

Some schools will accept test scores only during the first year of enrollment, or during the time before a certain number of credits are earned. Others will be open to accepting transfer credit (either coursework or tests) after admission *only* if permission is asked and granted before taking the course or test. The likelihood of your receiving this acceptance increases if the course is not available on that campus or if it is endorsed by your faculty advisor.

What kinds of assessments will not be accepted?

You already know that assessments have to be college level, a determination that is made by the faculty and the registrar. There may also be courses that you absolutely *must* take because of their significance, rigor, or relevance to other coursework. For example, many colleges require the completion of a capstone project that brings together all of the things you have learned during your classes. This project would necessarily be a requirement that cannot be completed before you have neared the end of your degree. Other coursework may emphasize a team approach to problem solving and require interaction with members of a class to assure satisfactory completion.

Is there an appeals process for evaluation?

In the cast of standardized tests, if you do not score high enough to earn a credit recommendation, it means that you do not know it as well as you thought you did. If it is a required class, you will just have to take it. If not, at least you learned something and now you will have the opportunity to learn something else.

What if the credit you request for your portfolio of prior learning is not granted? There are a number of reasons why portfolios could be rejected. The advisor or faculty working with you during the preparation phase will help keep risks to a minimum. Still, it does happen. If your assessment does not turn out as you had hoped, the reasons should be clear (CAEL says so). You may have an opportunity to resubmit your essay or provide further documentation. Work with the assessment advisor to determine what is necessary.

What are the costs associated with assessment at your school?

Course transfer should be included in the application process; you will already have paid for the assessment process if you have taken tests elsewhere. However, there may be fees associated with transferring course credit into a program *after* you have become an enrolled student. The registrar will be able to answer questions about evaluation fees, but may refer you to other offices for other questions, especially those regarding financial aid. For fees regarding portfolio evaluation, contact the experiential portfolio advisor.

If you choose to participate in an experiential portfolio program, there is likely to be a limit to the amount of time you have to complete and submit your portfolio. Ask the experiential program advisor about policies and procedures specific to the institution. Also ask about informational workshops that can help you determine whether you are a good candidate for portfolio evaluation at that institution. The informational workshop should clarify many questions specific to that school, including:

What are the fees for portfolio evaluation?

Some evaluation fees are based on the specific number of credits requested, some fees are based on a percentage of the tuition you would pay to take those courses in a classroom. Still others may be based on the number of different subject areas requiring evaluation. The fees must be reasonable, but many yardsticks can be used.

What is the average length of time between submission and notice of evaluation results?

Because individual faculty must look closely at each portfolio submission, the process can take several months. This is why it is often necessary to complete your portfolio as early as possible in your degree study. In addition, if any of your requests are denied, you will have time to prepare additional documentation (if permitted) or modify your academic schedule to incorporate classes you had hoped to prove competency in.

What kind of help is available?

Assistance can range from sample manuscripts to specialized writing courses, and vary from school to school. Knowing your own needs, as well as the resources provided by the school, will help you decide if this route is for you.

To Sum Up. . .

In this chapter, we have looked at the many different ways and processes for receiving credit for the learning you have acquired outside of the classroom. You learned that your ability to obtain college credits in this way will be determined by its designation as college level, by how well your learning fits within your selected program, and by how well you can document that you have acquired it. Whether you choose tests, evaluations, or portfolio, it may seem like a great deal of work. And it is. But this work can be rewarding on many different levels and help speed you on your way to your chosen goals.

Did you know that the question most people ask regarding their education is, "How much?" In the next chapter, we will examine the ways to fund your education so that you can relax and pay attention to learning.

Remember to use the School Decision Checklist provided in Chapter 11, "Choosing an Educational Provider", to keep track of policies at schools that interest you. These resources, and others, are also available at the Online Resources Web site at <www.delmar.com>.

Notes to Yourself

Are there other questions you need to have answered? Perhaps there are specific workplace training experiences that you wish to ask about, or you have other concerns about how your experiential learning will be evaluated. Write them down here, so that you will remember them when the time comes:

_____

_____

_____

_____

CHAPTER 10

Financing Your Learning Journey

THE COSTS OF LEARNING

Many adult students assume that there is no possibility of financial aid for their learning endeavor and give up before they even try to find out. Do not let this be you! In fact, there are many sources available to help you pay for your education.

The first step in determining how much money you will need to achieve your educational goal is to add up all the costs on an annual basis. The basic formula for determining your financial need is: Annual School Cost − Personal Contribution = Expected Need.

The costs for on-line instruction may actually be less than costs for traditional college study. The items included, however, are only a bit different. These include tuition, books, fees, supplies, computer/printer, Internet service, study area, and any other costs you may need to include, such as residency requirement travel. You can use the School Costs Worksheet in this chapter to determine how much you will need to set aside or finance.

You know that education is changing at all levels. Many people believe that this is a long-term societal change that signals a fundamental shift in the way all people will learn throughout their lifetimes. You may already have heard that the Department of Labor currently estimates that every worker will change careers (not jobs) five to seven times during his lifetime. Workers, the trends show, will be required to upgrade skills every three to five years to even *maintain their current jobs*. Yet the financial aid rules continue to be written as though the majority of college students are between 18 and 24 and attend one school full-time until graduation is achieved. It is no wonder that you may believe that there are few resources for you, the adult distance learner. Yet with ingenuity and persistence, you can find a way to pay for the learning you desire.

"Do what you can, with what you have, where you are."

—T. Roosevelt.

The basic formula for determining your financial need is:
Annual School Cost −
Personal Contribution =
Expected Need.

Finding financial aid can be a time-consuming task. Even with advances in streamlining paperwork processes and providing instant information on-line, the federal financial aid *guidelines* have not kept pace with technology. This can have dramatic impact on the distance learner. For example, you may be able to find the perfect arrangement of courses and guidance through an on-line consortium of colleges, which allows you to choose classes that originate from different colleges around the country or the world. The present financial aid guidelines, however, expect students to go to *only one school at a time.*

Federal aid is paid directly from the federal government to the 'host' institution at the time of this writing. Legislation is pending, however, to allow aid to be paid directly to the student. This would allow students to use financial aid and divide their coursework between several institutions to meet their educational and career goals. This is legislation that you can support by writing to your elected officials and being aware of other pending legislation that supports adult and lifelong learners.

GRANTS AND LOANS

Each year, more money becomes available for on-line learning. In the United States, Congress recently passed legislation allowing students who participate in on-line education programs to receive financial aid through their institutions. However, because most adult students attend school part-time, much of the aid (which is still targeted at full-time students) is not available to them. There are exceptions to this rule, however. Be sure to ask the financial aid officer at your selected institution about rules that may effect you.

To receive **grant** aid, which does not need to be repaid, federal income guidelines must be met. This requires filing a federal application called the Free Application for Federal Student Aid (FAFSA). You may have already completed this for your children, if they are of college age. Tax return disclosure is part of this process. The FAFSA is available on-line at <www.fafsa.ed.gov>, as are many other forms of financial aid information. Links to financial aid assistance sites are listed on the Online Resources Web site, as well.

Although you may not qualify for grants, nearly everyone is eligible for some form of guaranteed student loan, regardless of income. If you have had a student loan before, you may remember that these are low-interest loans that usually do not come due until after you have completed your coursework. In some cases, you may have to pay only the interest portion during the time you are enrolled in school and for a short period thereafter. Any defaults on old student loans will endanger your eligibility for these programs. Credit history can also have an impact on whether you will receive a student loan or not. Before applying, obtain a copy of your credit report and be sure that all of the entries are correct. Modifying your credit report is not difficult, and it is better to know in advance where potential problems lurk, than to be surprised by a loan rejection.

 Start your financial aid search early. Deadlines are not extended!

If you decide to apply for a loan, be sure to include in your calculations all of the costs of education, including a computer, estimated cost of books, and fees. Do not forget to include childcare costs, if applicable, and any other necessary expenses, such as the costs for travel, meals, and lodging to attend required residency seminars. All of these can be included because they are related to the cost of your education. Keep careful records, as well, to avoid spending loan money twice.

SCHOOL COSTS WORKSHEET

School _____

TOTAL COSTS:

1. Tuition per course _____ X courses taken per year_____ = $_____

2. Average cost of books per course ___ X courses per year _____ = $_____

3. Computer /Internet service provider per month: _____ X 12 = $_____

4. Annual cost of education(1+2+3): = $_____

ONE-TIME FEES

Application fee $ _____

Graduation fee $ _____

Exam fee(s) $ _____

Other fees(s) $ _____

5. Total fees: $ _____

AVAILABLE RESOURCES

Employer reimbursement $_____

Savings $_____

Gifts $_____

6. Total available $_____

To determine the amount needed annually,

subtract line 4 from line 6. $_____

This is the amount you will need to finance annually.

To determine the *total* cost of education,

multiply line 4 X the number of years needed to

complete your degree, + line 5. $_____.

 If you do receive a loan rejection, the agency *must* provide a reason and free access to the credit report used.

Most college loan programs involve payments made directly to the institution once a semester or quarterly. After applying the loan amount toward your tuition and fees, any remaining balance will be sent to you. Then you can apply this amount toward the cost of books and other supplies.

OTHER SOURCES

Tax Strategies

You may not be able or choose to participate in a loan program. You can still defray some of the costs associated with education through an adjustment on your tax return. Since 1997, taxpayers have had the ability to deduct some or all of the costs of education through the Hope and Lifelong Learning programs. These provide adjustments to annual taxes based on cost of education and income level. See the IRS information regarding higher education payments on-line at <www.irs.gov/prod/forms_pubs/pubs/p97001.htm> or ask your tax return specialist for further information.

Payment Plans

In addition to this tax return adjustment, you should be able to manage your educational costs on a monthly basis. Most schools, including on-line learning institutions, provide payment plans to ease the burden of tuition and related expenses. Most also accept credit cards in payment of tuition bills. See your school for eligibility information and relevant forms. Be sure to calculate the interest costs of credit-card payments, if you choose to use this method. A loan could prove to be less costly and easier to manage than credit-card debt!

Employer Benefits

You may be one of the millions of working adults eligible for employer-sponsored tuition benefits. In some cases, your employer may pay the entire cost of schooling. Employers are finding that desirable employees value current knowledge and seek this benefit during the job search process. As employees are becoming more involved in planning their own careers, more and more employers are including costs of education and training as a regular addition to benefit packages. After all, an employee who actively seeks to improve is one the employer wants to keep!

Most of these benefits are in the form of tuition reimbursement programs, meaning that you must pay for education in advance and your employer repays you when you have shown proof of satisfactory completion. The definition of "satisfactory completion" can vary greatly from one company to another. Many benefit programs are grade related, but this may not be the case at your place of business. Check with your human resources officer to determine your company's policies on tuition reimbursement.

Also be aware that there may be other policies that govern educational reimbursement. Your employer may require preapproval of degree plans based on relevance to your job description. Repayment may be limited to a set percentage of your salary or an annual cap, or available in different percentages in different departments. Because many institutions that cater to adult learners give grades only when asked, be sure to find out whether a particular grade achievement is an employer requirement, so you can ask for grades at the beginning of a course.

Getting Creative

As an adult, you also may have resources at your disposal that most younger students do not. To finance your education, you might consider any of the following:

- a home equity loan
- a secured loan against your savings or life insurance
- a portion of educational funds originally established for your children (if they are still young)
- a portion of your retirement account (educational expenses may be penalty free)
- church or community organization loan or gift-for-service programs

Another sure way to save money is to consider a state-approved, but unaccredited, university. If such a school can meet your personal, academic, and career goals, you will likely save a great deal of money on tuition. Some of the bigger state-approved schools even offer interest-free monthly payments after an initial down payment.

DEVISE A PAYMENT STRATEGY

Once you have determined how much your education will cost and the time required to complete it, you can devise a strategy to pay for it. You may decide to take one of the conventional approaches listed above, or you can decide on other ways of fitting your learning endeavor into your budget. You may decide, for example, to limit involvement in a hobby or activity and divert those funds to your educational enterprise. One learner I know quit smoking and saved the money he would have spent on cigarettes to improve his mind, along with his health! Another used some of her inheritance to keep a deathbed promise to her father to finish the degree she had started years earlier. One even sold a highly desirable motorcycle he had lovingly restored to finance his educational dream.

For further ideas, seek out Web sites and books that cater to helping on-line learners find money for school, such as "Finding Money for College," by distance learning experts John and Mariah Bear. This text includes a number of unusual strategies, including barter and real estate investment, for financing your own or your child's education. Many of these can be applied to your own educational payment strategies.

Most adults continue to work while they are pursuing further education, but you may decide to take time off from work to complete your degree more quickly. Be sure to factor in the financial costs (health insurance and lost wages) and savings (commuting costs, business lunches, wardrobe, child care) that such a change will bring. You certainly would not be the first grown-up to become a full-time student!

To Sum Up. . .

In this chapter, we have briefly touched on the ways that you can fund your educational pursuits. Whether you choose to save, apply for financial aid, take advantage of an employee benefit, or combine other strategies to fund your education, do not put it off. With forethought, planning, and persistence, you can find what you need to get what you want, right now.

Find additional information and ideas for paying for your learning on the Online Resources Web site at <www.delmar.com>. Links to the FAFSA, other federal government sites, as well as strategies specifically designed for adult learners can be found there.

In the next chapter, we will examine the many resources you can use to find and choose the educational provider that best meets your learning needs. We will reexamine all of the questions you should ask, as well as some you have not considered yet. In addition, you will find a School Decision Worksheet that provides a convenient way to organize all of the information you find. Before that, though, take a minute to think about how you will choose to fund your education.

Notes to Yourself

Are there particular costs that you are concerned about? Do you have ideas for creative strategies to finance your study? Write them down here, and share them with others at the Online Resources Web site:

_____

_____

_____

_____

CHAPTER 11

Choosing an Educational Provider

Up to now, this text has provided information on what you can do and what you can ask to assure yourself of finding an option for education at a distance that can meet the goals you have identified for yourself. You should now be able to make informed decisions about the institutions that interest you. So, if you turned here first, looking for a quick way to decide on a course of on-line study, go back and read the earlier chapters!

Choosing a provider is basically a two-step process: First, you must obtain information on which providers offer the learning you are interested in. Then, you must narrow the possibilities down to the ones most likely to meet the needs that are important to you. What on the surface seems like a pretty straightforward procedure quickly becomes confusing. You realize that there seem to be as many information texts and Web sites about distance learning as there are schools that offer it. And more of each seem to appear every day.

Most of the discussions thus far have highlighted learning provided by individual institutions. Yet these are not the only sources of on-line learning. You can receive training from noncredit skill providers, where you can acquire learning in short tutorials or longer, self-paced classes. Degree programs can also be completed through **consortia** of schools, which consist of groups of schools that join together to offer all kinds of courses, programs, and degrees. By doing this, they save money that would have been spent in developing independent systems, keeping costs down for themselves and the students they serve. Some on-line sites provide just information; some provide both information and learning opportunities. Following are a few of the different kinds of resources you can access on-line to begin your exploration.

> "...if we make the praise or blame of others the rule of our conduct, we shall be distracted by a boundless variety of irreconcilable judgments, be held in perpetual suspense between contrary impulses, and consult forever without determination."
>
> — Samuel Johnson

ON-LINE AND PRINT-BASED DIRECTORIES

Learning-matching services such as on-line directories invite seekers to select several criteria as guides to search for prospective programs. After making your selection from a wide variety of pull-down lists and other options, the search software combs the database for options that meet your standards. With a simple click of a button, a list of available programs that meet those criteria is revealed. It is quite convenient, and usually quite easy. It is meant to be.

Directories can be helpful in the initial steps, but can also be missing crucial material. The selections available are only as good as the database and its contents. It is important to find out how the directory is organized and filled. Some directories include only those providers who have paid a fee to be listed. Some of them have very limited search criteria, or contain only a limited number of the thousands of schools that offer courses through distance learning. Some even have differing definitions of distance learning, so that studies that are entirely satellite-based, on-line, and those requiring a month-long residency are lumped together. Although they *may* have more individual pieces of information that is more recent than the print directories, the likelihood of being any more *thorough* than the paper options is low.

The published texts released by major publishing houses, or those recommended by distance learning specialists, are generally more thorough and reliable, as well as being reprinted on an annual basis. Printed directories almost always contain information that the Web sites do not. In fact, many of the guides offer a good deal of 'teaser' information on their own Web sites. They also provide a convenient link to the page on which you can purchase the book. Printed directories also have their own criteria, just as the on-line ones do. This may not reflect everything you want to know and will most certainly include information you could care less about.

Every time one major publisher comes out with a book on a topic, it seems that the others follow suit. This can be both good and bad. Good, because it forces the publishers to look for new information all the time. That means you will get the most comprehensive intelligence available. Bad, because each publisher's offering will be slightly different, and no one text will be likely to include everything you are interested in.

The major publications, like the Petersens' and Barrons' guides, are renewed annually. Many more are available, and most are housed in your local library. Other guides, covering specific subjects or degrees, are also available. A major bookstore will also carry a good selection of these texts, or you can visit one of the on-line booksellers like Amazon.com or Barnes & Noble <www.bn.com>. Here, you can search for and see reviews of each text and look for guides in more specialized areas, like divinity or law.

In choosing the guides to help you determine where to spend your educational dollar, look for an established publisher and a well-explained methodology. In other words, the book should contain a section on how the information was

 Do not rely just on the Internet to find distance learning programs.

gathered and who was consulted in the gathering. This will help you to understand the audience for which the book is written and decide whether that audience includes you.

A combination of on-line and print-based resources will probably serve your needs best. One of the most popular databases is Petersen's LifeLongLearning site, where you can search by degree, subject keywords, and delivery medium (i.e., satellite, on-line, etc.). But this site does not presently link directly to any schools, only to a page in its own directory, which is a summary of the Petersen's print guide. Still, there is a great deal of information available in these directory sites, and they are a good place to start. A list of these, and links to others, is included at the Online Resources Web site at <www.delmar.com>.

LEARNING PORTALS

You might also look for information at one of the recently developed distance learning "portals" or "hubs" on the Internet. More than just directories, these sites often include a wide array of services and information to enhance your educational search. This is also a good source for links to on-line consortia, noted above. Examples of services one can expect to find on portals include links to financial aid information, study skills advice, articles on distance learning, textbook vendors, and more. Like directories, some are better than others. Most of the on-line portals are geared toward the younger college students, with links to music sites, shopping areas, discount travel information, and food vendors.

Caveat emptor (let the buyer beware) is the rule, rather than the exception, with all on-line resources. Some sites list programs from schools that are not accredited, or of questionable academic depth. These will be listed right along with highly respected, fully accredited programs. It is important to pay attention and verify everything you see before investing any time or money in a particular program.

Another recent and developing trend is the proliferation of institutional portals, sort of an electronic front door to the college. Most of these are seen at colleges that have both a campus-based and on-line presence. The best of these Web sites allow students, faculty, alumni, and parents to find the specific services and information they need with just a few clicks. Often, pages are made secure with a password system, so that you would need to be a registered student to gain access to certain pages. From the portal page, for example, you could get to your academic department, leave an e-mail for the financial aid department, find out the score of the game and the top news stories, visit the library, or register for a class. You can even register to vote!

Overwhelming research has shown that this 'one-stop-shop' orientation is the way in which the college experience will continue to develop, as both distance and on-campus students demand greater convenience from every aspect of their college experience. But not every institution designs their site or portal in a way that is clear to the uninitiated. Sometimes, you have to *guess* which links lead to your desired destination. Be aware that vocabulary definitions and organizational structure can change drastically from one school to another, and these differences will often be reflected in site design. In other words, be patient!

SEARCH ENGINES AND COMMUNITIES

Many people who are just beginning their exploration use search engines to seek distance education options. Most of the major search engines, including Yahoo and MSN, organize indexed material into **channels**, or categories of information. These can be searched or simply browsed by clicking on the channel of interest.

Orders of descending depth, like outlines, organize material from the general to the specific, for example: Education/Adult and Continuing/Noncredit. In this way, you can find listings and direct links to information on distance learning options, and visit the provider's sites directly.

Because the channels are developed by the search engine software and personnel, the listings may be more comprehensive than sites that only list paying providers. However, there is often little effort made to review or regulate what appears. This is also true if you simply run a multiple-engine search for "distance learning providers." The results you receive will include everything from Ivy League institutions to diploma mills, as well as every article on distance education ever written!

Community sites, which employ guides with a background or interest in a topic, are often a good bet for beginning a search. These sites will usually provide background articles, listings, cautions, and general information, just like portal sites. What makes them different is that they will also include either bulletin boards or chat rooms (or both) to provide a forum for questions and answers. The opportunity to interact with others can be extremely helpful in narrowing your search and learning the reality behind the marketing. Bulletin boards and chat rooms are discussed in greater detail in Chapter 15, "Online Listening and the Educational Community."

Another community source for on-line information can be found in Usenet newsgroups, or forums. These message board-only sites have been around since before the World Wide Web and browsers, when the Internet was entirely text based. Here, you can read postings that are archived and search by keyword for the topic you have an interest in. Interchange is often lively and assertive, so it is always best to **lurk** (just read without posting) for awhile to understand the rules. There are newsgroups for every conceivable interest. One of the best for distance education discussions, <alt.education.distance>, can be accessed on-line through Deja.com. This and other Web-based options are listed on the Online Resources Web site.

Doing your research responsibly may seem like a lot of effort, but it will pay off in money and time saved later.

Doing your research responsibly may seem like a lot of effort, but it will pay off in money and time saved later. Links to and information on many of these options are organized and listed on the Online Resources Web site for your convenience.

GO TO THE SOURCE

When you have finished your review of guides, Web sites, portals, and other resources, and figured out which programs bear further scrutiny, it is time to approach the educational providers directly. Review each provider's Web site to confirm that the information you have found is verified there. If you are seeking a degree or other credit-based program, the next step is to contact each institution by e-mail or telephone and request an application package. This material should arrive in a timely manner and include course and program information, services

If you have not gotten the message by now, here it is:

• Use more than one resource.
• Do not rely only on Internet sources.
• Check all information thoroughly.

available, schedules, tuition information, and academic policies, and probably more. Oh, and an application. If you have requested information from more than one provider, be sure to keep the packages separate.

Using what you have learned from reading this text, go through the materials you receive and answer the questions that are important to you: program, timing, costs, aid, and so on. Use the School Decision Checklist provided at the end of this chapter to help you remember what to ask. When you have finished going through the materials thoroughly, review your checklist to see what questions are left unanswered. There will undoubtedly be some.

Even if you are not seeking a degree or credit-earning courses, some of the questions on the checklist, such as number of students per class and issues of time and structure, will still be relevant. Answers to these questions will help you determine which choices will be better structured to your particular needs. Review the checklist to see which questions are important to you, and add any others that are important to you, as well.

Now, it is time to contact the school and ask those questions that have yet to be answered. Get your pen and paper ready, and pick up the phone. Soon, you will have all the information you need to make a decision. After that, you will be able to use Section IV, "Get It Done—Managing the Educational Project," to find strategies for completing your chosen learning task. With them, your success as an on-line learner will be assured.

To Sum Up

In this chapter, we have reviewed the many options available for finding and selecting your distance learning experiences. We looked at both on-line and print directories, search engines, and moderated communities. We found that there are many places to find information about programs, but that not all information is equal. In the end, you were advised to use a combination of resources to make a selection, and then turn to the provider directly for verification and to begin the application process.

By using the School Decision Checklist, you can tailor your search to exactly what you need and desire. In addition to the copy here, an additional copy of the checklist is included in the appendix and on the Online Resources Web-site.

There, you will find direct links to many different portals, directories, and books to help you make your educational choice. You can visit the Online Resource site at any time by going to <www.delmar.com>.

Notes to Yourself

You have been offered many options here to help find the course of study you are interested in. Now, it is time for you to move on to actually undertaking your educational choice. Before you do, feel free to make notes or reminders here. Is there a particular book or site you like better than the others? Why? Have you visited many college portal sites? Which ones are the easiest to navigate? The answers to these questions will help you identify the way that you want to experience your education. What do you think?

_____

_____

_____

_____

FIGURE 11-1

School Decision Checklist

School Decision Checklist

Name of school_____   Date contacted_____

Web site URL_____   Name of contact_____

School

Offers program I want to study?

Accreditation—Regional assn.: _____ Program:_____

How long in existence?_____ How long accredited?_____

Credentials of faculty: %PhD_____ % that hold degree from this school:_____

How many students are enrolled?_____ Graduated?_____

Name, phone/e-mail of enrolled students or graduates to contact: _____

When are students admitted (i.e., January/Sept., rolling) _____

Program - Degree/Major: _____

What are the prerequisites for admission?_____

Any tests required?_____ Other documentation:_____

Letters of recommendation?_____ How many?_____ Who from?_____

What are the application deadlines? _____

Number of credits to graduate: _____ Allowed in transfer: _____

What are the transfer criteria? _____

How many courses can I take before applying? _____

Can I complete a certificate and later use those credits toward a degree?_____

Credit given for prior learning? How? _____

Graduation requirements: _____

Who teaches courses; what credentials do they have?_____

Will I have an assigned advisor?_____ Can I change advisors?_____

Are there residency requirements?_____

What is average length of time to complete program?_____

Is there a time limit to complete the program?_____ For each course?_____

Can I take time off if I need to? How?_____

What is the time limit before I have to reapply?_____

Is there a "real" graduation, where I can march down the aisle?_____

Courses

How are courses structured? (tutorial, classes, etc.)_____

How long before a class starts can I enroll?_____

Is class size limited? If so, to how many?_____

What happens if too many?_____

What are grading policies? (Pass/Fail, etc.)_____

How are students assessed (projects, exams, etc.)?_____

What are the policies on incompletes?_____

Support

How do I obtain textbooks?_____

How do I access a library?_____

Is there an on-line writing center?_____ Other assistance?_____

Is the Student Handbook on-line? URL:_____

Is there an on-line student directory?_____ Faculty directory?_____

Are there any career services?_____

Technical

What are the recommended technical requirements?_____

Is there a tutorial I can try out? URL:_____

How are technical problems handled?_____

What about an on-line support manual? URL:_____

Costs

How much does each course/program cost?_____

What is the application fee?_____

What is the average cost of books and materials?_____

Are there other fees (graduation, residency, travel, etc.)?_____

Is financial aid available?_____ What kind?_____

How do I apply?_____ What are the deadlines?_____

What credit cards do you accept?_____

Other Questions:

_____

_____

_____

_____

Action	Date received/Sent
Requested application materials	
Mailed application	
Requested recommendations	
Requested transcript(s):	
Accepted	

Notes:

Get It Done—Managing the Educational Project

This section supplies tips, techniques, and information that will help you progress steadily through all phases of your distance learning project.

The chapters in this section are:

PREVIEW

Undertaking a project like a course of study or a degree program can seem overwhelming. For many adults, the idea of investing time toward an achievement that can take years to accomplish is hard to even imagine. In our instant gratification culture, the conscious commitment to a long-term goal seems to run counter to everything we hear in the marketplace. Daily, we are bombarded with options that seem designed to confuse and urged to choose 'before it is too late!' Yet, a choice as potentially important to you and your family's future should rely on forethought and careful consideration of all alternatives.

You can avoid the lures and claims of marketing by choosing a goal that is based on your own needs and lifestyle. Achieving a long-term goal such as a college degree requires two basic tools: a plan and the motivation to achieve it. Those who do not succeed generally have no lack of intelligence or ability. What they do have is a case of bad habits overcoming good intentions. Knowing how to identify and overcome the habits that prevent you from reaching your goals and the outside pitfalls that can overwhelm you is a complex mixture of determination, understanding, and support. The information in this section will help guide you in developing an achievement plan that works for you and those around you.

In addition, you will find advice and techniques for increasing your study skills, constructing research papers, and maintaining clear communication, both in class and out. You will read about the importance of a support network and receive tips on nurturing yours, so that it will nurture you.

CHAPTER 12

Setting and Achieving Goals

If you do not really want to return to school, but are doing it to satisfy someone else's idea of what you should do, you will not maintain the motivation you need to succeed when things seem most overwhelming. If you do not have a plan to accomplish each task that is part of your ultimate goal, it will remain an unfulfilled wish forever. You must have the desire, a driving passion for achieving your goal, whatever that goal may be. Whatever comes along to tempt, dissuade, or discourage you, you must be able to picture your passion and say, "That is why I am going through all this."

KNOW WHAT YOUR GOAL IS

Think back to the last time you achieved something that was important to you. It could have been anything: quitting smoking, completing a 10-K run, losing 10 pounds, or mastering a language. Do you remember the moment that you realized that you had achieved your goal? Did it feel good? Did that feeling have something to do with how much planning and time it took? Did you also realize, perhaps later, how the process had caused you to change? Perhaps you are a different person than you were before you succeeded at this achievement.

Arriving at an important milestone like overcoming a bad habit or teaching yourself a new skill probably changed you in many small but meaningful ways. It also provided a viewpoint from which to examine the past and plan for the future. That is the power of accomplishment. Every time you attain something you have struggled for, you add to your faith in yourself. The more faith you have in yourself, the more you can accomplish. You may be uncertain that you can succeed with something you have not tried before, like distance learning, but remember that you have already accomplished many things that you could not do once. You are already learning, and you will learn more.

> "Success is not a place at which one arrives but rather . . . the spirit with which one undertakes and continues the journey."
>
> — Alex Noble

The reason that many people fail to reach a goal is rarely because they are unable to do the work. If we do not meet our goals, it is often because of lack of management skills, either in self-management or management of the environment around us. Sometimes, we neglect to devise a plan and commit to carrying out our goals. Sometimes, we commit to goals that are so general that we cannot be sure when we reached them. Moreover, we will often set goals for ourselves that are unrealistic, or that do not take into account the ways that we can undermine ourselves into failure. Thus, deciding on a goal to work toward requires an understanding of yourself as well as an understanding of the work entailed to reach it. Before committing to the project, you should be sure of these things: It is the right goal for you, and what will let you know when you have reached it.

Know Why It is Your Goal

Marketing for your educational dollar is fierce, and advertising research shows that buyers can respond strongly to messages that speak to our fears. The dire warnings of being 'left behind' in a changing economy, or admonitions to 'live up to your full potential' prey on the fears of inadequacy and failure that abound in changing times. Once activated, fear helps to create the illusion of crisis, forcing the decision-making process. It is in this crisis state, where decisions are expected to be instantaneous, that many people make choices they later regret.

To add to the sense of urgency, it is probable that you have been considering further education for some time, but may have been putting it off. There are many reasons why you may have been putting off learning. Maybe you are not sure that you can stick with something that will take so long. Perhaps you can only remember past failures. Possibly, you are not sure that you have what you need to succeed. Maybe you do not know what is available or how to access it.

All of the questions and possibilities may have been crowding your mind for some time. If you are like most adults, though, a significant event has pushed you to take a more serious approach to your education. This "trigger event," as it is often referred to, can be anything, from the departure of a child for school to a change in your relationship with a loved one. Here, one on-line learner reflects on her reasons for choosing her goal:

> "You asked how I got here [to this class]. I had been thinking about returning to school for awhile—it was something I had talked about a lot with my dad. He only finished the 8th grade and I think he felt bad about his lack of formal education. This was kind of funny, because he was one of the smartest guys I knew. Sounds corny, doesn't it?
>
> He wanted me to finish my degree, and I wanted to, but I hadn't gotten around to it. I was always making excuses: the kids, it was too far, or too late at night to go to class, you know, it was always too much of an effort. Then last year, my dad had a fatal heart attack. Two weeks after the funeral I really started looking for ways to finish, and I found this on-line program. I know I'm doing it for me, but knowing that I'm doing something that was important to him, too, keeps me going."
> Sarah H., personal e-mail

For Sarah, the completion of her degree is motivated by the importance of her relationship with her father. Family relationships and the ties between family members are a very important part of her life, and can be seen in nearly everything she does. Love of family, then, is one of her driving values. She visualizes the happiness her studies would have brought to her father, and that helps to motivate her when she feels like making excuses.

GOALS ARE SHAPED BY VALUES

Whatever motivates you toward your goal, whether it is the ability to pursue a dream in the future or to flee a bleak reality in the present, it should be strong enough to hold you to the course of study you have chosen. To do so, it will have to be based on one or more of your own core values.

Values are the traits and conditions that, through experience and culture, have become important to you. They are your measurements for judgment, for the way you act, and for what you believe. They are the underlying reasons why you choose to do the things you do. Some of your values were formed in childhood, including concepts like fairness and privacy. These you learned from your parents and your earliest experiences, from the way you were treated and expected to treat others. The earliest experience of values learning, they determine the expectations you have about the way life *should* be and how you exist in it.

Some of the values you embrace came to you through the society you grew up in. Through education and popular media were transmitted the ideals that shape your concept of what a society should be, concepts like religious freedom and civic responsibility. For example, the schools you attended might have had a strong environmental orientation, so you learned to think of protecting wild spaces and recycling efforts as important to society. This is a value orientation and governs the way you value other groups within society. These kinds of values determine the way that you and others act in the groups that make up societies, and determine the kinds of cultures in which you will feel comfortable.

Another source of values education is the workplace, where you learned and came to believe which behaviors are appropriate and can be expected in the 'good' workplace. This is your expression of a 'work ethic'. For example, your work experiences have probably taught you that the attributes you need for success in the workplace include the ability to solve problems and cooperate with others. Not surprisingly, these abilities are highly valued by employers, as well. Workers who do not exhibit these values in their actions may not do well—unless there are other value systems at work. One example of a different value system is often referred to as 'the good-old-boy network'. Another is 'favoritism', in which poor performance may be rewarded because of an employee's relationship to the boss, instead of their contribution to the workload. Workers in a company that has an embedded culture of favoritism come to learn that treatment is different for different people. This can cause high frustration and frequent turnover. If fair treatment is a high value of individuals who begin working in such a company, the same individuals will probably feel resentful and take the first opportunity to move to a company that they perceive as having fairer practices. You can see why it is no mistake that the environment in which you work is often referred to as the "company culture."

The decisions you have made about what to study and why you want to learn it may be directed by your needs, but those needs are expressions of the values you have developed over your lifetime. Finding a way to meet your need to learn that allows you to be available to your children may be an important need for you. In

Culture consists of the behavior patterns, arts, beliefs, institutions, and all other products of a particular group's thought and work. Everyone is a part of at least one culture, and usually several.

that case, your value of being a good and caring parent is the value yardstick by which you measure the available alternatives. Take a moment or two now to think about your needs and what values motivate them. This will help you to clarify your alternatives and choose a program that is right for you on every level.

Examples:

I need to use what I learn to help others, because
I value being helpful.

or

I need a program that will get me a good job, because
I value being responsible for my family.

What do you need from the learning opportunity you choose, and why? Enter as many items as you feel are important to you:

I need a program that will let me_____

because I value_____.

I need a program in which I can_____

because I value_____.

When I think of what is important to me about how I learn, I think of (for

example, adhering to a schedule, doing the best work I can, etc.)_____

_____.

When I think of what is important to me about *what* I learn, I think of (for

example, relevant to my career, challenging, etc.)_____

_____.

Add other ideas as you think of them. To maintain motivation, keep your values in mind and in front of you as you progress through your program.

Individual Values Differ

Perhaps you will remember the earlier discussion about Kolb's theory of adult learning. In Kolb's model, adults observe events, compare them to what they already know, and make judgments (hypotheses) about their interpretation of observations. Then, they test this judgment in action, to see if it conforms with what they have decided, and adjust their judgment accordingly.

On a very fundamental level, this is how we obtain the values that make us both similar and unique. When something occurs to make us question what is happening, it is often because our values have been called into question. Perhaps things did not happen as we expected or assumed they would. We might begin to wonder what is wrong, when the problem is often the result of a clash of values. If you picture each person, including yourself, as enclosing a sphere of beliefs, feelings, and ideas, as in Figure 12–1, it may be easier to see how conflicts can occur and why they are no one's fault.

If the people around you do not share your enthusiasm for learning, or if their priorities are different from yours, their own values may be clashing with yours. Maybe your partner or friends feel threatened by your desire to succeed, and may try to undermine your plans. They may even be *completely unaware* of these feelings.

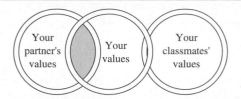

FIGURE 12-1

Your own values and beliefs will be close to those held by those around you, but classmates in distance classes may not share these values with you. Despite difference, you should respect what is important to others.

Contradictions can occur in work or family responsibilities. There will be times when your employer both supports your learning pursuits and insists that specific deadlines be met. There will be times when crises will interrupt your carefully arranged and fully packed schedule. There will be times when your need to turn in a perfect paper (if perfection is something you value) will be prevented by the time you have to complete it. There will *always* be conflicts. Learning to deal with them is a personal management skill.

Later in this chapter, we will explore ways to help deal with the inevitable conflicts and still stay on your educational path. However, the simple awareness that some unforeseeable events will interfere with your learning process will help to make those conflicts easier to navigate. If you are clear in your own mind about what you value, you *can* find appropriate compromises.

Knowing your values clearly can also make it easier to explain to others why you feel that pursuing education is important to you. It will, in turn, set the stage for others to share their own beliefs and thus minimize the negative aspects of conflict. You may not agree with each other on everything, but you can at least understand and reassure each other that there are values and beliefs that you do agree on.

When Values Collide

Value clashes can occur within us, as well. You may have noticed conflicting values on the list you made above. For example, you may value both safety and challenge. Perhaps you can satisfy both of those personal values by finding work that is intellectually challenging in an environment that is safe. The tension between the attributes and ideals that are important to you can be negotiated successfully. Awareness of what is important to you can help guide you in choosing a path that works for you.

You have already done your homework by finding out how you learn best, what is available, and even, perhaps, where you will obtain your learning. You have a learning goal. Your goal is motivated by your needs and values. What is it? Write it down here:

My learning goal is: _____.

This is my goal because: _____.

And because of that I will be able to: _____.

To help reinforce your commitment, copy these phrases and put them in a place where you will see them every day.

Every individual's response will be different. Moreover, your reasons for pursuing your goal can be stated in positive or negative terms, for example:

> My learning goal is: to complete my Master's in Education.
> This is my goal because: I will be able to attain my dream of being an elementary school teacher.
> And because of that I will be able to: help children prepare for their own futures.

Or,

> My learning goal is: to obtain Novell® certification.
> This is my goal because: I will be able to give up this dangerous job of driving a cab.
> And because of that I will be able to: work in a safe and secure environment.

CHECK YOUR LEARNING GOAL AGAINST YOUR VALUES

Take a moment to look back at what you wrote down when you completed the needs and values section. Do the goals you have for learning and the reasons you have those goals correspond with what you have identified as your values? If not, do you know why not? Do you need to reflect further on why you have chosen the goal you have? Make any notes you need here:_____

_____

There are many books and articles about setting and achieving goals. You may have some of them in your personal library. There are also resources on the Internet to help you work on identifying your dreams and working toward them. The most important component to setting your goals is you. No one can tell you what works best for you. Your learning is a decision you must make yourself. Do not let that stop you. Remember that you set and reach goals all the time without giving them much thought. Do you believe me?

Think back to the times that you learned something new, like driving a car. At first, it was something you had to think about all the time, but now it comes naturally. In some ways, you are like that car. You have the potential to 'drive' through your education, as long as you have the 'key' to start yourself up. Motivation is the key, plans and support are your fuel, and the destination is ahead. So get your map and hit the road!

 Make your commitment concrete. Write it down!

"I read an article about setting goals and wrote my impossible goal, getting a college degree. I placed this goal in my wallet and carried it around for several years. I decided to go for my impossible dream. In some ways it was incredibly difficult and in others it was easy. I now teach adult basic education students who want to get a GED . . . I guess I went back to school as a personal challenge, and it has changed my life dramatically."

—R., discussion board posting

ELIMINATE BARRIERS TO ACHIEVEMENT

Think about the reasons that have kept you from pursuing education in the past. How many of them are motivated by fear? Were they your own fears, or were they impressed upon you by others? Did you go ahead with your plans anyway, or let your or others' fears rule your actions?

As discussed in Chapter 3, any reasons that inhibit your pursuit of education can be categorized as *barriers, obstacles,* or *excuses.* To review,

- *Barriers* are events or circumstances that are beyond your control, such as a physical disability or the unavailability of a program you are interested in.
- *Obstacles* are circumstances that you can overcome with planning or practice, such as improving your writing skills or saving the money to attend school.
- *Excuses* cite circumstances that are easier to overcome, such as being tired or unable to study.

You might take a moment now to look back at those items you identified as barriers, obstacles, and excuses to your own educational desires, and the strategies that you identified to deal with them. How many of them can be attributed to your own fears of failure or change?

Take a moment to fill your own answers in the following blanks.

When I think about going back to school, my biggest fear is _____.

I think I fear this because _____.

Look again at what you have written. Is this really your biggest fear about returning to school? Is it realistic? In other words, is this thing you fear so much likely to happen? If the answer is "Yes," then you will need to find one or more ways to prevent it from happening. But at least you are aware of and better prepared to notice it if it does happen. If this fear is really not likely to transpire, tell yourself to stop worrying about it. It may also help to write "I am not going to worry about this," next to this unlikely event you fear. Use a brightly colored pen so that it really catches your eye!

The Importance of Attitude

Your success also depends on your attitude toward yourself as a learner. Do you think of yourself as having the ability to learn anything you set your mind to? Are you able to find the energy to study even when you have had a busy day? Do you enjoy learning new things? Or are you prone to self-doubt, feel you may be too old to learn, or give up when things get difficult?

If you ask people who have been successful at achieving a cherished goal what their secret was, they might say 'motivation', 'passion', or even 'focus'. Those are great words, but the expression of each of those terms is personal. You may already know why you need to pursue the educational plan you have chosen, but you will probably need to have a solid and very personal way to deflect temptation and banish doubt. There will be many situations and people who will doubt you or try to turn you away from your choice. You can ignore them, but they can be persistent. When they get under your skin, you will need to be able to tell yourself something to decrease their power. Having something specific to say when the negative people and thoughts try to make you pay attention can mean the difference between success and failure. But what *can* you say? What can you tell yourself that will deflect fear and strengthen your resolve? Here are some examples that have worked for others:

You hear: "You never finish anything."
You say: "That may have been true in the past. Will you help me change that?"

You hear: "You do not have what it takes to go to college."
You say: "Actually, I do, and I can learn the rest."

You hear: "You are trying to be something you are not."
You say: "You are wrong. I am going to be what I *can* be."

You hear: "You will never graduate."
You say: "Just watch me."

You can always avoid the company of those who would wish you to fail, but you can not avoid your own mind. Is there a little voice in your head that gets your attention and convinces you not to try? You need to tell that dark voice the same thing that you tell the people who thrive on others' failures: Not me. You are wrong. I *will* succeed.

Make a Contract to Succeed

Here it is. Your space to state your intention to be successful at distance learning. Write down your intention here and sign it.

Learning Success Contract

I, _____, being ready and able to learn, do hereby state my intention to succeed as a distance learner.

I promise to listen to people who encourage me and take energy from their good wishes.

I promise to do the work that is necessary because this goal is important to me.

If I am tempted to diverge from this goal, I promise to review my reasons for learning.

If anyone tries to tell me I cannot succeed, I will say:

_____

(Fill in a phrase that is special to you.)

I swear to keep these promises to myself and my loved ones.

I will succeed.

Signed:_____

On:_____

FIGURE 12-2

Your learning journey entails many stops. This is no express train!

PLANNING TO ACHIEVE

Now that you have identified your goal and your reasons for choosing it and made the commitment to success, you will need to devise a plan that will help you achieve it. Knowing your goal and the reasons behind it will help to give you the encouragement to attain it. One way to keep on track is to refer back to that note to yourself when your enthusiasm drops. That will help you remember why you have undertaken this journey. But it is a long journey, with many steps. Each step can be thought of as a stop on the journey, sort of like a train trip.

In Section II, "Know Yourself," the attributes of the self-reliant learner were discussed. One of these attributes is *the ability to set goals and standards. Goals* relate to the milestones and accomplishments you expect of yourself; *standards* relate to how you achieve and measure those goals. Achieving goals requires planning and organization. This is something you already know how to do, whether it is the steps you have gone through to plan a vacation, buy a car, or complete a work assignment. It does not happen overnight or because you are "lucky."

Goals Must Be Measurable

If you do not know where the finish line is, how will you know when you have reached it? For goals to have a possibility of success, they must be measurable. For example, you can say you will lose weight, but this statement does not include how much weight you want to lose, nor does it give you a time frame or plan to achieve it. A more manageable way to state this would be: "I will lose 10 pounds over the next three months by increasing the time I spend on exercise by a half hour each day." This is both a plan and the measurable steps toward achieving it. The standards for this goal are clearly stated and easily mapped, and you will know immediately if you are not sticking to the plan, and when you have reached your goal.

Set Learning Goals

Setting learning goals is very much the same. As noted earlier, all successful goals arise out of those values that are important to you. These are your own personal standards. For example, if you value flexibility in your work life, you may set a goal of finding a job or career that allows you to set your own hours.

Personal learning standards you might set for yourself could be to read all the assignments a week ahead, or complete all course requirements by a week before the deadline. Standards might also include expectations regarding the quality of the work you completed. For example, you might expect yourself to review all work before making it public, and to be sure that anything you post for people to read contains no misspellings. Other quality standards could include checking any URLs before posting to make sure they are correct and working, or the commitment to share your own knowledge with others.

If you value a feeling of 'being on top of' the technology necessary to fulfill course requirements, a goal you might easily expect of yourself is "to be familiar with how the instructional package works by the start of class." The standards to meet this goal could include understanding and being able to post messages in the class forum, knowing how to navigate around the class Web site, and learning how to contact other learners and the teacher easily. These are fairly simple things you can expect of yourself that will make your on-line experience more rewarding. Your learning goals will also change as your learning increases.

In many instances, certain goals and standards will be set forth in the **syllabus** for the course you take. This tells you what you will study, the books and materials you will need, and what is expected of you, often in great detail. For example, your syllabus might state that one of the requirements (goal) of the course is a written paper that must be at least 10 pages in length (standard); or that every student is expected to participate in the discussion forum (goal), making at least one posting per week (standard). Then, all you have to do is devise a personal plan based on your own values to meet the goals of the class.

COMMIT TO YOUR GOALS

Obviously, you will have goals that are both short-term and long-term. Perhaps you have committed to the long-term goal of achieving your master's degree by the time you are 40. How will you plan to achieve that goal? By breaking a large project down into smaller mini-goal components, you can build upon successes toward achieving that major goal.

What *learning goals* have you made for yourself? To graduate alongside your oldest child? To be the first person in your family to earn a master's degree?

What *standards* will you use to tell you that your goal has been reached? When you walk down the aisle, or see that piece of paper on your wall?

What *actions* will you commit to so that your goal becomes a reality? Will you set aside at least half an hour a day to study? Find three Internet sources for every discussion topic?

Committing to a learning goal is very much like making a promise to yourself. Like the commitment to succeed at distance learning, seeing these goals in writing will help to reinforce your determination. Write your personal learning promises here:

_____

_____

_____

_____

Goal Commitment Exercise

To help you keep track of each goal or promise and the standards and actions that will assure your success, use the Committing to Yourself form in this chapter. You can post the form near your computer to remind you of what you have promised to yourself. Repeat this goal and standard-setting exercise for every class you take to make it a normal part of your lifelong learning practice.

MANAGE TIME TO MEET YOUR GOALS

To make your trip a manageable one, break it into sections, and add sections together. Easier said than done, you say? Then one of your first stops (or steps) should be to develop a time management strategy that works for you. If the idea of time management seems laughable or unnatural, you are not alone. Lots of people do not have effective ways for getting the most out of that limited commodity. Lots of people also do not have your desire to succeed. If you want to succeed at

In the first column, state the goal you have identified. In the second column, set out the parameters so that you will know when you have reached your goal. In the third column, make note of the actions you will take to achieve the desired goal result.

FIGURE 12–3

Committing to Yourself

Goals	Standards	Actions to take

distance learning or any other goal, you will have to budget the time you have available to accomplish your goal.

Any successful student will tell you that the most important study skill is time management. This is especially important in an on-line study, where it is easy to procrastinate and lose momentum. After all, the computer is just sitting there, right? It is especially important with on-line learning to make sure that your motivational key is driving the car. You do that, in part, by controlling and making effective use of the time you have.

You have already read about setting your goals and the need for establishing the steps in the plan to achieve them. The first step is gaining control of your time. The next step is eliminating unnecessary or inappropriate tasks. Part of that step is determining what your most common time wasters are.

Time management is really about control. Time wasters can be internal or external; that is, they can be self-generated or environmental. You can let the events of life and the demands of others control you, or you can assume control of your time. It is, after all, yours to use. And yes, there are even ways to negotiate certain demands that you think you cannot. Once you get into the habit of a regular schedule, you will wonder what the problem was. Of course, scheduling is not the only piece of the puzzle. We will also look at ways that you can do what you need to and still have time left for yourself. Incredibly, even with more to do, you may find, as others have, that a habit for organizing your time allows you to fit in even more tasks. But now, you will be the one deciding what to include.

There are many strategies to help you regain control of your time, but first you should be aware of what you are up against. What are the factors that steal your life away and keep you from maintaining mastery of your own time? Hints and suggestions for dealing with the "thieves of time," noted in *italics,* are noted here.

Internal Time Bandits

Are you disorganized? Do you spend hours searching for items that have been misplaced? Is your work and study space effective? *Disorganization* is one of the main culprits for wasting time. Some people can work very effectively with clutter, so if you are one of them, there is no need to become a 'neatnik'. But if you find yourself regularly buried in paper and unable to find crucial items quickly, it will be especially important to get organized before you begin any on-line study.

Despite the fact that the majority of communication in distance learning occurs through the computer, any studying requires even more paper than you are dealing with right now. Yes, even more. Journal articles, textbooks, classmates' printed-out responses, class schedules—all of these will add to the desktop mess. You will be required to write papers, which are often easier to edit and revise if they are printed out. You may want to use commuting time or other off-line (away from the computer) time to read items you have been sent. Organize your work and study space now, and commit to organizing it regularly.

Procrastination is one of the problems cited by the majority of on-line learners. The simplest way to overcome procrastination is to set up a schedule and stick to it. Easier said than done, you say? If you use one of the many popular calendar programs, such as those that are part of Microsoft Outlook®, you can program reminders into your computer. Or, you can rely on post-it notes or a pocket calendar. Write yourself a pledge to study and post it on your refrigerator, as you might have done with your goal statement. Ask family members to follow up with you. If you put off assignments because they seem overwhelming, break them down into smaller, more manageable chunks. If the task is one you are not particularly looking forward to, set a deadline and decide on rewards for completing it. And, of course, to keep from focusing on what needs to be done *manana* (tomorrow), *do it now*!

One of the most common time wasters, especially for women, is the inability to say "No." Remember that most people will not be aware that you are on a time budget. They can not read your mind; tell them. You can thank them for thinking of you, or tell them when you will be able to give them time, just clearly state your need to focus on your education. The majority will understand, and may even become loyal supporters.

If you seem to be wasting time because you are experiencing a *lack of interest,* it is time to examine why you are taking this course. This is almost always a case in which your attitude is undermining your desires. If you can identify what the problem is, see if you can resolve it. Maybe your attitude is shared by your classmates. Perhaps you can communicate about it and discover ways to overcome the barriers and approach the topic in a different way. If the lack of interest is temporary, perhaps a short break is in order. With on-line learning, you can take time to do other things when you need a rest or reflection break!

Environmental Time Bandits

Time wasters in your environment may not be caused by you, but your time is used *reacting* to them. Thinking of them as time wasters implies a connotation that they are worthless or bad, but these are often things and people that you want to spend time on. It is important to realize, though, that some of the things that you want to do will take time away from your educational goal.

In Chapter 3, you used the Time and Activity Analysis Worksheet to determine how to fit learning into your life. This worksheet helped you to identify where your

Strategies for Dealing with Internal Time Wasters

Disorganization

- Review your work area to save effort.
- Have a designated place to keep only school-related work. Keep it all in one place.
- Make folders for classes before you need them.
- Have your references easily accessible.
- Practice planning and completing tasks.
- Resume working after interruptions.
- Limit the number of tasks you are working on at one time.
- Read all of the directions before starting.

Procrastination

- Set a deadline and stick with it.
- Plan backwards from the deadline. If doing the task for the first time, allow additional time.
- Write notes to yourself to remind you not to put off study and post them prominently.
- Build in rewards so that you have something to look forward to when you finish a task.
- Break the task into smaller pieces.
- Schedule regular times for studying, reading, and research.
- Do it while you are thinking about it, instead of thinking about doing it later.

Inability to Say 'No'

Be honest, but nice. Some nice ways to say no are:
- "That sounds interesting, but I am working on this now."
- "I am sorry I do not have time for that right now. Can I let you know when my schedule is less hectic?"
- "I will have time on _____. Can it wait until then?"
- "I am sorry, but I just can not do that right now. Have you asked _____?"
- "Thank you for asking me, but I will not have any time until _____."

Lack of Interest

- Incorporate something that is of interest as part of the task.
- Read more about it to find a perspective that is more interesting to you.
- Create a personal connection to make the topic or task relevant to you. Who *would* find this topic interesting? Look at it from that person's point of view.
- Make up a story about the topic that helps you want to learn more.
- Imagine it as a business venture. What would the product be; how would it be advertised; who would the customers be; and so on.
- Focus on how to *do* the task rather than the task itself. For example, think about ways that represent the topic in pictures or a song, or challenge yourself to find at least 10 references or at least three supporting arguments, or try to imagine how you would teach it.
- Talk to a friend and listen to suggestions to get a fresh approach.
- Review your notes for something you may have missed or want to explore further.

Which strategies do you think you will use most?

time was being used on a weekly or monthly scale. Be sure to also pay attention to the little time bandits that steal minutes away throughout the day. Once those minutes are gone, you can not use them for learning. Consider, for example:

Do you have a large number of *visitors*? Do you spend time talking with neighbors, just shooting the breeze? How many times have you found yourself saying, "Where does the time go?" If you want to visit with friends or coworkers, choose shorter meeting times and avoid the impulse to hang around.

What about your use of *technology* tools? Do you spend hours talking on the telephone, watching television, or surfing the Internet? Limit exposure to all of these tools and reallocate your time to schoolwork. Be honest with yourself about computer time. Obviously, distance learning on-line will mean extensive use of the computer. Just be sure that the time spent is mostly spent on classwork, and not just aimless surfing. An additional benefit of this kind of self-regulation can be that you begin to lose interest in nonproductive information seeking. Will that happen to you, do you think?

Do you spend a lot of time *waiting*? Use this 'empty' time wisely. Always have a textbook or project with you, use commuting time to read or listen to books or notes on tape, or carry a tape recorder to dictate notes for that next paper. While waiting for a meeting or the doctor to call you, review your notes. If you spend time waiting while sitting at your computer, use that time to organize your bookmarks or course folders. If you are waiting for 'Tech Support', this activity will have the additional benefit of helping to keep you calm!

There are environmental time wasters in the workplace, as well, like unnecessary meetings and duplicated tasks. Although these may not directly impact on your educational project, effective management of these time users can provide clues to dealing with the time that does.

Finally, there is the inevitable *crisis*. There will always be crises. Some can be avoided before they happen, however, with adequate planning. If you notice that the same events are happening over and over again, a pattern may appear. Determine the steps that are necessary to plan ahead so that crises do not become a habit. Never react to a crisis by having another crisis! Instead, use a trick that many successful project managers use when planning a task. Ask yourself:

- What can go wrong?
- When will I be aware of what is wrong?
- What will I be able to do about it?

If you find yourself dealing with crises more than you think is appropriate, serious self- and process evaluation is in order. Is it possible that you are not the person who should be dealing with the event for which another is responsible? Ask yourself if you have gotten into the habit of being the 'problem solver' because you like and value that role. If that is the case, designate another problem solver and resume your focus on your studies.

Is the crisis one that is triggered by a particular person or situation? Maintain a focus on the situation as a problem to be solved, rather than an opportunity to place blame or instill guilt. Everyone makes mistakes and deserves a chance to learn how to avoid them. Get everyone associated with the crisis situation involved in devising a crisis-avoidance plan or designing a disaster recovery process. Like planning to achieve, planning to avoid time-consuming problems will save time in the long run.

Delegating to 'Find' Learning Time

By examining your priorities and enlisting the support of family and others, you can delegate or discontinue duties you may not have time for any longer. For

Strategies for Dealing with External Time Wasters

Visitors

- Limit visitors, if possible. If not possible, go to them and keep an eye on the time.
- Stand up when someone comes into your office. Remain standing to talk.
- Schedule visits for times of the day that encourage brevity. For example, get together for breakfast instead of evenings or weekends.
- Close your door or use a "No Interruptions, Please" sign.
- Use a 'do not disturb' signal. One learner wore a red hat to tell her children that she was studying and would talk to them later.
- Say 'Hi,' and keep walking!

Telephone, Television, and other Technology Tools

- Use the answering machine or voicemail instead of answering the phone when it rings.
- Return calls in blocks, or while you are doing something else.
- Turn the TV off or, better yet, do not turn it on.
- If you can not give up the TV or telephone, schedule its use as a reward for getting work done.
- When the program you want/need to watch is over, turn the set off.
- Limit Internet time to research: Ask yourself how the time spent is related to school.
- Time Internet surfing (browsing or grazing) and telephone calls by using a timer.
- Think about what you want to find or talk about before you go online or pick up the phone. Stop when you have reached the objective.
- End subscriptions to e-mail lists and newsgroups that rarely generate helpful information. (You can always join again later.)

Waiting

- Always carry something to do with you. Plan ahead and expect to wait.
- Tape your notes or textbooks and listen to tapes while waiting or commuting. This also reinforces your learning.
- Keep a notebook nearby to jot down ideas.
- Use a microcassette recorder to develop ideas for papers or for interviews.
- Restate the major points of your last reading assignment.
- Review the remaining requirements; check to see if you have missed anything.

Crises

- Reflect on past crises to determine if a pattern emerges; take evasive action to prevent crises.
- Take a deep breath. Stay in control. Consider alternative remedies in a methodical way.
- Treat crises as problems to be solved, not situations to be reacted to.

example, because you now need to use some of your time to study, you may not have the time or energy to cook a full dinner every night. Or, you might not have time to be solely responsible for doing the family laundry. You may decide to curtail participation in some of your social or community activities. When you have decided that your education is a priority, you will find it easier to decide which other activities are necessary and which are not.

Be sure to include family and other supportive individuals in planning, so they understand how important these choices are to you. Sharing with others your goals and the planning process to achieve them will reinforce your commitment and demonstrate the importance of your desire to achieve.

Time Allocation Activity

Help your supporters to help you. First, read the portion of this chapter entitled "Share Your Goals." Use the worksheets provided in this book to agree together on the tasks that need to be done and who will be responsible for them. Discuss what responsibility means to everyone, and how you will know if the plan is not working. Remember that you do not have to make all the decisions yourself. Consultation with your family, friends, and coworkers may yield ideas for excellent alternatives that you had not considered.

First, get together and look at the Time and Activity Analysis Worksheet you completed earlier. This will establish the pastimes or tasks you can delegate or delete during the time you will be pursuing your studies.

Then, use the Time and Task Adjustment Worksheet in this chapter to identify tasks and activities to delegate, change, or temporarily delete from your schedule, so you can use that time to do schoolwork. For example, you may delegate pet care to an older child, change your housekeeping pattern, or decide to forego television on weeknights. Be sure to leave time for yourself and your family, as noted earlier.

You can copy the worksheet as many times as you need to meet the fluctuating needs of your and your family's schedule. An extra worksheet is included among the other worksheets in the appendix, and on the Online Resources Web site.

SHARE YOUR GOALS

As you are no doubt aware, people often say things that are different from what they mean. You have probably done it yourself! If you ask about what is behind a statement, without simply reacting to what you have heard, you can often find the underlying meaning and address that. For example, it is not uncommon for partners of adult learners to feel threatened by the changes that school may cause. Some of these partners fear that the learner will become 'smarter' than they are and no longer find them interesting. Some will foresee a change in the balance of the relationship and feel their worth, authority, or power shifting. Some will even sense a competition developing and rush to join in. Yet all of these very different feelings may be voiced as worries about how school is to be paid for!

Children will have specific concerns, as well. They may want to know whether you will be able to drive them to activities or attend sporting events, as in the past. You will see what is most important to them by listening to their questions. Realize that young children are less able to visualize long into the future. That is what you are there for! Remember that their perceptions of life are often far more immediate than yours, but that they can be your greatest source of support. You, in turn, will be giving them important lessons in group decision making, as well as being a dynamic role model for their own learning endeavors.

Parents, too, can have an impact on your ability to achieve your goals. They may be willing to help by caring for children to give you time to study or by help-

Write down the tasks or activities that can be adjusted to provide time for your studies. You may make multiple copies of this worksheet as the demands of your school schedule fluctuate. Be sure to share this worksheet with your family and others when delegating responsibilities!

FIGURE 12–4

Time and Task Adjustments

Activities/tasks to delegate	Person responsible	Time saved
Activities to change	**How to change**	
Activities to delete temporarily	**When to resume**	
	Total time saved →	

ing to fund the costs of education. It is just as likely, too, that they may hinder your efforts by sending doubting messages or by being otherwise unsympathetic. Everyone has different perceptions and experiences. It is always a possibility that the ones who should care most about your success may also feel threatened by it in some way.

Part of achieving your educational goal, then, has to include discussions with the people who are likely to feel its impact. They will be the ones to be directly influenced by your goals. They are your support network and safety net. They will be the ones to support you through the difficult times and celebrate the achievement along with you. Help them to help you by including them in the planning process and by being clear and consistent in your messages. Then, even those who do not encourage you will be less likely to hinder you.

Choose the Right Time to Share

Begin by setting aside a time for everyone to discuss the ways that they think your educational goal will affect them. Make sure it is a time when everyone will be as relaxed as possible. Do not try to sandwich this important discussion between other events. Deal with each question and concern directly and honestly. Try not to predict what each person will say, because that will only decrease communication instead of fostering it. Avoid responding to anger or insults in kind. In fact, if anger or other strong emotions persist, reschedule the meeting for another time and deal with whatever is causing the outburst first.

If you have a regular family meeting, that will serve as a good framework for your discussion. If not, you may want to use dinner or after-dinner time to begin the educational discussion. Use the Time and Task Analysis Worksheet form to stimulate discussion and decision and help you to illustrate how you have already thought about the influence this undertaking will have on everyone.

If it is the first time your family will be talking about the impact of your education, do not try to cover all bases. Depending on their ages and personalities, children will have different reactions. One approach is to simply tell children that you are thinking about going back to school, and ask what they think. Another, more inclusive method, is to involve them in the process as participants. For example, you might begin this discussion by saying, "I/We wanted to talk to you because Mommy (or Daddy) is thinking about something that will affect all of us." This approach, at least, will pique the curiosity of even the most jaded teen.

Decide What to Share

Like most adults, most children will immediately think of how this announcement relates directly to them. Most school-aged children will be curious about your teachers or classmates, because they think of any school as the kind of school they go to. Ask them to listen first to you and promise to listen to them when you have finished. Then, before you become overwhelmed with questions from the talkative ones (or have to drag responses out of the reticent ones), you can tell them why you have decided that this is a good thing for you to do. Let them know, at a level that is appropriate, about the things you have thought about and your hopes for your own—and their—future. Expect to say these things many times in the future.

Reassure them that you will not be leaving them alone to go to class, but will be learning on the computer, over the Internet. If you have already done your research and chosen your learning provider, tell them what you expect. If you are not sure what to expect, it is all right to say so. Because so many schools are integrating technology—including the Internet—into classroom activities, you may even have a resident guide, who is likely to be your biggest supporter. This is also an opportunity to tell your children how much you hope to learn together and how much you count on their help.

Instead of trying to answer all questions or providing solutions to any problems that may be revealed, ask children what *they* think should be done. In addition to alleviating the pressure for you to come up with something, it will help your children learn to think problems through and apply their own reasoning to them. This is a skill that they will need to succeed in their own right. Listen to what they say and make sure everyone has a turn to speak.

 Do not interrupt or minimize the feelings stated in the family meeting. Doing that will only cause problems later.

Establish a Regular Time to Talk

Leave the issue of learning open. Adults are not the only ones who think of things to say or ask after the meeting is over. Consider setting up a regular time to talk about school, activities, and other issues. Middle school children, especially, will relish the opportunity to ask you whether you are done with your homework! At the first meeting, you may want to suggest that each person write down questions or concerns as they think of them, rather than expecting reactions to something new at the moment it is revealed. Follow the first discussion with one-on-one talks so that issues that may have been forgotten or been embarrassing to air around siblings are also confronted. The comments, questions, and concerns you hear will tell you more than you realize about your children and their perceptions of you.

Take time as well, if it applies, to get your partner's impressions of the meeting. You may both be surprised at the way your interpretations complement one another, with a more enriched picture emerging from both your observations combined than would have been possible for one of you to see alone.

Family meetings, as well as discussions with friends, will reveal the people you can count on to be the most helpful. These are the ones you will turn to for encouragement when your own enthusiasm flags. *This is your personal support network.* Later in this chapter, we will discuss methods for maintaining your support network through the journey ahead. There will be times when you will need them, and you will want to be sure they are there.

By sharing your commitment to self-improvement, you put your dream on display. Now your dream is a goal known to many. It is a goal, though, that only you can actually accomplish. Be sure that you have discussed with *yourself* any problems or concerns you have, as well.

By sharing your commitment to self-improvement, you put your dream on display.

ACHIEVEMENT REQUIRES MOTIVATION

Motivation to learn should be sustainable. The way to assure that your desire will continue to fuel your progress is to know the restrictions you face and have a plan to deal with them. As you are probably aware, there are forces counteracting your very rational desire to succeed and make the best possible life for you and your loved ones. These barriers, if outside your control, can impede your progress and cause frustration.

By now, you will have identified your possible pitfalls to distance learning success. You have read about the characteristics that are required for success in distance learning and the restrictions that can impede that success. You know the problems that might prevent you from achieving your learning goals, and you have a plan to achieve them and the help and support of others.

Blueprint for a Family Meeting

1. Choose a time when everyone is relaxed.
2. Communicate the issue clearly.
3. Give all relevant details.
4. Ask for questions and comments.
5. Solicit solutions to questions and perceived problems.
6. Agree on solutions or actions.
7. Ask for support.
8. Follow up individually, as necessary.

When the time comes—and it will—when you feel you can not stand to go on, when you question your resources and your abilities, you will need to remember why you undertook this learning journey in the first place. Return to your notes in this text and wherever you have posted them around your home study area and elsewhere. Keep your goal in front of you by picturing it in your mind so that every time you close your eyes, you can see yourself achieving. Visualize your success. Perhaps you can find a picture in a magazine that represents your goal—cut it out and tack it to your bulletin board. These things will help you to remember the values that made you choose distance learning as a means to success.

To Sum Up. . . .

In this chapter, we looked at the ways to define and manage your educational goal. We discussed what shapes the values that drive our goals, and how each person's values can differ. We also examined concrete ways to discover whether your goals interfere with those around you, and how to manage those disruptions to keep them to a minimum.

Further, we investigated barriers to achievement and considered methods of dealing with the ones that may plague you. The importance of making a plan to meet your goals, including strategies for dealing with time, was also mentioned. Because it is important to make your commitment to self-improvement public, we spoke about sharing your goals with those around you.

Practice and small successes will help you to gain confidence in your abilities and assets. To practice learning, you have to learn. Now, it is time to actually get to work. In the next chapter, we will look at ways that you can complete your school assignments effectively and efficiently by learning to study effectively.

Notes to Yourself

This chapter may have raised issues that are hard to face: issues around support and encouragement, that many of us did *not* experience as youngsters. Help yourself to succeed now by writing down here those messages that you tell yourself because you heard them so often. Notice that written at the end of the line is 'NOT'! You no longer have to be a slave to those internal enemies. Say no to them, now.

_____ *NOT!*

_____ *NOT!*

Okay, now prove that you *can* do it!

CHAPTER 13

Learning to Study and Studying to Learn

For most of us, studying is a dim memory of sprawling on the bed or reviewing illegible notes the night before a test. You may have been one of the 'lucky' ones who did not have to spend too much time studying to get good grades. You may be terrified that you are too set in your ways to overcome your bad habits or, worse, too old to learn anything new.

PREPARE TO STUDY

First, forget the myth that your memory or intelligence deteriorates with age. You are just out of practice. You have plenty of mental capacity to do what you need to learn—on-line or anywhere else. The first thing you should do to prepare yourself for studying is to start an exercise program—a mental exercise program—as soon as possible.

Any course of study will require a good deal of reading. If you are not used to doing a lot of reading, start now. Therefore, what you get from coursework is directly related to how well you read. Choose materials that you are interested in and read critically. What does it mean to read critically?

Rather than being negative, reading critically has very little to do with making nasty remarks. It means, instead, that you question what the author says, asking why she says what she does, and looking in the text for support of her ideas. This is a skill that is absolutely necessary for college-level study. In addition, critical reading skills can help you in the workplace and in all other aspects of your life. Being able to judge whether messages contain truths or falsehoods is a core critical skill. It is the method you need to separate concrete facts from mere allegations, and worthwhile information from advertising. If you are a good but slow reader, consider a speed-reading course to help you keep up with reading assignments. Critical reading and study skills are discussed in greater detail in the next part of this chapter.

"God gave us two ends. One to sit on and one to think with. Success depends on which one you use; heads you win— tails you lose."

— Anonymous

If you are not used to doing a lot of reading, start now.

Here are some other things you can do to get your mind and memory 'back in shape' and prepared for school:

- Go to the library. See how things are organized and get used to looking for material.
- Watch educational channels on TV instead of sitcoms.
- Take a memory improvement course, or look for books on memory techniques. Practice the techniques.
- Get your kids to teach you how to play some of their computer games. Many require a different way of thinking and acting than most adults are used to.
- Try learning a new skill that you have always been interested in learning. You do not have to become a master to try it.
- Open yourself to possibilities! Think of yourself as a learner.

REMEMBER WHAT YOU READ

There are many ways to improve your retention of course material. Now that you know what your own learning style and strengths are, you can devise ways to remember that capitalize on those strengths. For example, if you are an auditory learner, reading your chapter assignments into a tape recorder and listening to them when you drive to work will reinforce the material as you both see and hear it. Here are some other strategies for remembering and thinking about what you are learning:

Skim the material first to get an overview of the topic. Then go back and read for detail.

Ask yourself questions about the material as you are studying it. What more do you want to know? How does what you are learning relate to what you already know? What is confusing? Write your questions down after you skim before you read in depth. Often, the instructor will post directed questions that you will be required to respond to. These questions will help your brain search for information automatically.

Make notes of key ideas and concepts. If you are a visual learner, you might draw a diagram or build a model that illustrates these ideas. Or, think of an example from your experience that illustrates the key points. In that way, you will be able to hold them in your mind more easily. Do not highlight as you read, as this tends to interrupt the flow of ideas. If you want to highlight as an aid to review, go back and do it separately after you have identified the main ideas.

Test yourself on the material. Try to figure out why the instructor chose this material and how it fits into the rest of the course material.

Restate what you have read by making up a story or analogy to illustrate complex concepts.

Some teachers provide directed questions, which force you to look for material in the reading assignment that answers a question. Unfortunately, many students read only enough to answer the question, and may miss entire concepts. If directed questions have been provided, do not read them until after you have skimmed through the material to get the main ideas.

Tell others about your studies. Make it a regular habit to discuss key ideas you have discovered during your family's dinner hour. These discussions may yield different points of view, as well as having the benefit of including your loved ones in your endeavor. It will also reinforce to your family the seriousness you feel about learning.

If you follow these steps with your studies, you will find that your memory—and your understanding—will improve in no time, and you will be well on your way to becoming a powerful learner. To deepen your learning experience even more, you may want to keep a learning journal.

THE LEARNING JOURNAL

The learning journal, or learning log, is a personal record of your class experiences. Its purpose is to help you make connections between what you are learning and what you already know, by charting your impressions, opinions, and reactions to the material taught in the class. Learning journal entries help you think about how to apply what you are learning and incorporate it into your day-to-day reality. They can be thought of as a sort of 'thinking out loud' process.

Learning journals are being used increasingly by teachers of adults. It is a generally held belief among adult educators that adult learners need to see the connections between what they are learning and their experiences, and shared journals help to do this. Most teachers who use this method to reinforce learning will ask questions to stimulate your reaction. They may ask you to share your observations with them on a regular basis, or require a 'reaction paper' as part of your overall coursework.

The discussion board participation in an on-line class can take the shape and flavor of a learning journal. Here, you will post your reactions and observations about the course materials and readings, often using examples from your own experiences. This narrative reaction, especially when shared with others, can make on-line learning a collaborative and reinforcing adventure. You might choose to keep a separate learning journal in a folder within your word processor, and cut and paste entries into the discussion board from there. Even if your teachers do not ask you to compare what you are learning to your work and life experiences, you can choose to do it yourself and increase the return on your educational investment.

The Learning Journal Template

By reading your learning journal, you and the teacher should have an impression of what you think and feel as a result of the course. In addition, your writings will reveal to both of you how what you have learned in the course can lead you to act and think differently at work, and in life.

You can use the template following to help guide your learning journal development. Follow the directions to an influential way to help you learn even better. Additional copies of this template are available in the appendix and on the Online Resources Web site.

ADOPT A 'STUDY MENTALITY' FOR SUCCESS

Part of your preparation for each study session should include getting into the right frame of mind to study. It is unfortunate that many people have the attitude that studying is drudgery, a necessary evil to be passed through. Yes, learning does take time, but it can (and should) be interesting and exciting. If it is not, you might want to review your goals or values in choosing the topic you will spend so much time on!

To make the most of your study time, create a positive attitude. Look forward to learning something new or reading someone else's ideas. Actually, this is usually not difficult. Many on-line learners report such a high degree of interest in the on-line class interactions that they access course boards and e-mail several times a day. Curiosity about how others have reacted to your comments and interest in what others have to say about assignments can be incredibly motivating.

If there is a portion of the class assignment that does not interest you as much as some others do, approach the task by asking questions prior to undertaking the assignment. Try to predict what the author of the textbook or the instructor of the class will say next. Perhaps you can make this into a game with yourself, seeing how many ideas or facts you can 'guess' before they are revealed in the text.

Learning Journal Template

Directions: Choose a concept or idea from class readings and record your thoughts, feelings, opinions, or personal experiences about them. Include reasons for your reactions, supporting your points. As possible, your entries should contain ideas for applying what you have learned to your daily life. Write in a descriptive way, and as freely as possible. Do not limit or censor yourself. This is not a research paper! Be yourself.

Include:

- observations
- descriptive examples
- realizations
- reflections on the realities of your life
- other reactions you feel are important

Make journal entries at least once a week. Keep them in separate folder or notebook. At the end of the class, read through all of your entries and complete the journal by summarizing them in a final entry. Feel free to construct a learning journal for more than one class.

Name of class: _____   Date:_____

Concept or idea:_____

How I feel about it: (Write as much as you wish.)

Describe why you feel this way. Use examples, if applicable:

Tell how this concept or idea may influence your behavior in the future:

Imagine a story explaining a concept before reading a chapter. For example, instead of just launching into an explanation of the economic principles of supply and demand, imagine an example that illustrates how you understand it before reading. Maybe you can visualize a lemonade stand and its pint-size proprietor on different points of operation, one on a sweltering July afternoon and another on a frigid January morning. See if what you read reinforces or refutes your own visualization and understanding. Be sure to write down the items that you have learned, too.

To additionally stimulate your study mentality, make a conscious resolution to be open to new ideas. This is especially necessary when you are learning about entirely new concepts or ideas that are foreign to your experience. Such a resolve to be open minded can also be invaluable when dealing with other learners who may be hundreds of miles away and see things very differently than you do. Use those critical thinking skills: Reserve judgment until all information is made available. Decide to weigh information based on facts presented instead of your feelings. (Put your personal feelings into the learning journal, instead.) Approaching the task of studying with this point of view, and practicing it consistently, will help to assure your success as a learner.

HAVE A STUDY PLAN

It is good to have a plan for studying that entails more than staring at pages in a book. One popular study effectiveness plan is known by its steps as **SQ3R.** The steps in this plan are very similar to the memory steps outlined earlier. The steps for this study effectiveness plan, from which it gets its name, are *Survey, Question, Read, Recite and Review.*

In the *survey* step, you bring together all of the information you need to complete your assignment, whether that is simply reading a chapter, reviewing a classmate's project, or anything else. Following the way you are most comfortable with, begin to form a mental picture of the information you are scanning. For some people, this will take the form of a mental outline, with main ideas listed prominently and supporting information ranked beneath. For others, a mental map showing relationships between ideas will work best. Yet others will find that bullet lists or charts will help them to remember. Use the survey step to decide what kind of organization will work for this assignment and for you.

As you survey the material, look at all pictures, graphs, and other learning aids. This will prepare you to take the next step, in which you *question* what you have read. This does not mean that you are looking for loopholes or mistakes. Instead, formulate questions to focus your mind and help you find the important concepts. If the text states that an event took place, ask yourself "Why?" Seek other questions that the text prompts. Look for the answers to your questions. Knowing the reasons for an occurrence or the conditions of experiments on which theories are based will help you to remember them.

Adopt a Successful Study Attitude

- Look forward to new information.
- Cultivate curiosity.
- Use your imagination.
- Keep an open mind.
- Seek out facts and proof.

As you actually *read* the material at hand, keep those questions in mind. Pause often to evaluate what you are reading. Does it make sense to you? You have to be able to make sense of the basics before you can build on it to advance your knowledge. Read to fill in the sketchy outlines of the picture you have formed. As your questions are answered, note them.

When you have finished reading the section or chapter, stop for a moment. Compose your thoughts and *recite* to yourself what you have learned in the reading. The voice that reads in your head will be the same as the one you hear through your ears. If you are an auditory learner, this is a particularly powerful opportunity: Tape your recitation to reinforce what you have read, and to use as a review later. Hearing this information in your own voice cements it in your mind much more securely, because you are both seeing and hearing the same information, with the same voice.

Finally, *review* the material to be sure that you have it right, and to firmly embed it in your memory. Complete your notes or rewrite and embellish the ones you have already made. Date or number your notes (or both) so that you can keep track of what you have done and when you did it. Keep all of your notes together in one place.

For even more study effectiveness, look over the notes you have made at this point before you begin the cycle again with the next assignment. This will help to quickly prepare you for optimum learning.

SCHEDULE STUDYING FOR LEARNING EFFECTIVENESS

Regularly scheduling your study sessions will help you to succeed. First, scheduling will help overcome any tendency to procrastinate. Secondly, by getting into a regular habit of studying, you will keep up to date on your coursework and minimize ineffective last-minute cramming. Scheduled study times also reduce stress, increase understanding, and enhance your feeling of competence.

For best results, choose times to study when you are most alert and relaxed. This will assure that you will absorb maximum information and get the most from your limited study time. If you function best in the morning, for example,

---

The SPQ3R Study Method

SURVEY—Gather the information necessary to focus and formulate goals. Notice any headings, graphics, or charts and build a mental structure for comprehension.

QUESTION—Help your mind engage and concentrate.

READ—Fill in the information around the mental structure. Keep the questions in mind as you read.

RECITE—Repeat key concepts after each section. See if you can answer the questions you had without referring back to the text.

REVIEW—Make notes of your reading to begin building memory.

Learn to follow this plan when you are studying and it will soon become second nature. Also, see the end of this chapter for a link to other study strategies available through the Internet on the Online Resources Web site, at <www.delmar.com>.

your most effective time to study might be in the early morning before the rest of the family awakens.

Making regular study sessions habitual will also make your mind more receptive to learning. When you have scheduled the time you have available in a routine set aside for studying, you will be ready and able to retain your readings more easily and you will begin to learn more each time you study. You will learn more quickly and with greater persistence in memory. Practice regular studying to establish a habit of lifelong learning.

Remember that if you are just reading and not able to recall what you have read, your reading time is wasted time. Check out the Online Resources Web site link at the end of this chapter for other hints and tips on increasing your study-time effectiveness and managing your time so that you can accomplish everything you have set out to do.

Learner Profile, Continued

Greg chooses a study path

I found out right away that it was easiest for me to learn while I was doing something physical, so I taped many of my class readings to listen to on my walks. I also found that it helped prompt my thoughts to tape myself thinking out loud about the ideas in the lessons. The teacher had introduced the SQ3R method at the first class, and I had thought at the time, 'great, another dumb acronym to remember.' But it really works. I think, though, that some pieces of the study process work better for some people than they do for others. For me, the reciting part helped the most.

Someone asked me the other day what advice I would give to students that were thinking about distance learning. Here is what I said:

- Practice reading. Just because it's on-line doesn't mean it's not hard work.
- Read all the assignments before you start posting in the discussion area.
- Get ready for changes in yourself!

MAKE NOTE TAKING WORK FOR YOU

Just as the SQ3R method is one way to retain what you learn, there are many different ways to organize the material you cover for later review. Many of the study effectiveness links on the Online Resources Web site also provide tips for writing notes and organizing what you have learned. The main purposes of taking notes are to cement the information in your mind and to find it quickly when reviewing. Choose a way to organize your notes that works for you, whether it is a mental map, an outline, a series of lists, or some other method.

Just as there are many different ways to keep track of your time, there are many note-taking 'systems'. Several preparatory steps are common to all of them, whether you are taking notes from a classroom lecture, participating in an on-line course, or reading a textbook. Remember, these are all just different ways of delivering education.

First, be ready to learn. Deal with any distractions ahead of time and decide to handle other responsibilities later. Even if you are remarkably skilled at multi-tasking, you will need to be able to concentrate on what you are doing. Put on the phone machine, make sure the kids are being looked after, and get comfortable.

The main purpose of taking notes are to cement the information in your mind and to find it quickly when reviewing.

FIGURE 13-1

Organize your notes in a way that works for *you*.

Be sure to read whatever material has been assigned prior to connecting with your on-line class space. This will go very far in helping you to understand what is going on, yet many people neglect this important step. Have the main ideas written down. This can be the beginning of your note-taking system.

If information is given in an ordered, sequential way, or if you are a concrete or detail-oriented learner, the Cornell note-taking method may work best for you. In this method, the notebook page is divided roughly in half, with one side of the page used to state main ideas and the other to fill in details. This method can be used to provide an outline of the course, chapter, or lecture, and used as a study tool for review. For example, the left, or main idea side, can identify a concept, which is explained on the right, detailed explanation side. The format and an example are shown in Figure 13-2.

Not every course, teacher, or learning experience is sequential and orderly, though. If the teacher's lecture or your own ideas seem to jump around all over the place, you may want to use a mental map to keep track of the "big picture." In this method, you construct a network of interconnected information organized by main ideas and subtopics. Mental maps and semantic webs use a web-like network to help you keep track of ideas and concepts that jump from one area to another. That way, you can get a quick overview of main and supporting ideas. An example of a mental map is shown in Figure 13-3.

Mental maps are designed to limit the amount of detail that can be included. Particulars can be filled in later with a more organized approach like the Cornell system or another detail-oriented approach. Mental maps are also extremely helpful in identifying where further detail or investigation is required. In this way, they can serve as study tools to remind you where you need to direct further exploration to round out your understanding.

As you can see, there are many ways to organize your notes and many reasons for getting into the habit of taking them. It is certain, though, that taking good notes is a necessary component to success in any learning endeavor. Clear, organized notes are particularly important to success in distance learning, where the limitations of space and time can prevent you from seeing class participants and the teacher. Other methods and study strategies can be found on the Online Resources Web site, noted in the summary at the end of this chapter.

The Cornell Note-Taking System-Sample

FIGURE 13–2

The Cornell system allows as much detail as you wish. It is sequential and yields good study notes.

Subject: PLA 001   **Date:** 8/15

Main Idea	Details

1. Prior Learning Assessment is for learning, not experience.	1.1 College - level
	  A. writing
	  B. depth of understanding
	  C. Theory + practice
	  D. Transferable
	
	2.1 Standardized tests
	  A. CLEP
	    1. lower - level
	    2. inexpensive
	    3. study guides
	  B. DANTES
	    1. Military
	
	2.2 Evaluated training
	  A. A.C.E. - Employer
	    1. costs employer $
	    2. updated annually
	    3. Co. + public util.
	  B. Military - A.C.E.

2. Methods of PLA for credit.	

On-line Notes Are Especially Helpful

On-line learning, particularly in the retention of course materials, can actually be superior to other, more traditional, methods of learning. One of the specific bonuses to on-line learning is that everything that is written in the on-line class space is **archived.** This means that all of the notes, comments, and other information provided as a course of the class experience remain available for you to look at again and again. Most, if not all, of the thoughts and responses can be reviewed before you reply, so that you can be sure you are responding to what was written, instead of having to rely on what you think you heard in a crowded classroom. Moreover, any—or all—responses can also be copied and downloaded to your own computer's hard drive so that you can save them with other course materials for later retrieval.

FIGURE 13–3

Mental maps and semantic webs organize large amounts of data well and show the relationships between the individual pieces.

Mental Map Note-Taking Example

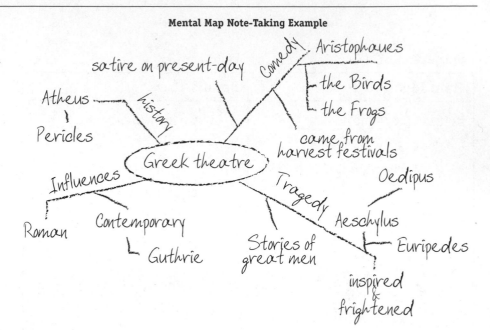

These saved responses can form the framework for very detailed notes that you later distill, as well as serving as a precise record of the class. This record can be reviewed or annotated in the future, giving you a concrete record of your learning experiences. Then, you will have a resource on which you can build at a later date, or simply review to refresh your understanding. Along with this text, the complete record will also become an enhanced educational autobiography of your lifelong learning journey.

To Sum Up. . . .

In this chapter, we examined the important study skills necessary for success in any learning enterprise. We learned that adequate preparation and the right attitude were as important as—if not more so than—following through with study strategies. We also determined that the learning journal exercise can be a helpful method to increasing understanding and integration of your learning.

Like much of everything else in life, effective studying requires a study plan. We reviewed how such a plan is made and carried out in an effective way. We examined several different note-taking systems and discussed the special challenges and opportunities for note taking with on-line learning.

The Online Resources Web site, at <www.delmar.com>, provides links to a vast array of study skills and academic resources. Use this resource when you are looking for new ideas to make your learning experiences as effective as possible.

In the next chapter, "Researching and Writing the Research Paper," we will look at the steps and tasks needed to successfully complete one of the most dreaded items associated with college attendance (aside from Public Speaking!). With the information there, you will be able to confidently begin writing for college courses. Before you turn the page though, take a moment to reflect on what you have learned here.

Notes to Yourself

Does any one study strategy or note-taking method appeal to you? Are there other strategies you have used effectively in the past? Why not take a moment here to record observations that are particularly relevant to you. You might also visit the Online Resources site and note here study guide links that you want to remember. Make your notes here:

_____

_____

_____

_____

CHAPTER 14

Researching and Writing the Research Paper

The research paper is merely a structured process for determining the answer to a question.

Whether you choose traditional or on-line methods to pursue education, sooner or later you will be asked to restate what you have learned *in your own words*. Was there ever a phrase that struck greater terror into the hearts of students? Maybe you remember being in class when the teacher announced this dreaded assignment. Did ears prick, listening for the guidelines that would chart a course between acceptable regurgitation and abject failure? Did you glance around to see who might take this requirement calmly and, therefore, become a good study partner? Or did you immediately tune out anything else the teacher said as your mind frantically flipped through possible topics to find something both acceptable and well documented? Like it or not, research papers are still the primary measurement upon which learning is evaluated. That means writing a research paper.

This requirement is a barrier that keeps many adults from returning to school, even if they desperately desire a college degree. Some students fear they will not be good enough, or feel they have nothing interesting to say. Some think there is some mysterious talent to writing research papers that they never learned. These fears keep potentially wonderful students from exploring topics of interest to them, from interacting with other inquisitive minds, and from sharing the knowledge and experiences they have had. Even worse, these fears keep adults from achieving a better life for themselves and their loved ones. But there is nothing mysterious about writing a research paper. The research paper is merely a structured process for determining the answer to a question. Like any process, it can be learned and mastered.

WHAT A RESEARCH PAPER IS NOT

Perhaps you remember a time when you waited until the night before a paper was due to begin it. Do you also remember why you put it off so long? Did you feel that writing was just a boring exercise that had no relation to you? Well, it may have seemed that way to you because of the way you were taught or because of what classmates said. It is not the view held by the majority of teachers.

If you put off writing, maybe it was because you could not think of anything to write about or did not have the first idea of where to begin. Now that you are an adult, you probably have plenty of ideas that you would like to explore further. This section will help you learn how to find information on topics of interest to you.

Papers are not assigned as punishments, nor are they make-work to justify a teacher's salary, in spite of experiences in your past that might have made you feel that way. In most college courses, papers are opportunities to show your knowledge of a particular idea, concept, issue, or state. They are also a measure of your understanding. To understand something well enough to write about it coherently takes time, thought, and energy.

Research papers are not opinions. You may start with your opinion as the basis for your exploration of a topic, but good papers rely on sound research that supports the writer's ideas with proof and examples.

WHAT A RESEARCH PAPER IS

A research paper is your account of the material available on a topic you have chosen to investigate. It is your exploration into what others think of the topic and a summary of that thought. Most importantly, it is an opportunity to learn something for yourself, by yourself, without the teacher's constant direction. In the best cases, the paper-writing process provides a means to interact with knowledge in a way that enriches you and challenges you to think in new and different ways, questioning old assumptions and reevaluating past experience. And the more you do it, the easier questioning assumptions and evaluating facts becomes. Subsequently, it becomes easier for you to adjust to change with flexibility instead of fear.

Writing a research paper is much like completing any project. You must decide on the boundaries of your project, plan the steps to be sure you are covering all the requirements, and carry out the planned steps in logical order to bring the project to fruition. It is generally required that you write in a particular manner and cite resources so that those reading your written work can find the articles you use to support your arguments. One of the primary conditions that defines a research paper is that writers must substantiate the claims they make by saying, in effect, 'and these people think so, too.'

The particular manner that is used to write papers is different from letters or novels, and is referred to as a 'style'. Writing style covers everything about putting a paper together: how a paper is organized and structured, the kind of grammar that is used, the way that references are written, and even the spacing and margins preferred. There are manuals available that make the process, if not simple, at least simple to follow. A style manual should be part of every student's personal library. For many undergraduate term papers (a research paper in other words), two of the most often used style manuals are Turabian and Strunk & White. Be sure to determine which style manual is preferred at your learning institution, so you can be prepared. Complete information on both of these titles is listed in the annotated resources at the end of this text.

A style manual should be part of every student's personal library.

Your educational path may lead to graduate study, where the research paper style requirement will be different from those you may have become used to as an undergraduate. If so, you may already have read some articles in scholarly journals, where you will have noticed that these articles are very different from what you see in reading the evening paper. Journal articles must conform to certain style standards too, which include the way they are written, how other writers are given credit, and how they are organized. You are not expected to know these standards automatically, and there are style manuals for these requirements, as well. Even the scholars who write articles regularly refer to them often. The most frequently used styles for the vast majority of academic research papers are that of the MLA (Modern Language Association) and the APA (American Psychological Association). There are specialized style manuals, as well, for topics like engineering and statistics. Each educational institution, and sometimes divisions within them, will have its own requirements for written submissions, so find out which style manual is preferred and purchase a copy of the specified manual.

There are also specific requirements for conducting and submitting the results of scientific or biological research or any other kind of research for publication. We will not discuss conducting research studies here, a topic to which entire books and courses are devoted. Here, we will explore the process of finding and writing about research done by others.

WHERE TO FIND INFORMATION

You may be able to attend class, interact with classmates, and carry out every other requirement for completion of your study over the Internet, except for one thing. Although more and more information becomes available on-line every day, not everything has been translated to the Web. If the topic you are researching is at least 10 years old, there is a very good chance that there will be more available in hard copy than on-line. In other words, do not expect to limit your researches to on-line resources. This may seem like a royal pain, but you will ultimately learn more and suffer less frustration by utilizing the services of a good public or university library in addition to your on-line exploration.

Do not expect to limit your researches to on-line resources.

The best source of information and help is a librarian, who will often have ideas and suggestions that you were not aware of. Take some of the time before your classes start and get to know what is available in your area. Ask at the local public library if there is an interlibrary loan process in place with area colleges, and what informational databases are accessible. Many libraries also now offer the availability of searching their on-line catalogs and databases from your home over the Internet, which can save valuable time.

Even if time is at a premium, there are good reasons for spending time doing research on-site in the library. Almost anything you are looking for will be there, and you can preview the resources to determine whether they will help you before you check them out and carry them home. Searching through the stacks for books can also yield surprises, as when books appear that you did not even know about, but which are perfect for your study. Photocopy machines and research assistants are just a few steps away. Further, a library, with its quiet spaces and ample seating, provides a good place to study with few distractions.

If there are no good libraries in your area, be absolutely sure that your distance learning provider has made arrangements to meet your research needs. Many on-line institutions form partnerships with large university libraries to allow their students access to the same resources that on-campus students have. In fact, many institutions that offer both on-campus and on-line courses have a librarian specifically devoted to the needs of the on-line student. In this way, you can either download or borrow articles and books from the convenience of your home or office. Be aware that borrowed articles are sent through the mail, so it is especially necessary to plan ahead so that your research can be completed with plenty of time left to organize and write your paper.

Learner Profile, Continued

Ellen's advice for library users

With kids in middle school, a job, and an on-line degree to complete, I thought I would never have time to do the required library research. What I discovered was just the opposite; going to the library seemed to give us all time to do what needed to be done. My kids could do homework, find stories to read, and surf the Web at the same time. That last situation alone did wonders at reducing the argument level at home! Going to the library on a regular basis also helped us all get organized. We had to decide beforehand what we were going to do when we got there and take the materials we needed to make notes (I took my laptop, but I could have used a regular paper notebook, too.).

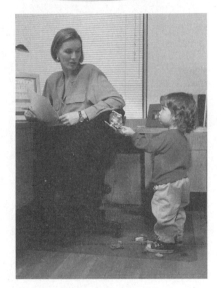

The regularity of our visits also became known to the librarians, who helped all of us out from time to time. Missy even helped the children's librarian by volunteering to read to some of the younger children. Mark's class was working on making their own Web sites (They get it so quickly, it is scary!), so he was really happy with the faster download times available at the library. Luckily, we live pretty close to a major library, so we would plan to spend several hours on a Saturday and then have a nice meal and share what we had found. Other than the meal, all of the resources were free, so you could not beat it. And even though we spent money on an outing, it was far more relaxing being served and listening to each other. Much better than if we had rushed around to fit everything in! So going to the library really turned out to help us all to do what we needed to do, and become closer as a family, too.

So, if someone were to ask me what I would suggest as the most helpful things to include in an on-line study, I would say:

- Get to know your library.
- Get organized.
- Make learning a family affair.
- Plan ahead.

You know, even when the degree came to a close, we decided to keep going to the library. It had become a special time for all of us, separately and together. Maybe I will be able to read that novel I have wanted to get to!

Prepare by Organizing

Before you go to the library or turn on your computer, decide how you will organize your information gathering. Using a binder to list all of the references you discover will help to keep everything in one place in the manner you will need to cite in your paper. Each citation consists of the author, title of the work, the publication date, volume, and page in which it appears. If you leave ample space between each entry, you can also note what was especially helpful and what was not. Further, if you must request some of the sources through mail or interlibrary loan, you can note which have arrived and when they are returned. You can use the reference pages to develop your bibliography without having the actual sources all over your desk, and keep the pages of reference notes with your final paper when it is completed in case you wish to go back and reuse the articles for other coursework.

You can also keep your material organized in a Palm® organizer, if you have one, by altering slightly the same fields you use to store business cards. This has the added advantage of being downloadable to your PC when it is time to actually commit your research to paper. Some learners find that it works well to begin the paper by building the list of resources, or bibliography, first. If you are careful about keyboarding your citations, and be sure that you place paragraphs in the text only for new citations, you can utilize the sort function of your word processor to alphabetize. That way, you can enter whole lists of books and articles in any order you wish as you review them, and organize only the ones you eventually use to support your paper.

Another method to organize references is to keep each citation on separate file cards. This may seem like a low-tech solution, but file cards do have several advantages for those who do not have or can not carry their electronic equipment with them. File cards are easy to organize and have lots of space on the back for additional notes. They are easy to carry around in a pocket or purse. Using file cards also allows you to discard resources that are not helpful without creating a mess.

It may take some time to develop the method of organization that works best for you. Perhaps it will be a combination of the organizational strategies listed above, or you may develop an entirely different method. The method you choose should be easy for you to maintain and understand, even when you interrupt your studies with work and home responsibilities. So, to be successful in your educational effort, get organized and stay organized.

THE RESEARCH PAPER PROCESS

Once you have figured out where you are going to get information and set aside time to do your research paper, the process of completing it can be divided into four major steps:

1. Identify and develop the topic.
2. Find information.
3. Evaluate what you find.
4. Write and cite in the preferred style.

First, Identify and Develop Your Topic

State your topic as a question that your research will answer. For example, if you are interested in finding out about how drinking alcohol during pregnancy affects the fetus, your topic question might be: "How does drinking alcohol during pregnancy affect fetal development?" Identify the main concepts or keywords in your question: These will be the words you will use to search for information. Some people like to use colored highlighters at this point in the process to identify the key terms to search on.

Test your topic by doing a library database or Internet search on the keywords. If you are finding too much information and too many sources, try narrowing your topic by joining two or more of the keywords together using 'and' in your search. For example, 'pregnancy and alcohol'. Finding too little information may indicate that you need to broaden your topic. Check your topic words against a thesaurus or subject heading list to find more search keyword possibilities.

Next, Find Information

This step has several parts. First, find and read background information. Your instructor will most likely provide lecture notes, textbooks, and reserve readings in which background information may be found. This is a good first step. In addition, you will find that the better public and most college libraries include many different kinds of encyclopedias in their collections, encyclopedias that cover specific topics such as engineering, biology, education, and others. Look up your keywords in the indexes to subject encyclopedias in your topic area. (Ask a librarian for help, if you need it.) Read the articles in these encyclopedias to get a general context for your research. Pay attention to the bibliographies at the end of the encyclopedia articles, where you will find where the information was condensed from. This background information will also help you to generate ideas for future papers, as well as giving you an overview of the subject. Reading background information also helps you to determine early in the research process whether your chosen topic is either too broad or too general.

Use the same language in thinking about your topic as you find in the indexes and catalogs you use. This will help you to understand the material more quickly so you will catch nuances that you might otherwise miss. Next, find books on your topic by searching the library's catalog. You can choose to keep this information in a specific binder, on individual cards, or some other method that helps you keep track of the material you need. Use keyword searching and print out or write down the citation. The citation includes the author, title of the article or book, the publication information, including date, volume, and page. Also note the library location information. This includes the **call number.** The call number is the number the library uses to keep track of each piece of material, and the specific collection in the library, if applicable. Note the circulation status, as well, to be sure that the book you want is listed as available. You do not want to waste time searching for a book that is checked out!

When you pull the book from the shelf, scan the bibliography for additional sources. Be especially watchful for resources that include book-length bibliographies and literature reviews on your subject. These list citations to hundreds of books and articles in one subject area and are a wonderful source of additional material.

Then, use indexes to find periodicals on your topic. One index for articles in popular magazines is *The Reader's Guide to Periodical Literature,* which lists articles by subject, author, and magazine title. This and other indexes and abstracts may be found in print or computer-based formats, or both. Ask at the library's reference desk (different from the main circulation desk) about the resources available. Many libraries subscribe to on-line search services like EBSCO®, which are designed to search several on-line databases at one time, based on your search criteria. Some on-line indexes contain the entire text of the article you need, so you can preview it to see if it meets your needs and then print it, or e-mail it to your own computer. EBSCO® notes whether the material you seek is available on-line in a full-text version, or if only as an abstract or summary. In either case, you will be

Test your topic by doing a library database or Internet search on the keywords.

Use the same language in thinking about your topic as you find in the indexes and catalogs you use. This will help you to understand the material more quickly so you will catch nuances that you might otherwise miss.

given the complete citation for the work so that you can find it and credit it accordingly. The results of your search will also include whether that library owns a copy of the journal. If not, there is always a way to discover which area libraries do own it, and often you can request that it be sent to your local library through interlibrary loan. This is another good reason to start working on papers as early as possible!

In conjunction with your library searches, check Internet resources. The instructor for your on-line course will probably provide a bibliography of background material for the course. This material will most likely be linked to full articles that you can read at your convenience. The best time to check out and scan these resources is at the beginning of the class, before you have to begin working on a paper. In the course bibliography, you will find hints for topics and the means to find out whether the topic you choose will fall within the scope of the course.

Do not forget alternative media resources. In many cases, the library will also house films, television shows, radio programs, photographs, and other visual materials related to your topic. Do not overlook these resources. These can all add greatly to your final presentation. Ask your librarian about media catalogs and CD-ROM archives.

Beyond the materials prepared for the course by the teacher, use Internet search engines (not just one!) to locate materials on the Web. Search on-line academic journals and their databases. Links to lists of resources, academic journal databases, and other research assistance tools are included in the Online Resources site. The site address is noted at the end of this chapter.

Evaluate What You Find

Learning how to quickly evaluate a given resource is one of the core skills of the research process. The evaluation of your resources entails two parts: evaluating the source and evaluating the content.

Evaluating a source can begin even before you have the source in hand. You can initially appraise a source by first examining the bibliographic citation, the written description of a book, journal article, essay, or some other published material. Bibliographic citations generally consist of three main pieces of information: author, title, and publication information. These components can help you determine the usefulness of this source for your paper. For example, an initial appraisal should examine the author's credentials in the topic area. Does the author appear to have solid credentials to be knowledgeable in the topic? These will include the author's education, previous writings, experience, and associations. Respected authors are frequently referred to by other authors, so you will see these names often.

After an initial appraisal, you should read to determine the author's intentions, point of view, and possible biases. What is the author's purpose for writing

Do not limit your on-line search for material by using just one search engine. Maximize what you can find by using various resources.

the article? Look over the table of contents and index, in the case of a book, to determine how the author approaches the topic. This can also be useful when scanning a journal article, because looking at other articles published in the journal will give you clues to how the publishers approach the topic, as well. Always review the bibliography at the end, which will reflect the depth and care authors have taken with their work. You should ask several questions while reviewing your articles:

1. What is the author's intended audience?
2. Is the information fact, opinion, or propaganda? Is the reasoning objective and can the facts be verified?
3. Is the reasoning valid and supported?
4. What material is covered? Is it up to date; does it update others' work?
5. Is the author's style logical, clear, and easy to read?
6. Is the book or article considered a valuable contribution to the field?

Check the reviews in a reviewing source. Many academic journals are peer reviewed before publication, which means that they have been critically read by others in the field. These journals often include articles or letters that respond to a writer's views. These rebuttals can be enlightening. Web-based review sources that publish evaluations of on-line information are also available. Pay attention to what reviewers say about authors' works and train yourself to ask the same questions. This will make your critical thinking skills extremely powerful!

Write and Cite Using the Preferred Style

Here is where your style manual will come in especially handy! To minimize problems, be sure to organize your paper in the manner that is preferred. If you have not spent some time looking through the style manual to determine how you will begin to organize the paper, do it now, before you write even one sentence.

Although the style manual will guide and determine the final outcome of your paper-writing experience, the way you chose to draft the research you have found is more flexible. As with note taking, what you are comfortable with and what works best for you depends on a combination of your learning styles, the teaching style, and the topic in question. Some people like to work with outlines developed during the background-reading phase, and fill in detailed information as their research progresses. Some like to keep reading until that magic moment when the paper begins to 'gel', and then write a draft from start to finish. Yet others like to meticulously craft one paragraph at a time. There is no one 'right' way to get your paper written, only criteria for the final paper to meet. Whichever method you choose to do the work of writing your research paper, leave time for revisions and editing.

Pay attention to what reviewers say about authors' works and train yourself to ask the same questions.

There is no one 'right' way to get your paper written, only criteria for the final paper to meet.

The Four Steps for Completing a Research Paper

Step 1: Identify and develop your topic.
Step 2: Find information.
Step 3: Evaluate what you find.
Step 4: Write and cite using the preferred format.

Revisions, which are major changes in scope, attitude, or organization, take the longest time. Editing, the rewriting and rearranging that makes the paper flow well, the purpose clear, and the grammar and spelling correct, can take almost as long to finish.

Make sure you have someone available to review your paper for coherence and to catch those little typographical errors that are so easy for the one writing to miss. Consider pairing with a classmate to review each others' drafts. You will both learn more! If pairing up with a classmate is not practical, ask a member of your support network—a colleague, family member, or friend—to critique your papers before you submit them. Choose your reviewers from people who have good writing skills themselves. It may well be an additional bonus that these personal editors will become your most ardent supporters. Do not be surprised if they follow your lead and begin to take courses themselves!

Consider pairing with a classmate to review each others' drafts. You will both learn more!

As you can see, there is far more to completing a good research paper than you may have realized. But rather than being a source of fear and frustration, or a boring piece of make-work, the paper-writing experience can be a robust learning event in its own right.

THE FUSS ABOUT PLAGIARISM

There are few things more upsetting than realizing that you have been the victim of robbery. Yet it happens every day, and the thievery is often committed by people who consider themselves good, law-abiding citizens who would never consider stealing even a pack of gum.

Simply stated, plagiarism is the use of another's ideas as your own, whether the use is intentional or not. It is stealing, and in academic work it is often grounds for expulsion. The wide availability of resources on the Internet, coupled with the ease of 'copying and pasting' and the pressures to perform despite too many responsibilities, make plagiarism a temptation. Be alert for evidence of plagiarism in your own work and in the work of others.

It is sometimes difficult to determine whether you are actually plagiarizing when reporting on another's ideas, although style manuals provide guidelines. There is software available to help teachers discover incidences of plagiarism in papers submitted. There are also Web sites that help you to determine how you can meet research requirements without running the risk of claiming another's work as your own. Several of these are listed in the Search and Research section of the Online Resources Web site. Use them to help you be sure that the words you use are your own.

Following these steps and tips will help make your paper-writing experience a positive one. Like anything else, writing research papers becomes easier with practice. Soon, you will wonder what the big deal was. There are many sources of additional information and support both on-line and for the asking through your educational provider.

To Sum Up. . .

To help you keep the summary of this chapter in mind, copy the box below and commit it to memory! Of course, it will always be here, with additional resources to be found at the Online Resources Web site at <www.delmar.com>.

Notes to Yourself

In the next chapter, we will look at the skills necessary for effective on-line communications and building your virtual community. First, though, check out the sources and links for research, search engines, and other helpful resources and the Online Resources Web site, at <www.delmar.com> and make a note of your favorites here:

_____

_____

_____

_____

_____

_____

_____

_____

_____

Summary of Research Paper Writing Steps

Follow this general framework to successfully complete a research paper: identify the topic, find information, evaluate resources, and write your paper using the preferred style.

In addition, follow these guidelines:

- Work from the general to the specific. Find background information first, then seek more specific sources.
- Write down what you find and where you found it. Write out a complete citation for each source you find, even if it seems like unnecessary work. You may need it again later.
- Keep everything in one place. Whatever system you choose, stick with it and keep it organized.
- Get to know the libraries in your area. Find out which ones are most likely to have the resources you need, and which ones can be accessed over the Internet. Use them and do not be afraid to ask questions.
- Give yourself plenty of time to research and write. Make a schedule and stick to it! You will be happy you did.

CHAPTER 15

On-line Listening and the Educational Community

Y ou might think it silly to talk about improving your listening skills when you are considering on-line study, but many of the same techniques you would use to remember what you hear will be used in an on-line environment. You will just be listening with your eyes, instead of your ears. Say what?

CRITICAL LISTENING DEFINED

Think about it: When you read, is it not your own voice you hear saying the words you are reading? Are you paying attention to what your voice is reading and evaluating the information with an open mind? Or do you focus, instead, on the differences between what you hear and what you believe?

To be sure that you get the most from your participation in on-line discussions, you need to use the same skills you would use to listen critically to the teacher and classmates in a traditional classroom setting. Remember, it is the information that is important, not the method in which it is transmitted. For optimal understanding and retention, you need to be:

- mentally awake, aware, and prepared to participate;
- willing to ask questions when you do not understand; and
- aware of your 'filters'.

Filters are those biases, judgements, and attitudes that affect what you hear and may cause you to react before thinking, because they are so deeply rooted in experience and belief. They can cause misunderstanding and confusion. And because nonverbal communication such as facial expression, tone of voice, and posture cannot usually be seen on-line, you must rely entirely on what you read.

"A good listener tries to understand thoroughly what the other person is saying. In the end he may disagree sharply, but before he disagrees, he wants to know exactly what it is he is disagreeing with."

—Kenneth A. Wells

The emphasis on verbal expression in a text format can make small misunderstandings seem much larger, and make it difficult to forge rapport. Participants who begin interaction by reacting to their filters can contribute to an uncomfortable on-line atmosphere in which people choose not to share ideas for fear of being attacked or ignored. It takes practice to listen to another's point of view with an open mind. Do you know what your filters are?

Activities: Filter Awareness

We are more likely to take seriously those people who 'act serious', and be most comfortable sharing information with people we identify most closely with. But what constitutes 'acting serious'? What makes us most comfortable? Try the following exercises when doing the activities listed below and ask yourself these questions as you perform them:

- Do I feel I can believe what this person is saying? Why or why not?
- Does this person remind me of someone? Are the memories good or bad?
- If I met this person at a party, would we be likely to enjoy talking to each other? Why or why not?
- If this person asked me for help, would I be likely to give it? Why or why not?

Now do it:

Activity A, Part 1: Turn the television on to a discussion or news program, but listen only to the voices: Do not look at the picture. How do you answer the questions above?

Activity A, Part 2: Now turn the sound off, then view the picture. Are your reactions the same, or different? Are you aware of biases based on voice, tone, accent, or vocal delivery?

Activity B, Part 1: Now, think of someone that you like. Imagine that they are telling you a joke or funny story. Now answer the questions above. Are you smiling?

Activity B, Part 2: Now, ask the same questions while thinking of listening to the same joke or funny story told by someone you *do not* like. What makes the experience different?

Now, note here the filters you want to be sure you are aware of when engaged in on-line listing:

_____

_____

Be sure to review these now and then to keep yourself as 'filter free' as possible.

LISTENING SKILLS FOR ON-LINE STUDY

For most of us, the educational experiences of the past occurred amid familiar surroundings, accompanied by classmates and teachers that had many of the same expectations, experiences, and attitudes that we had.

 Do not let misunderstanding overtake you. Read with an open mind.

In on-line study, the likelihood is very high that your classmates and your instructor will have less in common with you than if you were all part of a traditional class at a local college. Members of your classes may live in other parts of the country or world, speak diverse native languages, have unfamiliar customs and beliefs, and live guided by values that may be unlike your own. The ability to overcome these differences and interact, share, and learn with those outside of our day-to-day life is one of the challenges of on-line learning, and one of its greatest benefits. So it is especially important to internalize those skills that help us understand new ideas and be open to new experiences.

The attitudes of a critical listener listed above—mental alertness, willingness to ask questions, and awareness of how your own attitudes effect participation—are only part of the listening skills you should bring to the classroom or meeting room to get the most out of the time you spend listening to others. Those who do receive maximum benefit from the information available utilize both comprehensive and critical listening methods.

Comprehensive listening skills are needed in order to understand the message that is being conveyed. This is the kind of listening you do when you need to follow directions or grasp a complex concept. This is the kind of listening most commonly practiced in the classroom or office. It is very important but different from critical listening, which, like critical reading and thinking, involves a process of evaluating a message for the purpose of accepting or rejecting it based on the proofs and support supplied. With critical listening, you listen not only to the message, but for the evidence that tells you it is true. Without the proper evidence, you will reject the message, judging it as false. This is the kind of listening used to evaluate a classmate's argument or a sales pitch.

Beginning students may have difficulty and lack confidence in their skills. Studies have suggested that those who lack confidence do not learn as deeply or do as well as those who are comfortable with their abilities. Specifically, beginning learners tend to focus on facts and memorization instead of what is meant by those facts. They have trouble understanding concepts and applying them to their experience. They struggle at integrating new material with what they already know, and cannot see the relationships between what they are learning and everyday reality. They tend to view assignments as tasks imposed by the instructor, rather than essential components of the topic. Does this sound familiar?

It takes time and effort to build confidence and to relax and "let the learning come," but the more you practice, the better you will become. This is true whether you are listening to a presentation in a meeting, a classroom, or on-line. Awareness of the point of view you bring with you is important, as is awareness of the possibility of possible differences in interpretation. In a face-to-face interaction, you can look at the speaker to catch nonverbal clues and see if what they say is intended as serious or sarcastic. Or, you can listen for tone of voice to hear if either humor or anger is the intended response. This is less possible on-line, and is one of the reasons why on-line learning is perceived as less interactive than traditional teaching methods. Despite this perceived drawback, learning on-line provides rich opportunities to learn, both by its nature and by the responsibilities it places on teacher and learners.

With critical listening, you listen not only to the message, but for the evidence that tells you it is true.

Two Important Ways to Listen:

Comprehensive = Listening for understanding (comprehension)

Critical = Listening for evidence (evaluation)

Learner Profile, Continued

Someone told me when I first started looking into finishing my degree that the application process would be the hardest part. They were not kidding. Not that it was the school's fault or anything, there were just so many papers to get, write on, and sign. You would think I was buying a house or something. After awhile, I actually started to think of it as my personal remodeling project. I felt like the contractor without a clue. Ha, ha.

Anyway, once all that was taken care of, I got down to work. The requirements were clear and I could map out my future pretty easily. The distance classes fit right into the middle of everything else I had to do. Now that I have been at it for a year and a half, it seems like I have always been doing it. Almost half-way there; well one-third of the way, at least. This has been much easier, logistically, than trying to go to a regular class was.

It did not take too long before I got into a regular schedule, even managing to tuck little "family moments" in there to keep us all going. The twins have been fabulous, and I almost cry when they insist that we all have to spread our homework out on the dining room table together. Of course, I promised them that when I'm done, we are all going to celebrate by going to Disney World, so that could have something to do with it.

The classes have really been interesting. You know 'interesting', it is one of those words that can have a lot of meanings. Yes, I am learning about the business world and business practices, but I am also learning a lot about myself. Like that what I know already is valuable. And that other people in this class are really smart, too. There is a woman from Texas who has a son that is the same age as my twins. She has been through difficult times, and she keeps coming up with the most incredible observations. I have learned as much from the other people in the class as I have from the teacher—maybe more! It really gives you a different perspective talking to other people, you know? What really floored me was when someone mentioned that *I* was smart! I just never thought of myself as 'smart'—resourceful and practical, yes, but not 'smart'. And yet, as soon as I read that, I was filled with pride. It is like I could suddenly see myself in a different way. Kind of took my breath away.

After that, it was not just one day after another anymore. Everything looked different all of a sudden. It was like I noticed everything with such clarity. Even my mom noticed, and that is saying something! That is when the connection with the others in the class really clicked for me and I really began to feel that we were working together. Think of it, here I was, clicking away on the keyboard at some late hour up in the spare bedroom, and I felt like my mind was everywhere at once. Creepy, huh? But that was the turning point for me. That was when I knew that I would stick this out and finish. The interaction has become so much a part of my life, I can not even imagine being without it anymore.

You know, anybody could do this. The classes are not that hard, it is more that you have to be open to bending your mind around the reasons behind the rules and regulations. Boy, are there a lot of them in healthcare! And it does not look like it is going to get any better in the future. The future has really begun to interest me, too. Not just my own and the kids', but the way that people will take care of themselves, and how doctors and hospitals will use technology to take care of patients. It is not going to be cheap, I will tell you! But exciting, yes.

There are so many questions about what will come, how things will look, and how we in healthcare will manage them. I can not wait to learn more.

Because of the technology available, 'listening' can be easier on-line, because everything written can be saved and reread. Have you ever found the exact right response to a question or comment—three hours later? Have you ever thought of something to say, and then had it evaporate from your mind as it started to come out of your mouth? Have you ever missed making a great response, or the next thing the teacher said, while writing down your notes?

In the traditional classroom, once something is said, it is often forgotten. On-line, you can review it, print it out, and think about questions and possible answers before you reply. You can write your reply and review it to be sure it is what you mean to say before you send it. You can even include pieces of the statement you are responding to, so that your reply is as clear as possible. This opportunity to reflect before responding is the way many educators believe real learning takes place. In addition, the reflective pause demanded by on-line technology makes it easier for those learners who would be less likely to speak up in class to be 'heard'. They are not drowned out by the few classmates who always speak up first and loudest, as can happen in a traditional class. In fact, reticent learners report a high satisfaction rate with on-line technology for just this reason.

Even if you are reluctant to 'speak up', you have responsibilities that, if fulfilled, assure that you receive maximum profits from your educational investment. As a participant in an on-line class, it is your responsibility to concentrate and read your classmates' and teacher's postings closely. Are you sure your understanding is the right one, or are other interpretations possible? If you are not sure what the writer means, it is important to ask. Use active listening techniques to clarify what you understood. Here is an example of an exchange that utilizes active listening to clarify what is being said:

C: . . . and then he consolidated the government by eliminating the other party.

G: You say that he eliminated the other party. That sounds like he could have had people killed. Is that what happened?

C: No, I didn't mean that. He eliminated the control that the members of the party had by liquidating the party, by revoking its charter. But it was the equivalent of a political killing (!).

If 'G' had not asked, it could have been assumed that 'C' meant that the party members were murdered. That is quite a different circumstance than 'G' meant! Because it is easier to react to what you *think* you see when it is written on-line, it is especially important to clarify what you understand. Just as important is the practice of clarifying what you write, as well. Develop the habit of rereading what you have written before you press the 'Send' button.

Clarify what you have learned, as well. Restate for the group your understanding, using examples that show others that you have grasped the meaning of the lesson. In many cases, you will be given formal opportunities to show that you understand in the form of directed questions, presentations, and papers. Apply

Develop the habit of rereading what you have written before you press the 'Send' button.

the same thought processes to class interaction, and everyone in the class will benefit along with you.

Clarification Strategies

One of the most common strategies used to demonstrate concepts are examples. Examples illustrate ideas in a concrete way and help to relate what you are learning to what you already know. You have undoubtedly used them many times, yourself. Your teachers will use examples to help you to comprehend complex ideas. They will tend to be examples from the teacher's own experience, and may not relate well to yours. If the teacher uses examples that you do not understand, ask for others or offer your own examples to test your understanding.

Clarify what you have heard by:

- offering examples
- making analogies
- restating concepts in your own words
- asking a question and then answering it yourself (rhetorical questioning)
- making and asking for suggestions
- giving feedback to others

You will probably find that you learn as much from the other class participants as you do from what the teacher provides. Good on-line teachers will help you to interact with others so that this collaborative learning activity is emphasized. Still, it remains your obligation to actually interact with others. Instead of waiting for someone else to organize an activity or assignment, offer your ideas. Request feedback on your ideas and give it openly to others. Tell others how you perceive the problem to be solved and submit suggestions. This is not the same as telling others what to do. Your classmates do not have to follow your suggestions, but your submission will help them frame their own ideas, and perhaps be the impetus to creating even better ones. Participate in the act of creation.

It may be uncharacteristic and uncomfortable for you to extend yourself in this way. *Remember: this is your education, not someone else's.* You are more than likely paying for it yourself. Presumably, you want to get as much out of it as possible. In order to do that, you may have to behave in ways that are different from what you are used to. How lucky that you have chosen a safe environment like the on-line classroom to experiment with increasing your assertiveness! Here, you can offer your opinion knowing that your right to do so is supported by all, even the ones that do not agree with you.

If you recall, the characteristics of successful distance learners were mentioned in Chapter 3. Successful learners, it said, are "active learners who take part in learning instead of sitting back and absorbing it." Be sure to take an active part in your learning. Be sure to do the following:

- Ask questions when you are not sure what is meant.
- Clarify what you have learned by restating your understanding of the topic.
- Interact with classmates with an open mind.
- Give and receive feedback with respect.
- Take the initiative with enthusiasm.

Confidence will come with practice. Soon, you will forget to worry about what you can not do and recognize the strengths you have and what you *can* do. You will acknowledge your ability to learn, and your satisfaction in learning will increase tremendously. The more practice you get in being an active participant in your own learning, the more comfortable it will become and the more you will want to learn.

INTERACTION = LEARNING

As noted earlier, effective learning often occurs when learners interact with each other. Discussing a topic in a group or solving a problem as a team presents different points of view and spurs creative activity. Reading what others have to say makes you realize that others have thought about similar things, that they have similar challenges and hopes. Sharing your ideas, and seeing them accepted by others, makes you realize that your ideas are worthwhile. Sharing and discussion also reinforce your learning. As the anecdote goes, you really do not learn something until you have to tell (or teach it to) someone else. This homespun truth is actually borne out in educational research.

The most effective and satisfying educational experiences, then, grow out of interaction between participants. We all know how this is done in the classroom, but what are the technologies that support interaction in on-line study?

"I have had some wonderful experiences on-line, learning about learning as well as life from fellow students and respected educators."

— Steve Lesh

TECHNOLOGY FOR INTERACTION AND EDUCATION

The technologies available to interaction, both in real time and asynchronously, are undergoing rapid change and constant development. Discussed here are a few of the technologies currently in use for educational purposes.

E-Mail

The oldest computer-based distance learning programs began as purely e-mail transactions, sometimes supplemented by telephone conferences. E-mail, as you know, allows contact with large groups or individuals, is quick, and does not necessarily require an Internet connection. It is still the most prevalent means of interactivity in distance learning, used as a supplement to Internet-based or other educational technology. E-mail allows students to receive feedback on assignments from instructors. It supports students' problem-solving activities, no matter where the students are located. It allows learners to share ideas and comments privately (sort of like passing notes in class) and it is always there, ready and waiting to perform the interaction you desire. Like most of the asynchronous (anytime, anywhere) learning opportunities discussed in this text, it can be accessed and used at any time of the day or night that is convenient, from any computer with a modem connection.

As with any technology, it is wise to be aware of the drawbacks and opportunities for misinterpretation. Just as there are differences and similarities between talking in person and on-line, e-mail is both similar to and different from postal mail.

E-mail is more like conversation and can be, therefore, grammatically sloppier than something you might send by postal mail. Because of its nearly instantaneous nature, you may be less likely to spend hours slaving over content. You and your reader(s) can respond to each other quickly and easily. Like postal mail, but unlike conversation, e-mail cannot easily convey emotion. This reality encouraged the development of **emoticons,** also called 'smileys', those little keyboard strokes that are shorthand for feelings. Here are some popular emoticons:

:-) happy, smiling
:-(sad
;-) winking
:-| indifferent, "I don't care."
:-& tongue tied
:-(crying

FIGURE 15–1

E-mail can follow a long and twisting path and find the right 'mailbox' in seconds.

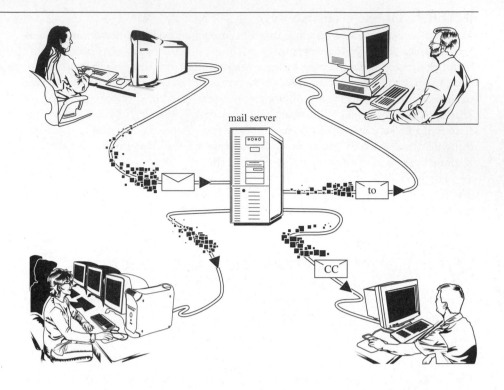

How many of these emoticons have you used? Some people use them sparingly, and some use them constantly. Whether you like them or not, they do help to convey and clarify a feeling associated with a written message. But showing feelings in a text format has its difficulties. Sarcasm is particularly dangerous, and can lead to hurt feelings and e-mail **flaming,** which is the e-mail equivalent of a hate letter. Correspondents who do not follow e-mail etiquette are likely to be flamed, sooner or later. Without the nonverbal component of visual communication, text messages can easily be misunderstood. Emoticons help to inject a 'visual' component to the communication process.

If you are considering on-line distance learning, it is likely that you have used e-mail extensively. You have probably corresponded primarily with people you know and who know you. They will have some idea of what to expect from you, and may know your voice and appearance as well. When you interact with members of your on-line classroom, that will not be the case. Increased importance will be placed on your need to be clear, and to realize that your messages may look different when viewed by someone else's e-mail software. This simple difference in appearance can lead to misunderstandings. Remember that there are still people whose e-mail programs cannot accept attachments and that, for those that can, word processors are not universal. It is common courtesy to ask first what your correspondent's system requirements and limitations are. Good on-line instructors will include this information in the orientation materials. If it is not included, ask!

Being a considerate correspondent is one of the ways that you can make the interactive portion of on-line classes enjoyable and productive for everyone. Links to further information about using e-mail and understanding e-mail etiquette (also known as **netiquette**) are available at the Online Resource Web site. That on-line address is noted at the end of this chapter.

Bulletin Boards

Many years ago, software developers realized that using familiar terms to represent software functions made nontechnical people using those functions more comfortable. Familiar terms can often be used to indicate familiar functions, even if the technical functionality is actually very different from the way the software actually works. An example of one of these 'cross-functional' terms used often in on-line education is the bulletin board. Like the cork article of the same name, electronic bulletin boards allow you to **'post'** your information for all to see. They also contain the discussion areas, which represent and provide a visual area analogous to classroom space. Instead of using thumbtacks, though, you post your comments with keyboard commands.

Imagine, though, if a dozen or more people started writing messages and asking questions, with no way to organize them. You would never know what question pertained to which comment, or vice versa. To keep the course interaction from becoming completely confused, then, the design of many popular courseware packages includes threaded bulletin, or discussion, boards. These bulletin board discussions are usually organized into **threads,** which organize different topics into easy-to-follow groups. There may be threads for different assignments, subjects, work groups, or any other component utilized in the class. It is usually the method of choice to allow all class participants to see the topics under discussion, who has participated, and when.

Electronic bulletin boards are available outside of class activities, as well. Leaving a message on a public electronic board usually uses the same procedure as you would in class, so it is much like leaving a note on a cork board, only safer. (Most on-line communication forums are still free at this time, though you must register and receive a user name and password.) Because you do not have to give your e-mail address, anyone who responds will not know your real name or be able to contact you other than through the forum, unless you give them that information. Anyone who wants to respond to your question or message can, and everyone who subscribes to that discussion can read it and respond—or not.

An example of what a bulletin board looks like is shown in Figure 15–2, in a board developed for the Online Resources Web site. A similar bulletin board is available for you to interact with other readers and the author of this text on the Online Resources site, at <www.delmar.com>.

Some on-line educational options are "delivered" to your PC through courseware packages that institutions have purchased from developers, and some software has been developed by the institution itself. Just like the options available in word processing and Internet browser software, each option will have its own identifying characteristics. For example, some packages allow you to send personal e-mails directly from within the courseware. Some will include audio or video functions that may require **plug-ins.** (See Chapter 6, "The Technical Connection," for a discussion of plug-ins and technical requirements for on-line learning.)

Some packages will include personal pages where learners can post information about themselves, their interests, goals, and, perhaps, pictures. This feature, which allows you to put faces to names and ideas, can also add a sense of connection to your fellow learners. The package your educational provider has chosen will include enhancements to allow you to interact with your teacher and classmates in a way the provider thinks is important. Then, you can forget about the technology and get on with the business of learning.

As noted earlier, it is important to be confident in your abilities in order to learn effectively. One of the components that can add to your confidence is for you to make sure that you are comfortable with the technology used to teach the

"Those who have never tried electronic communication may not be aware of what a "social skill" really is. One social skill that must be learned, is that other people have points of view that are not only different, but *threatening*, to your own. In turn, your opinions may be threatening to others. There is nothing wrong with this. Your beliefs need not be hidden behind a facade, as happens with face-to-face conversation. Not everybody in the world is a bosom buddy, but you can still have a meaningful conversation with them. The person who cannot do this lacks in social skills."

—Nick Szabo

FIGURE 15-2

Bulletin boards can help connect you to others for problem solving, information, and other communication.

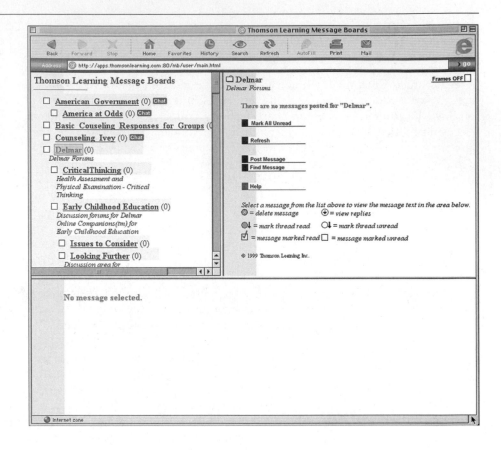

Make sure that you are comfortable with the technology used to teach the course, before the course starts and you get caught up in discussions and assignments.

course, before the course starts and you get caught up in discussions and assignments. To do that, be certain that you have given adequate time to the orientation and tutorial for your course. Even if you are continuing courses with the same institution, it is a good idea to review the tutorial to see whether changes have been instituted and what additional functions you can use to enhance your learning experience.

Newsgroups

The real power of the Internet is that it allows people from all walks of life to communicate directly about whatever they are interested in. Before the World Wide Web, the Internet was dominated by Usenet, a collection of thousands of discussion groups, called **newsgroups,** on topics ranging from abnormal psychology to Zeldas®. Usenet is accessible through your Web browser and works like a bulletin board. Here is how it works: Once he has arrived at the Internet address unique to the newsgroup, a member of the group posts a message that all other members can read. Messages remain on the board; they are not sent like e-mail. Through Usenet newsgroups, people who previously had not had the means to state their opinions publicly now have the ability to voice their comments and concerns instantly and at virtually no cost.

Like Web-site URLs, which have domains like .com and .edu to identify their classification, newsgroups are classified into standard sets. These are indicated by the first letters of the address. For example, one of the most popular newsgroups for discussions relating to distance education is alt.education.distance. The major newsgroup sets are:

alt.	alternative, the largest group
comp.	computer
rec.	recreation
sci.	science
soc.	society/culture
misc.	miscellaneous

Newsgroups are, by definition, not controlled by any moderator. The members of the group are also those who control it. There is complete freedom to state whatever you believe. But this absence of official control does not mean an absence of regulation. As you might imagine, communication options that are open to the immediate world could quickly devolve into anarchy if some rules did not apply. So, with freedom comes responsibility.

As with e-mail, the use of newsgroups implies the adherence to codes of on-line etiquette (netiquette), those few simple rules that help Usenet to remain a valuable resource to many. Some of the most important rules include:

1. "Lurk" first. Spend some time just paying attention to what is being said, how it is said, and how things are structured by 'lurking', without posting any messages. This will help you learn the group's 'culture' so that you will be able to be an effective contributor.
2. Read the FAQs. Most newsgroups have a list of "Frequently Asked Questions" that will cover basic information for new users. If you can not find one, ask your question.
3. Be prepared for disagreement. No matter how mild you feel your message is, someone will eventually take exception and flame you. It happens in a free forum. The best way to respond to a flame is no response.
4. Do not flame. Be nice. It will be noted by other readers, whether they say so or not. What goes around, comes around.
5. Post your message in the right place. Stay within the thread and group that the message belongs.
6. Do not represent someone you are not. Unless you have permission to share a private message in public, do not do it.
7. Post only your own thoughts. Not only is it unethical to post copyrighted or private information as your own, it can be illegal.

These are only the general rules for Usenet activities, but also apply to other activities on the Internet. Remember to check the FAQs for each newsgroup for rules specific to that group. To learn more about newsgroups and to find opportunities to discuss your favorite topics, go to the Online Resources site.

Chat

Chat also offers the ability for individuals to discuss on-line topics of interest, but with one important addition: immediacy. Unlike newsgroups and bulletin boards, people who participate in chat (or chat rooms) do so in real time. It is a way that groups of people can converse privately, leading to the analogy of a group existing in a 'room', also called a channel.

Chat is usually more social than the other interactivity options, and can often involve downloading and installing a small software program, called a plug-in, to run. Chat room software will prompt you to enter your preferred nickname, your e-mail address, and perhaps other information like a personal Web site that other chatters can visit. This is your 'log-in'. Once you have logged in, you will be diverted to a virtual space, the actual chat room. To communicate, you type what you want to say and press 'Enter'. Your message and other people's comments appear on your computer's screen, prefaced by names senders have chosen to identify themselves. It could look something like this:

<Harpo> Cop1, did you say you'd been to Jamaica?
<Cop1> yes, harpo, I went last January to Ocho Rios.
<Sue> Hi, harpo, cop1. Thought I'd check this chat out.
<Harpo> Hi, Sue. Welcome. we were just talking about vacations. I'm trying to find a good place for a honeymoon.
<Cop1> The waterfall there was great!
<Sue> Harpo, I really liked St. Lucia. It's really romantic.
<Cop1>GMTA-me2!

In many chat rooms, you will often come in during the middle of a conversation. It may take a minute or two of watching the interactions before you can figure out what the conversation is about. Then, to start talking, just type! You do not have to type your nickname, because the program will insert it for you.

You can see that chat is just like, well, chatting. It can be ungrammatical and contain spelling errors. It is about speed, not accuracy. To help the conversation along without taking forever to type, acronyms are often used in place of entire phrases, as you may have noted above. GMTA, in chat parlance, stands for "great minds think alike." There are literally hundreds of acronyms, some specific to certain chats or groups.

The more commonly used chat acronyms include:

AFK - Away from keyboard
B4N/BFN - Bye for now
BRB - Be right back
CUL - See you later (also, CUL8R)
BTW - By the way
FWIW - For what it's worth
IC - I see
IMHO - In my humble opinion
LOL - laughing out loud
OTOH - On the other hand
TAFN - That's all for now
TIA - Thanks in advance (if you have asked a question that requires a reply)
TTT - thought that, too (when someone else types what you were about to)
WFM - Works for me

In addition to class bulletin boards, most on-line educational institutions provide semipublic chat rooms. Semipublic means they are open only to students and others who have a password. They serve as virtual social areas, where learners can interact about other topics that are not exclusively related to the class they are enrolled in. Most on-line institutions also provide chat areas that are always available so that learners can prearrange to 'meet' to discuss projects. This is a quicker—and can be an easier—way of interacting with your classmates when a specific issue needs to be addressed quickly.

Reading the on-line school newsletter or visiting the student services areas is usually a matter of accessing Web pages and simply reading. But these are official, static areas, solitary and not too different from reading handouts. With chat areas, you can talk directly with other students. Perhaps you can answer questions for someone who is even 'newer' than you. Many educational providers maintain chat areas that they call 'cyber cafes'. Here, you can exercise your membership in the student population beyond the specific class and post questions about instructors, swap textbooks, and even enter conversations about other aspects of collegiate life. If your school has a residency seminar, for example, you may visit the cyber cafe to see if you can arrange a ride or talk with someone who has attended the seminar in the past for suggestions.

Your on-line college experience may not give you a campus with trees and buildings to stroll through, but the technology that allows you to interact with students on-line does allow participation in a 'college experience.' The school's Web site is also a good place to find information about books, administrative processes, and other social activities. You can often complete all administrative requirements, including registration, payment, and grade checking, on-line. You can get together on-line in discussions with other students or participate in a live workshop. One school recently even launched a virtual football team!

Some options for trying out chats, message boards, and other forums are available at the Web site. All links provide 'how to' information to help make your on-line communication as pleasant and easy as possible.

Other Interactivity Technologies

After you have gotten used to e-mail and tried out message boards and chat, you may be interested in trying some other technologies that allow you to connect with others at a distance. What, there are more?, you say. Yes, and in addition to the technologies noted here, Chapter 18, "A Look into the Future" will review those technologies that are being developed and introduced now. These emerging technologies will shortly become the ways that all on-line learners connect.

Back before the Internet as we know it today, **MUDs** (multi-user domain/dimension/dungeon) were developed to allow text-based role-playing games to be conducted between multiple computers. Rather than using the browsers we use to access the World Wide Web, MUDs utilize a **file transfer protocol (ftp)** to connect directly between servers using a modem, much the same way as you use a modem to fax documents over telephone lines.

As we discussed earlier, the Web uses http, or hypertext transfer protocol, to connect you to Web sites when you type in an address, for example, <http://www.myhouse.com>. The people interacting using the ftp protocol (electronic process) access someone else's computer, or host, directly.

You do not have to be connected to the Internet to use ftp, but you do have to identify your computer to the host computer in order to receive files, using a set of passwords that give you permission to establish a connection. In other words, you must know the precise commands to make the computer open the door to the file cabinet, as well as the place on your own computer where you want the files to go.

Similar to MUDs are **MOOs** (multi-user domains, object oriented), which are gaining popularity in educational applications because they allow participants to role-play and learn through scenarios. MOOs allow people to meet, chat, and look at (or listen to) on-line presentations simultaneously through a software that allows split-screen presentations and interaction. For example, one panel could display a PowerPoint presentation that everyone can watch at once. Another panel could display references, while a third shows the transcript of an on going chat about the topic. Some MOOs include audio sections, so that remote learners can hear the instructor's words, see the presentation notes, and respond in the chat space. This technology, at least at this point, usually requires the download of a plug-in, although courseware packages that include this kind of functionality without downloads are being introduced.

Recent enhancements to e-mail allow any two people with Internet access and e-mail addresses to hold live telephone conversations through their computer. It is referred to as Internet telephony. Some of these services are even free! Using the microphone included with your PC and plug-in software, you can talk in real time for no more than the cost of your Internet connection. This technology allows two people to hold a discussion at the same time they are viewing a Web site or working on a project.

What will technological advances bring in the decade ahead?

To Sum Up. . . .

In this chapter, we discovered the importance of listening skills in the on-line environment and reviewed the specific steps you can take to assure that your communications are clear and direct. We examined those skills, in particular, that are required for critical listening and how being a self-reliant listener is a component of self-reliant learning.

We determined that public chat, newsgroups, and bulletin boards can be a rich source of interaction and information. We learned that support and encouragement can come from total strangers who live hundreds of miles away, who will offer help and understanding just for the joy of connection.

You may want to try chat or newsgroups before you even decide on a class, to get comfortable in an on-line space. In this way, you can receive support and encouragement from people outside of your class or your local support network. Links to several options can be found at the Online Resources Web site at <www.delmar.com>.

Notes to Yourself

Technology allows us to cheaply maintain connections and learn new things at any time and from anywhere. The implications for the future are staggering, but so are the changes we will all have to deal with. Expecting change and dealing with change are the subjects of the next chapter. Before that, though, take a moment to make a note actions you would like to take to make yourself more comfortable with on-line communication. Even if you just 'lurk' in a newsgroup space for awhile, the experience will help to get you ready to learn on-line.

What steps do you want to take to acclimate yourself to this crucial communication tool?

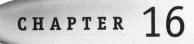

CHAPTER 16

Expecting and Dealing with Changes

It is one of Newton's Laws of Physics that 'for every action, there is an equal and opposite reaction.' Although we humans may not conform completely to all of the physical laws, there is no doubt that the introduction of something new into a system will inevitably cause changes. And if you did not realize it by now, there are systems within and all around you. Every time any one person or thing changes, other changes occur.

Going to school will change your life. It will take a good deal of your time. Some of the coursework and interaction will make you excited about learning in a way you may never have been before. At first, it may be difficult to keep your mind on your job when thoughts of class discussions intrude into every waking moment. You may even find it difficult to sleep when a particularly interesting project or class is underway.

Other changes may occur, as well. You may find that as you learn more, you have less and less in common with your friends and family. You may have less interest in what goes on in the office, because you are exploring an entirely new world.

You may also find yourself suddenly having much more interesting conversations with your children and your spouse. Their curiosity and your explanations will add a further dimension to your relationships and your learning. Many adult educators believe that discussions about what we are hearing and thinking is really how learning takes place.

"If we don't change, we don't grow. If we don't grow, we aren't really living."

—Gail Sheehy

CHANGES TO WATCH FOR

You may find that others treat you differently. They may be curious about your new status as a learner. Most will respect and admire your determination, although there will be some who are jealous and skeptical. Ignore them and concentrate on the positive ones.

It is possible that your coworkers may perceive you as being less committed to your work responsibilities. To help minimize this possibility, discuss your educational plans with your employer and colleagues before you start. Discuss how you hope to utilize what you learn in your work setting, as well as the financial and moral support you hope to receive from your employer and coworkers.

You should also be ready for some changes originating from your chosen school, where you are, after all, viewed primarily as a student. Even adult-centered on-line learning institutions will have some form of bureaucracy. Expect a certain amount of frustration, but be sure to ask those questions outlined earlier to minimize bureaucratic shock! Further unforeseen difficulties can be minimized by taking the following actions:

- Read everything the school sends you as soon as possible. Keep it all in a safe place.
- Ask questions about *everything and anything* you do not understand. Make notes of what was said and who said it.
- Know and adhere to deadlines. Be aware of all rules and program requirements.
- If something goes wrong, deal with it immediately.
- If you need approvals for changes, get them in writing.
- Be patient.

Earlier, we discussed the importance of including your family in your educational plans. Make sure that they understand the level of your commitment, the work involved, and that you will now be unavailable for things they might have taken for granted before you began your educational odyssey. Make it clear that you are not ignoring them, but need to concentrate on your studies to succeed. Ask for their support, and tell them how much it means to you.

Changes in schedule can be made clear by hanging a large wall calendar in a place where everyone can see it. Copy the information from your Time and Activity Analysis Worksheet, marking off your free time as well as the time needed for other commitments. You might even enlist the help of your younger children in filling in the blanks with colorful markers. Or, you might ask them to design an activity schedule of their own to mirror yours.

Take Care of Yourself

Be patient with yourself, as well. You may reach a point when no matter how strong your commitment to learning is, you just cannot look at another book. You know it is time then to take a short break and pay attention to your own emotional and spiritual needs.

Give yourself a chance to adjust to the momentous changes you are asking yourself to make. You may experience other feelings as you push yourself to achieve. It is normal for learners of all ages to feel at times overwhelmed, unable

 Be aware that the people around you will have different reactions to your new status as a learner.

Learner Profile, Continued

Brad's advice on change

We were about half way through the first on-line course when our first residency seminar came around. When I walked into the room, there were all these people who were older than me. I felt like a caddy trying to pass himself off as a club member, even though I had been talking confidently with these same people on-line just the day before! Who did I think I was kidding, trying to be one of these guys? Then, the faculty facilitator invited me to join the conversation, and the strangeness seemed to evaporate as I heard the same 'voices' I had heard on the screen. It was kind of weird, actually. Then Rich, a VP for a Big Six accounting firm, said the same phrase that he had been typing for several weeks. We all looked at one another and burst out laughing.

Later, after the initial class meeting, we were all talking about the things that we had done to make sure we could fit this degree program into our lives. Every single person had made changes that they had not expected to make just a few months earlier. Some had seen changes in the people around them, too. I decided to do a little informal survey, and came up with 'Change Advice from the Educational Trenches':

- Expect things to go wrong—the laptop breaks, there's a critical meeting, you get sick, something *will* happen—build in 'wiggle room'.
- Expect your thinking process to change—to deepen and become more enjoyable.
- Expect the people around you to be upset by your changes, but use the opportunities to make change positive.
- Remind yourself of your priorities regularly.
- Relax!

The evening was winding down, and we knew we had to be up early to tackle more management theory. Just as we were getting ready to call it a night though, a David Bowie song came over the loudspeaker. You should have seen us all, sitting silently, most of us smiling, as Bowie sang, "Time may change me, but I can't change time." I guess I belong, after all.

to 'make the grade', or isolated, feeling as if they are the only ones in the world with these problems. Remember that you are not alone, and reach out to your support network and your classmates. They are likely to be experiencing the same feelings and in need of a 'cyber hug.'

You may miss the things that you no longer have time for, even if you think you will not. Because you will have less time for everything, you must be careful to set aside time for yourself and for family relationships. Once the commitment to school has been made, it is often easy to let it overshadow other responsibilities. Remember that school is only one of the priorities you juggle.

Change is hard, but it is constant, whether we acknowledge it or not. Change is part of life. Fear is a barrier to change and growth, a barrier that is self-perpetuating. The more that you or those around you resist change, the more uncomfortable and rigid life becomes. Obstacles to change, whether real or imagined, can cause resentment, depression, and physical illness. Rather than giving in to fear of change, which will only guarantee a lifetime of fear, work to develop ways to address the fears within and without.

You may want to make a note here of the changes you expect your studies to bring. Remember to date your entries. When you return to look at what you have written later, you may be surprised at the differences between the things you expected and the things you experienced.

What do you think will be your 'change challenges'?

_____

_____

_____

STAYING MOTIVATED FOR THE LONG HAUL

Undertaking a long-term project as potentially life changing as a college education presents special challenges and requires special measures to achieve success. Some of the steps you can take to stay on track through all the ups and downs of your program were discussed in the chapter on goal setting and time management. You may want to review Chapter 12 from time to time.

The way that you structure and balance your learning with the rest of your responsibilities will help assure achievement. Yet there is even more that you can do to overcome those inevitable moments when your energy seems exhausted and you feel as though you just cannot go on.

Visualize to Attain Success

If you ask many successful people how they overcame the obstacles before them and achieved their goals, they would say, "I kept the goal in sight." This means that they had a mental picture that they could constantly refer to. A picture that embodied the feel, the look, and even the smell of success.

Performers, sports figures, and public speakers often use visualization to give them additional energy and enhance their performance. You can, too. Develop a daydream of that moment in your life when your goals become a reality. Make your dream of success as rich and complex as you can, and think about it often, adding embellishments as you do.

Before you even begin your educational undertaking, visualize how you will feel when you are able to say, "I did it!" See yourself mounting your diploma on the wall over your desk. Feel the swish of your graduation gown and the steps beneath your feet as you walk down the aisle to receive that degree. Imagine the admiring looks from your family and friends, who knew you could do it.

You may want to draw a picture of yourself in that future, or cut a picture from a magazine that embodies your view of the 'you' to come. Look at it often, and *act* like the vision of the person you see, to help you become that person.

Involve your children in your motivational quest, as well. Tell your dream to your children as an adventure tale, so they can see you as the hero of your own story. Or ask them to draw a picture of all of you in the future, when your education has borne the fruit of your goals. These pictures can often help renew your commitment when everything else fails. They will show the certainty that your loved ones have in your ability to succeed, even when you doubt it.

Share the Load

Reach out to your classmates, who will understand what you are going through as no one else can. Commiserate with your classmates about pet peeves and ask for advice. Others who have dealt with the same doldrums may have excellent ideas to share.

Develop a daydream of that moment in your life when your goals become a reality.

Several of the distance education resource sites listed on the Online Resources Web site allow you to chat in real time with students in other on-line programs, or leave messages for others to answer. You can also use the bulletin board on the Online Resources Web site to request other ideas for dealing with something that you are having trouble with. These discussions can help to eliminate the impression that you are the *only* one running out of steam.

Explaining how you feel and asking for assistance will help to distribute the anxiety you may be feeling about your ability to achieve. Review with yourself and those close to you the reasons why you have undertaken this project, and evaluate the changes that have already occurred. Look back at the notes you have already made in this journal to see how you have progressed. Reflection and the realization that you have come a long way from when you started will help to refuel the energy you need to continue.

Take a Break to Refocus

Periodic decreases in motivation are normal and happen to all of us at some time. After all, you can not maintain a fever pitch indefinitely as the once new becomes routine. Be aware of the reasons for your feelings. If you feel unmotivated at a crucial point in writing a term paper, ask yourself if you are afraid that you do not have something worthwhile to say. A dip in your enthusiasm for school is normal. Put aside your fears by promising yourself a small reward when you finish the paper. Perhaps there is an item you have been wanting or a bit of pampering you would like to indulge in. Make finishing your work the condition for your reward.

Plan for periods of boredom by scheduling occasions that break the routine and change the scenery or tone of the present. Take your spouse out for a romantic dinner, or just go for a drive or a hike in the country. Visit a museum or play a round of golf. Decide on the interim rewards that mean the most to you, and that you can look forward to when it is time to take a break.

Think of activities that leave you feeling energized and happy. They can be day long, or just take up a few minutes. Do you feel great after a visit with your extended family? After a trip to the zoo? An action movie? Clothes shopping? A trip to the gym? What activities help to both relax and rejuvenate you?

When the doldrums hit and motivation flags, it is often difficult to think of things that make you feel good, give you energy, and create a happy glow inside. So, take a moment *now* to make a list of activities that you can refer to when you feel the blahs taking over. Select boredom-busting activities that take a few hours or a day, or even just a few minutes, depending on the time you have available and the severity of your need!

When you return, rev up your motivation even further by looking back at the things you have written here. Remember what you have already done for school and how far you have already come. You can make it!

Visualization Ideas

- See it happening.
- Daydream about the future.
- Draw pictures together.
- Tell 'your' story.
- Imagine the feel, touch, and taste of success.

Ideas for Busting Boredom When I Have a Few Minutes:

_____

_____

_____

A Few Hours:

_____

_____

_____

A Full Day:

_____

_____

_____

The Importance of Support

The support of your friends and family becomes crucial when you feel a need for encouragement. Share the new experiences and ideas crowding your brain with your local support 'team'. Include them in what you are doing beyond asking them to shoulder new responsibilities. In that way, they will know how your studies are progressing and what they are supporting. This sharing will also help make it less likely that you will feel isolated in your studies. As if those were not benefits enough, you will also be providing a role model for your children and for friends who may secretly be harboring their own educational dreams.

No one is expecting you to be perfect except, perhaps, yourself. Being competent at assertiveness, one of those self-reliance skills, means that you should be able to tell others what you need without demanding that others make it their priority. Be sure to take the time to let your family, friends, and colleagues know how you are feeling. Take some time to focus on their needs, too. They may be feeling neglected and in need of a boost, as well. That may be a good time to savor a special lunch together or decide to take one of your 'delete for now' items off the list for the day.

In fact, include your family's 'energizers' in a list and plan to reward everyone for their perseverance and help along the way. In that way, you will all have something to look forward to regularly between the beginning and end of that long-term project. Get together during the next family meeting and make a list of activities that your children and partner or friends miss most and receive the most enjoyment from. Scheduling some happy times together will help the educational work move along more quickly and keep you and your entire support team together. What pastimes will you choose to experience together?

To Sum Up . . .

In this chapter, we reviewed the changes that education can bring. We looked at the changes that you might expect from yourself and the changes that those around you may experience. Be alert for indications of the changes in yourself and those around you.

You also learned that maintaining motivation is the key to persistence and success. With that in mind, we explored ways to maintain your own motivation and reenergize yourself when your energy or enthusiasm flags. Keep your list of 'motivation enhancers' nearby for those moments when it seems like you will never be done. Of course, these motivational strategies can be used to help you stay on task in any undertaking. The more you use them, the more you will accomplish!

Notes to Yourself

Soon, this educational journey will be done. In the next chapter, we will talk about the importance of celebration and renewal to help you take the greatest advantage of the learning you have just completed. First, though, take a moment to check the bulletin board or the links on the Online Resources Web site at (www.delmar.com).

In addition, go back a few pages and review the little list of rewards you made for yourself. Add a few more whenever you are feeling particularly good. Even a simple moment of reflection and a few deep breaths can help refocus and renew you. Just think how great it is that you live in a time when you can do your banking, shop, keep in contact with friends and family, gain information and wisdom, and even go to school without leaving your home. Amazing!

Instead of thinking about where you are, think about where you want to be. It takes 20 years of hard work to become an overnight success.

—Diana Rankin

CHAPTER 17

Wrapping Up

After perhaps years of toil, countless pages of readings, and seemingly endless registrations, you will finally fulfill all degree requirements and reach the end of this particular journey. It is a time for celebration, reflection, and renewed planning, as you decide what your next undertaking will be. Even if your learning journey has not included a degree, you will have made achievements that are worth noting. Take the time to congratulate yourself for reaching this goal.

CELEBRATING YOUR ACHIEVEMENT

Small rewards will help you get through the day-to-day frustrations and challenges. Along with all of your other planning, though, you should plan a major celebration to mark when you actually achieve your goal. Think about what you want that celebration to be.

If at all possible, *attend your graduation.* It may seem silly to parade around in a cap and gown, but it is an honor and a rite you *deserve* to participate in. But plan your own special celebration as well. Whether you decide on a big party, a family vacation or second honeymoon, a new wardrobe, or something else of special significance, a celebration brings closure to a long journey. Not a few learners have used the anticipation of this major celebration as a spur to help them through those last few months!

A special celebration gives you the opportunity to thank your supporters and to review where you have been and how you have changed. It does not have to be a lavish production, especially if your bank account is still recovering from the cost of education, but it should be clear that this is a moment of congratulations and thanks for all of the sacrifices you and your loved ones have made. It does not have to be closely related to your education at all, but something that will mean

"There are three ingredients in the good life: learning, earning, and yearning."

—Christopher Morley

something special to you and those around you. Some of the things that other learners have done include:

- holding a 'decide where the diploma should go' party
- taking the neglected hubby on a Caribbean cruise
- buying the 'perfect' designer interview suit
- ordering new business cards
- writing and sending personal thank-you messages to classmates and teachers
- spending a day at the spa
- taking another class, just for the fun of it!

What will *you* do to mark this passage in your life? Are there any things that spring to mind or that your family has mentioned? Maybe you should make a note of several possible rewarding events while you are at this point:

_____

_____

Learner Profile, Continued

Greg graduates

I was looking back over the things I said in what seems like years ago, now, and have to shake my head at the way things turn out. Next month, I will put on the cap and gown and march across the stage. But I will not be getting a degree in engineering, as I originally thought I would. Instead, I decided to major in political science. You probably wonder how I got there from engineering. To tell you the truth, there are several reasons. Part of it was that first distance ed course, in which I found out how interesting history is and how much of an effect the past has on the present and future. Part of it was that the way the credit worked from what I had done in the service. But the most important part of the decision came from something that happened at work.

You see, it is not a union shop where I work, but it has been something that the employees have kicked around now and then for a long time. Even with some of the new, good changes that the new management instituted, the little guy was not getting any protection or representation. I saw that things I was learning about that had happened in the past were happening right under my nose every day. So I got involved. Partly because of things I learned in classes, I was able to help organize the men. Now, at least, management is negotiating instead of demanding. They are probably a little mad at themselves right now for insisting that I go to school, too.

College has been a huge eye-opener for me. After completing the first two years' worth of credits, I was comfortable enough to move on to a completely distance bachelor-completion program on-line. One that had a real, live graduation. I made sure of that. Otherwise, nearly everything has been done on-line—papers, class bulletin boards, video presentations, everything. The better I got at negotiating the technology and connecting experience to what I was learning, the easier it got. And throughout it all, Sharon has been my rock, a real saint. After the graduation, we are going to go on a second honeymoon. After that, who knows what will happen? I wonder what Sharon will think of the idea of being married to a lawyer?

Reflect on Your Success

Your celebration can be ceremonial or festive, have the atmosphere of a rite or a holiday. It really does not matter how you choose to honor your success. But whatever event you choose to mark this milestone in your life, be sure that you build in the opportunity to reflect on how your educational undertaking has changed you and the ones around you. Acknowledge and respect the changes, and make them a permanent part of how you see yourself. As you have throughout your educational project, include your support network in your expression of appreciation, and vow to support them as they have supported you.

Take the opportunity, as well, to review what you have written throughout your learning journal and your school experience. How have you changed? Do you think differently about yourself and the things you read than you did before? Do you have more confidence and fewer fears? Let the alterations sink in and become a part of the new, improved you.

A Learner Reflects:

"Certainly the greatest feature that brought me to on-line distance education was the convenience factor. The professional literature continues to support the notion that many students no longer have the time to sit in traditional face-to-face courses. I agree with this premise! However, what challenged me to continue on-line distance education was even greater than the convenience factor! Whereas my initial goal was simply convenience, I soon began to learn about learning and experienced the metamorphic change from simply being a student to becoming a learner! Now, I know that sounds corny, but I really enjoy the ability to dig into topics and expand my cognitive horizons. I became both my own best and worst critic by developing themes and topics far greater than were "required" of any particular course. I empirically believe that the on-line learning component, and in particular the Internet, aided in part to this learning empowerment as there was a plethora of information at my fingertips. One investigation on-line led quickly to another, and to still another. I was able to develop and expand themes throughout my doctoral studies with the encouragement of the faculty who carefully guided my learning without dictating my studies. When it is all said and done, isn't the empowerment of the learner what education is all about!"

—Steven G. Lesh, MPA, PT, SCS, ATC
Assistant Professor of Physical Therapy
Southwest Baptist University

Celebrations also provide you with a benchmark you can look back upon, and from which to move forward toward your next achievement. In a sense, you are acknowledging that this phase of your life is over, and you are ready to commit to the next one. Allow yourself the closure that a special event brings. You will not be sorry you did.

UPDATE YOUR PROFILE

Studies and surveys have shown that the number one reason that most adults give for undertaking an educational program is to enhance or change careers. Presumably, you will want others to know that you are ready to assume greater responsibility and authority. You will especially want those in a position to offer you employment challenges to know about your achievement. Yet you might be surprised at the number of people who complete their learning and then neglect to follow up with these simple actions. If career enhancement is your prime motivation, the completion of your education is the perfect time to update all of your personal records and let people know that you are ready for the next challenge life has in store for you.

Revise Your Resume

Whether your education is job related or not, one of the first places you should make changes is on your resume. Check to make sure that all information and dates are correct. You may want to invest in the services of a professional to develop a resume format that will showcase your learning and experience in its best light. Prepare a number of spotless copies on first-class paper, to be ready when the opportunity to present your resume arises.

Next, make sure that all outdated information held by others is revised. Bring a copy of your new resume to your human resources office at work and request that it be added to your personnel file. If you have posted any resumes at on-line career sites, be sure to find and change those, too.

While you are in the updating 'mode' is a good time to make contacts with people who may be in a position to be aware of or offer you employment. Most people only think about looking for work when they are unhappy at their present position or unemployed. Yet employment experts say that this is the worst time to seek employment. Instead, take some of the time you will have now that you are finished with school to send updated resumes to recruiters and other employers in your industry. Be discreet, especially if your employer might hear of your search and react negatively. Let your cover letter state that you have completed a degree or an educational project. Take time to explain what you have gotten from completing this goal.

Perhaps your experience will be similar to Brad's. You will never know what opportunities might await you, until you take the time and effort to find out. So be sure to do your follow-up. This is not limited to sending out resumes. Follow through in some of the ways listed here, as well.

RENEW YOUR NETWORKS

If you are like most people, you have networks of influence, or groups that you belong to, that focus on work and personal interests. These networks often do not overlap, at least not obviously. Still, there are good reasons to renew both your professional and personal networks when you have reached the end of your educational enterprise.

Learner Profile, Continued

Brad, the executive

Even with completion of the program a mere three weeks away, I already think of myself as an MBA graduate. So much so, that I took the advice we received in last weekend's intensive and began reviewing and updating my resume, even while we were still in the room. In a very short time, I have become one of those people that can fit a tremendous amount of work and living into a very short space of time. I think I even talk faster than I used to.

While I was sitting there, revising, one of my classmates sat down next to me and cleared his throat. John works for a major IT firm on the West Coast, and I had learned so much just from listening to him, so I looked up immediately. "Brad," he said, "If you are looking for a chance to move up, I can pass your resume on to our HR people." He went on to tell me about the opportunities that were available at his company, and to tell me that he was impressed with my participation in the program. He thought I could go far, he said. I took a deep breath and said, "Sure," hoping he could not tell I was quaking inside. Within the hour, I had made the necessary revisions and printed off a resume for him to take back with him.

As luck would have it, my superiors were hatching some plans for me, too. When I got in on Monday, bleary-eyed from learning, driving, and spending a few more hours reading before work, I was summoned to the VP's office. I must have been distracted, because it took me a few minutes to figure out that he was offering me a promotion. It seems that he had seen a copy of a report I had done, mostly for a school project, analyzing some of the department's statistical data in support of some ideas I had for changing processes. It was a good offer, one that I had envisioned when I started this study. And yet. . . . and yet.

I said I wanted to think about the offer for a few days. There were suddenly more important questions to think about. Like what did I really want to do with my life? Did I want to take this offer, or see what other opportunities might arise? Was I selling myself short?

Well, the long and short of it is that John's company made an even better offer. Even though I had not actually received the degree yet, it seemed as though I had already earned it. All that concentrated effort was worth it. That, and choosing a program that put me in contact with other smart, goal-oriented people. So after graduation, I am going to pack up my things and move to California. After I get some sleep, that is.

Professional Network Renewal

If you belong to any industry associations or other business groups, inform the appropriate officers of your recent accomplishment. Accept any requests to speak about your on-line experiences. There will likely be a number of coworkers and colleagues interested in your experience, whether they are considering it themselves or wondering what the big deal is. This could be an opportunity for you to mentor another or provide much-needed information to help another make an educational commitment.

Your achievement can also provide the impetus for further openings that may have eluded you previously. Bringing a long-term project to completion is a valued management skill, and your accomplishment will indicate to others that you are a person that can get things done. So, the knowledge that you have completed your study, and not necessarily the subject on which it was based, may be the push that upper-level managers need to envision you in a leadership role. Pay attention to the manner in which your achievement is received. If this is a direction that interests you, make your interests known.

Personal Network Renewal

Pursuing and completing an educational goal will cause changes, but not fundamental ones. Your values and deep relationships will continue to be basic to your life and the way you live it. Now that your time is not completely devoted to study, you can return to some of the activities and recreations you may have had to curtail to make time for study. That is, if you still want to do them! If so, take the time to renew old relationships and catch up on the events in friends' lives as you share your own. Some of your connections with old friends may change, and some may initially be cool. Everyone has their own expectations about what education can do. If the friendship is an important one, you may have to take some time to assuage fears and reassure your friend that you are still the 'same old you'.

If you interrupted a volunteer position, you may want to return to your avocation in a different capacity, or merely resume where you left off. As may happen in neglected friendships, some of your former volunteer colleagues may have learned to get along without you and find it difficult to make room for you again. Watch for signs of conflict, but be patient and you will all be working together toward similar goals again soon.

Probably the most profound changes will occur in your home. Here, however, you have all been adjusting daily, adding and changing as needed, so you will perhaps be less aware of the differences. This is the time and place to stand firm on changes you want to continue. For example, if your teenager has taken over some of the household management chores, expect him to continue. Make your expectations clear. Do not allow yourself to resume old habits just because you can. This is also a good time to reevaluate tasks and rewards for all members of the family. You never know when you will want to learn something else. Soon, you may find yourself yearning for learning!

Learner Profile, Continued

Ellen returns

Look at me, a manager! And she thought she was kidding when Joan said I wanted her job! It turns out that she did go back to school, just as she had told me. The difference was that she decided to change careers and left the hospital to go to school full-time. So I was promoted to her position, because I was less than a semester away from graduation. Boy, was that ever a tough year. Finishing up my senior project, a promotion, and my mother's heart attack, all within three months. Oh, mom is all right now— better, actually, because she has been on this new medication. And we did all finally get to go to Disney World, too. But that is not the best thing, at least as far as I am concerned. I decided to go on for a master's, too.

The more management experience I got, the more I realized that I needed to know more than the bachelor's had taught me. My experiences coming up through the ranks were really important in making me good at what I do. But it was clear to me that healthcare is changing rapidly, and the industry needs people like me to look out for the interests of the patients, as well as the bottom line. It is a complicated system that is just going to get more complicated, so I decided that I wanted to focus in the area of healthcare technology management.

I am going to take it a little easier this time. After all, there are not as many credits to do as there were in the bachelor's, and I have my eye on that corner office. No, not really, but I found that I liked the classes so much on-line, and wanted to learn more in the management of healthcare technology, that it seemed to make sense to go right back. Of course, I got a lot of positive reinforcement, and not just from the teachers.

You see, there was this classmate that I started to talk to outside of the requirements of class assignments. After two classes together, we had gotten to know each other pretty well and had a lot of respect for the way each other thought.

If someone had told me before I started learning on-line that I would make really great friends with people I never saw, I would have said they were crazy. But you never know. I got to know some of the people in my class better than people I see every day. Not that everyone will be like me and meet a new friend, but it is certainly not the lonely experience I had thought it would be when I began. And I did everything I set out to do, too: Completed my bachelor's degree and got a better job so I can give Mark and Missy a better life. I just got a bit more than I bargained for.

To Sum Up. . . .

In this chapter, we reviewed the reasons why celebrating the completion of a long-term goal is as important as maintaining the motivation to complete it. We reviewed the steps you should take to update your professional and personal life when the project is done, and why those steps are important, as well.

So, if you have been studying and learning all throughout the course of this learning journal, by now you will have attained your goal. Congratulations! Be sure to share your achievement with others by visiting the Online Resources bulletin board, at <www.delmar.com>. We are all proud of you!

In the final chapter of this text, we will take a look into the future of learning at a distance. What will your future learning look like?

Notes to Yourself

Perhaps you have completed your journey—for now—and will learn more at another time. Look back again through what you have written in the text and see if there are trends that developed. Do you have more questions that you want answers for? Write them down here:

_____

_____

_____

Now, take a look into the future of distance learning.

A Look into the Future

Has your participation in distance learning seemed like magic at times? Yet it is you who were the magician in charge. Magically, you have learned to progress through all of the barriers that faced you to meet success on your own terms. You did it.

This final chapter will take a peek into the future of learning and the changes that technology will enable. Perhaps there is more yet for you to learn, too.

"Any sufficiently advanced technology is indistinguishable from magic."

—*Arthur C. Clarke*

CHAPTER 18

A Look into the Future

How will learning be delivered in the future? What can we expect to see as technology advances? Will distance learning supplant campus-based learning? Will changes in society require continuous training? How will educational institutions change in the future?

These are questions that many people speculate about every day, wager fortunes, and gamble their own futures on. It is certain that the technology will change rapidly, and many of the 'advancements' mentioned here may be in widespread use by the time you read this. Some will make a brief explosion, and others will become integral parts of life for many years to come. One thing is certain: Change will continue.

THE FUTURE OF LEARNING ON THE 'NET

In looking at the technology that will be used to deliver learning in the future, it seems clear that current cutting-edge applications and tools will become refined. Now available to just a few, for example, wireless PDAs (personal digital assistants) may become ubiquitous as tools to help busy professionals connect to their coursework, their teachers, and their classmates. Already, programs have been developed for Palm® users with which they can easily organize assignments or interact within class modules. Teachers can also use handheld wireless technology to prepare lessons and upload them to institutional servers, correspond with students, and manage administrative chores without being tied to a home or office computer. In the future, these devices will converge with others to provide on-demand, instant wireless access to knowledge and connections on a global scale. And they will become smaller and more portable with each generation.

Many of the most forward-thinking educators predict that distance learning and campus-based learning will merge, becoming seamless. They believe that

> "We live in a moment of history where change is so speeded up that we begin to see the present only when it is already disappearing."
>
> —R. D. Laing

partnerships will continue to grow, change, and flourish, as the needs of the learning society impels them. More and more, knowledge will become modularized; it will be broken down into pieces that can be reassembled into training classes, courses, or programs as the needs of the learning population dictate. Like electricity, learning will become something that is always available and therefore taken for granted. We will not think about it much, just access it as we need it. Perhaps the virtual assistant that our PDA has become will remind us that it is time for our next educational moment, much as it will remind us of our daily appointments and responsibilities. Or, with a mere vocal command, entire 'worlds' of virtual learning will open for us. Imagine being able to experience life-like simulations of a scuba dive in Belize or a bridge repair high above San Francisco harbor. What would it be like to use software programs to forecast the outcome of a major construction project or to retrace George Washington's steps? Yet these very applications are well beyond the planning stages and may be appearing at a university near you soon.

Already, the medical community is using distance learning technologies to train doctors and nurses at remote locations. These medical personnel are receiving training from the top talents in the medical community. Already, future managers are using virtual reality-based programs to develop leadership and supervisory skills, so they will become effective administrators in the global workforce. Already, automotive technicians in India can interact with their counterparts in Detroit while learning together on the corporation's intranet training site. So many changes, so quickly. Changes that were fueled by need and demand. And demand and need will continue to grow.

Working with the Web can be frustratingly slow, as transmission of large data packets, like graphics, can seem to take forever to appear on the screen. New technology promises to address this problem in the near future. Connecting through fiber-optic lines and via cable TV is already available in many areas, and the increased carrying capacity makes the Web more powerful. As this power increases, educational applications will also become more powerful, with desktop video-conferencing, virtual environments, and elaborate scenario-based learning being delivered right to your screen, or whatever appliance you will be using to access learning and information. Perhaps holographic displays and wearable personal learning environments are not too far away, either.

The programs, hardware, and infrastructure to power an instantaneous, just-in-time connection are also being developed today. The next wave of the Internet in current development is Internet2. A partnership of universities, corporations, and government agencies, Internet2 is an experimental breeding ground for networking development. It is being designed to transmit hundreds of times more data, at faster rates, than the Internet we have come to know. From this project, we will likely see new interactivity and learning technologies that are not yet even dreamed of, as well as the infrastructure to support them. In development since 1999 (just nine years since the WWW was born!), this next generation of the Internet will offer commercial use within a few years. Then, you will see an explosion of data services such as interactive television (ITV), movies on demand, virtual medical offices, and much more. Much is already happening.

As part of the Internet2 testing, the consortium of universities is currently seeking applications designed to push the system to its limits. In the future, we may see total immersion learning applications reminiscent of the Star Trek holodeck, where holographic representations meet and interact. You will be able to choose your own 'avatar', or virtual personality, to act out your virtual existence. Who—or what—will you be?

The first likely users of the Internet2 will be digital video producers and cable TV stations, who will use it in addition to satellite feeds. With the commercial

"We live in a time of such rapid change and growth of knowledge that only he who is in a fundamental sense a scholar—that is, a person who continues to learn and inquire—can hope to keep pace, let alone play the role of guide."

—Nathan M. Pusey,
President, Harvard

development of Internet2, look for highly developed 'information appliances' that combine high-definition TV, web connectivity, and personalized media to become available for home use. Internet2 may also change the way that people interact, much the same way that the Internet did. With increased bandwidth and speed, the average person will be able to produce his own videos and distribute them freely, using similar technology to that used now with MP3s.

MP3, short for M-PEG3, is a compression standard for audio files that allows music to survive the download interruptions that may affect a cellular phone. Because it is a standard, it can be easily recognized by and shared between a number of software applications. The compression rate is so high that any little missed transmissions are undetectable to the human ear. No wonder the people who make money from audio recordings are annoyed!

Just as MP3s have the potential to change the music industry, MP4 is set to do the same for video technology. This video standard will allow video that appears to be full motion, even when it is not—quite. The programming of MP4, like MP3, allows for an appropriate frame to be substituted when transmission is interrupted, and minimizes the amount of data that is sent. The substitution is designed to be undetectable in normal viewing. With this technology, for example, you could follow a complicated demonstration and see clearly the crucial items. All of this would be fluid because the camera would focus on the important items and float them over less critical data such as backgrounds or long shots. This would allow for greater clarity in a smaller package.

Another development is in the area of third generation wireless video. With 3G, or IMT-2000, as the standard is called, users of wireless devices will be able to add video to their connectivity. With this technology, for example, executives would be able to view video feeds of financial reports in the taxi on the way from airport to meeting. Emergency medical personnel would be able to send video of crash victims to physicians at distant hospitals, and teams of managers would be able to hold virtual and visual meetings from their respective manufacturing floors. Third generation wireless video technology will soon be available in Japan, where the infrastructure changes necessary are already underway, but it will not be long until it is available elsewhere, too.

The Impact of Technology

High-speed networks and compression technologies will make it possible for even more people to engage and learn without leaving their homes or offices. Moreover, these advancements will allow more meaningful and higher-quality professional development, and access to a just-in-time skill training network that we can only dream of. Soon, everything from your car and telephone to the walls in your 'smarthome' may be connected to the network, enabling you to communicate with others and learn, wirelessly.

It is hard to believe that the World Wide Web has been around only since 1990. In just a few short years, millions of people have learned how to connect with others around the globe. Millions have built Web sites, and few could have envisioned the success of e-commerce. Technology and society are changing rapidly, and each affects the other. Because of changes in the marketplace, the majority of workers on the job today will perceive a need for skill enhancement and education just to maintain their present jobs. This is even before they consider or attempt advancement.

Most experts in technology feel that the speed with which things change will eventually slow, at least until the next major leap forward (believed to be the workable development of nanotechnology). Still, it will take many more years for human nature and society to adjust to the explosive changes that are occurring now. This means that stress and uncertainty about the future will probably continue to plague humans for some time to come. We had better learn to cope.

Some of the visions of the future may seem fantastic to you now. As you have discovered, too, change can be positive. Each new technological development has brought positive change, as well. Connection brings understanding and tolerance. Collaboration brings peace. People who were never able to access learning before, now can. People from all walks of life, all cultures and backgrounds, can communicate and learn together. Perhaps the greatest gift that distance education promises is the empowerment of community. And now you have joined.

YOUR FUTURE LEARNING

You have learned to work with others, and by yourself. You have thought deeply and considered well. Among the skills you have become competent in through learning and experience are skills in dealing with change and stress. Do not let the end of your educational project mean a return to old habits. Review the skills you have learned and the experiences you have had and *decide* which practices to keep as part of your life. Perhaps you have found a good way to release stress or a great way to use technology to get more done. Do not forget them!

Similarly, do not be tempted to fall back into old habits . . . if you can even consider it! As you have probably found out by now, completing a learning project has changed you. You may not even *want* to participate in activities you used to hold dear, or renew acquaintances with old friends with whom you now have little in common. Remember that you have accomplished something to be proud of.

After such an endeavor is over, it can leave a hole. Be sure to take time during your celebration to say good-bye to the good times, the heartaches, and the friends you made during your journey. It may seem strange how much you can miss people you never see. But now it is over and it is time to apply what you have learned. Time to get back to some of the activities and people you did not have time for. Time to relax.

But you may be surprised. You may come to miss the interaction and sense of adventure that accompanies learning new things. As bizarre as it may seem, you may begin to think about jumping into further learning. You may wonder whether you need to learn more, or what it would be like to add another certification to your list of accomplishments. Soon, you may be looking forward to another course, and another.

> *Do not let the end of your educational project mean a return to old habits.*

"Aim for success, not perfection. Never give up your right to be wrong, because then you will lose the ability to learn new things and move forward with your life. Remember that fear always lurks behind perfectionism. Confronting your fears and allowing yourself the right to be human can, paradoxically, make yourself a happier and more productive person."

—*Dr. David M. Burns*

Like the learning that slowly changes the way you view the world, the technologies that will shape the future will become a part of your experience at what seems like a slow pace. When you look back, though, you will be amazed at how quickly you—and the world—have changed. Welcome to the world of lifelong learning, your world. Greet the future!

A FINAL WORD

By now, you know more about the special challenges of on-line learning. You have everything you need to identify your strengths, overcome your weaknesses, and build and maintain your support community. You know how to find information and evaluate it. You know that all barriers can be overcome. You have the tools to join the on-line learning revolution, a revolution that will soon become commonplace.

You know by now that you can find tools and resources to help you meet your goals at the Online Resources Web site <www.delmar.com>, and elsewhere on the Web. Just because you have reached the end of this book, does not mean you have reached the end of the road. You can still visit the site to make note of changes and, perhaps, help others to attain their own educational goals. If you find other wonderful resources, let us know by posting a note on <www.delmar.com>.

You must feel great. You have accomplished what you set out to do. Congratulations! You have proven to yourself and those around you that you can do anything you set your mind to, even distance learning. You have become a successful lifelong learner. You have proven that success is up to you!

GLOSSARY OF SELECTED ON-LINE LEARNING TERMS

A

academic advisor   The person, usually a faculty member, who helps guide students in the classes to take to compete a program of study in a particular area.

academic year   Period used by colleges to measure a full year of study, usually beginning in the fall and ending in the spring.

accreditation   A process of institutional review and determination of academic and administrative quality and solvency. Accreditation can be completed for an entire institution and/or specific programs, it can be regional or state based. Different criteria are followed for technology-based programs than those for academic programs.

analog   A signal that is received in the same form in which it is transmitted, although the amplitude and frequency may vary.

application   (computer) A self-contained program that performs a well-defined set of tasks under user control. Web browsers, mail readers, and FTP clients are examples of applications commonly used on the Internet. (college) Part of the official paperwork for asking an institution of higher education to accept you as a student in a degree program.

archive   (computer) Information that is saved from a chat or e-mail utility. (educational) Part of a library or building where records are kept.

assessment of prior learning   Refers to several methods, including standardized tests, course challenges, and portfolio assessment, through which adults gain college credit as a result of their learning outside the classroom. Also known as 'prior learning assessment'.

associate degree   Degree given upon completion of two years of full-time study or the equivalent. Most associate degrees are awarded by two-year colleges, although some four-year universities also offer associate degrees. Some associate degrees transfer to four-year universities; others are for career preparation.

assumptive   An expectation on the learners' part that there will be a choice of format available for every learning experience.

asynchronous   Communication in which interaction between parties does not take place simultaneously.

Asynchronous Transfer Mode (ATM)   A method of sending data in irregular time intervals. Allows most modern computers to communicate with one another easily.

audioconferencing   A way of interacting in real time that involves linking participants through telephone or speakerphone.

audiographics   Refers to addition of audio enhancements to Web-based or video conferencing.

authentic assessment   Refers to the use of methods other than standardized tests to measure achievement. These methods include portfolios, projects and the like.

B

bachelor's degree (baccalaureate)   Degree given upon completion of four years of full-time study or the equivalent, also referred to as a *baccalaureate* or *undergraduate* degree.

backbone   A primary communication path connecting multiple computer users.

bandwidth   Information-carrying capacity of an electronic communication channel.

binary   A computer language developed with only two letters (numbers) in its alphabet.

bit   Abbreviation for a single binary digit.

bookmark (Netscape)   A browser routine that allows you to save a reference to a site or page that you have already visited so you can return to that page at a later time.

browser   Software that allows you to find and see information on the Internet (i.e., Netscape or Internet Explorer).

Bulletin Board Service (BBS)   A computer service that allows users to access a central 'host' computer and read or post messages electronically.

byte   A single computer word, generally eight bits.

C

call number A library's unique identifier for material housed therein.

Central Processing Unit (CPU) The component of a computer in which data processing takes place.

certificate A credential awarded for completion of a specific educational program. Certificates are often applicable toward degree credit.

channel The smallest subdivision of a circuit, usually with a path in only one direction.

chat A form of interactive on-line communication that enables typed conversations to occur in real time. When participating in a chat discussion, your messages are instantaneously relayed to other members in the chat room while other members' messages are instantaneously relayed to you.

classical conditioning A behavioral training that takes advantage of natural instincts to effect training. Contrast operant conditioning.

CLEP Acronym for College-Level Examination Program, administered by The College Board, which provides standardized tests in college subjects and recommends college-level credit for successful completion.

college Higher education institution that generally offers two-year or four-year degrees, but does not offer graduate-level programs.

compressed video When video signals are downsized to allow travel along a smaller carrier.

compression Reducing the amount of visual information sent in a signal by transmitting only changes in action.

Computer-Aided Instruction (CAI) Teaching process in which a computer is utilized to enhance the learning environment by assisting students in gaining mastery over a specific skill.

computer teleconferencing Computer mediated interaction in real time, usually allowing participants to see and hear each other through the use of streaming audio and video.

consortia Entities (singular, consortium) formed by and among schools and other learning providers to meet a specific need outside of the normal practices of any one member.

contact hour The unit of measurement used to determine credit granted, one contact hour is equivalent to one hour per week, per term, spent in classroom instruction.

Continuing Education Unit (CEU) A nationally recognized system of measurement for continuing education programs. One CEU is defined as 10 hours of instruction (contact hours) by qualified instructors in a responsible program.

cookies Usually, small files that are downloaded to your computer when you browse certain Web pages. Cookies hold information that can be retrieved by other Web pages on the site. Some cookies are programmed with an expiration date so that they are automatically disabled after a period of time

core Relates to fundamental courses at a given institution that are required for all students to pass in order to graduate; also referred to as *general education requirements*.

cornell system A popular note-taking system.

correspondence study Individual or self-guided study by mail from an educational institution. Credit is earned through written assignments and proctored tests.

courseware Software consisting of instructional modules that can be used to present lessons.

credit Unit of value assigned by institutions upon successful completion of courses.

curriculum The combination of courses making up a particular area of study. The courses are arranged in a sequence to build on what has gone before.

cyberspace The nebulous "place" where humans interact over computer networks. Coined by William Gibson in *Neuromancer*.

D

database Loosely, any aggregation of data; usually a large collection of data that has been formatted by some defined standard.

degree plan A listing of the courses and expected schedule for completion that will lead to degree achievement.

desktop videoconferencing Videoconferencing on a personal computer.

dial-up veleconference Using public telephone lines for communications links among various locations.

digital An electrical signal that varies in discrete steps in voltage, frequency, amplitude, locations, etc. Digital signals can be transmitted faster and more accurately than analog signals.

Digital Video Interactive (DVI) A format for recording digital video onto compact disc allowing for compression and full-motion video.

diploma mill Term for a scam that promises a degree credential for a payment, with no work necessary.

dissertation Culminating product of doctoral study, recording the student's research and conclusions on a specific and unique topic.

distance education The process of providing instruction when students and instructors are separated by physical distance.

distance learning   The desired outcome of distance education.

doctoral degree   The highest academic degree awarded in many subject areas upon demonstration of mastery, including the ability to perform scholarly research. Usually, a master's degree is a prerequisite to pursuit of a doctorate.

download   Using the network to transfer files from a remote computer to another, usually your own.

E

elective   Indicates a course choice outside requirements.

e-mail   Sending messages from one computer user to another.

emoticon   The use of keyboard characters to express emotions :−) = happy :−< = sad, etc.

enroll   Become an official student by going through the application and admissions process.

enrollment   The total number of students officially participating in programs at a given institution.

experiential learning   Learning acquired from experiences outside of a classroom, also 'assessment of prior learning'. There are several methods for obtaining college credit for this learning. (Please see chapter on prior learning assessment for detailed descriptions.)

F

favorite (microsoft explorer)   A browser routine that allows you to save a reference to a site or page that you have already visited so you can return to that page at a later time.

File Transfer Protocol (FTP)   A way to move files from a distant computer to a local computer, using a network such as the Internet.

flame   A public post or e-mail message that expresses a strong opinion or criticism against another.

Free Application for Federal Student Aid (FAFSA)   The application students must first complete in order to apply for virtually all forms of financial aid assistance.

frequency   The space between waves in a signal. The amount of time between waves passing a stationary point.

Frequently-Asked Questions (FAQs)   A collection of information on the basics of any given subject, often used on the WWW.

full-motion video   Signal that allows transmission of complete action taking place at the origination site.

fully interactive video (two-way interactive video)   Two or more locations that are connected electronically to allow full interaction with audio and video.

G

GED   Acronym for General Educational Development program, or the instruction that prepares individuals to obtain a high school equivalency diploma.

graduate   Study or degree beyond undergraduate, or a student who pursues such study.

grants   Financial aid that does not have to be paid back is awarded to students based on financial need.

H

Herrmann Brain Dominance Instrument (HBDI)   An assessment instrument that classifies people's preferences for thinking based on how the brain functions physically. Four quadrants are identified, each with its own specialized functions.

higher education   Education beyond high school.

hit   A single web page address provided in response to a search engine query.

homepage   A document with an address (URL) on the World Wide Web maintained by a person or organization that contains pointers to other pieces of information.

host   A network computer that can receive information from other computers.

hypertext   A document that has been marked up to allow a user to select words or pictures within the document, click on them, and connect to further information.

Hypertext Markup Language (HTML)   The programming code used to create a home page and to access documents over the WWW.

Hypertext Transfer Protocal (HTTP)   The protocol used to signify an Internet site is a WWW site, i.e. HTTP is a WWW address.

I

instructional preferences   The ways a learner prefers to receive knowledge. Preferences can include study space, media, social interaction, organization, and other factors.

Integrated Services Digital Network (ISDN)   A telecommunications standard allowing communications channels to carry voice, video, and data simultaneously.

interactive media   Frequency assignment that allows for a two-way interaction or exchange of information.

Internet   An international network of networks primarily used to connect education and research networks begun by the U.S. government (Dept. of Defense).

Internet Protocol (IP)   The international standard for addressing and sending data via the Internet.

Internet Service Provider (ISP)   The company that provides connection to the Internet and World Wide

Web, either through a dial-up access number or other method (cable modem, T1 line, etc.).

internet telephony   Allows people to conduct a telephone call using the Internet and PCs.

InterNIC   The entity that controls the registration of most domain names on the Internet. The InterNIC is a cooperative activity between the National Science Foundation, Network Solutions, Inc., and AT&T. Its home page is http://internic.net/.

Intranet   A private network that uses Internet-related technologies to provide services within an organization.

L

learning journal   A personal record of reactions to classroom learning.

learning objective   A statement of the skills, abilities, and knowledge that students will be expected to achieve as a result of a course.

learning outcome   The skills, abilities, and knowledge that students actually achieve as a result of a course.

learning styles   The strengths and preferences that people exhibit in the ways they take in and process information.

listserv   An e-mail program that allows multiple computer users to connect onto a single system, creating an on-line discussion.

Local Area Network (LAN)   Two or more local computers that are physically connected.

lurk, lurker   The term used to denote the action of a person who visits and reads the postings of a newsgroup, but does not participate in discussion.

M

major   An academic subject area, such as economics or geology, in which students take many courses and can earn a degree. Usually constitutes one-third to one-half of the credits needed for a bachelor's degree.

matriculate   Official admission into a degree program.

mental map   (study skills) A way of note taking that shows the entire topic as a web, with subtopics grouped by relationship.
(learning theories) Piaget's term for a way of understanding children's emotional development. He believed children acted based on structures of thought, which changed as children grew and became more sophisticated.

microwaves   Electromagnetic waves that travel in a straight line and are used to and from satellites and for short distances (i.e., up to 30 miles).

minor   An area of interest studied at the same time as a major. It requires fewer courses than a major and allows a student to refine or incorporate a specialty.

modalities   Used to indicate ways of processing information in Gardner's theory of multiple intelligences. Also called "preferences."

modem   A piece of equipment to allow computers to interact with each other via telephone lines by converting digital signals to analog for transmission along analog lines.

MOO (multi-user domain, object oriented)   A MUD with additional functionality that appears like a browser.

MUD (multi-user domain)   Text-based program that allows interaction from multiple PCs to one server. Originally designed for role-playing games.

multimedia   Any document that uses multiple forms of communication, such as text, audio, and/or video.

Myers Briggs Type Indicator (MBTI)   An instrument that assesses personality preferences according scales derived from psychologist Carl Jung's theory of psychological types. Thirty-six combinations are possible.

N

netiquette   Network etiquette, or the set of informal rules of behavior that have evolved in cyberspace, including the Internet and on-line services.

Netscape   An example of browser software that allows you to design a home page and to browse links on the WWW.

network   A series of points connected by communication channels in different locations.

newsgroup   A public electronic forum where messages are posted and responded to.

O

off-line   Doing work while not connected to a network.

on-line   (computer) Active and prepared for operation. (education) Utilizing a computer network to complete course requirements.

operant conditioning   Trains behaviors through reward or punishment. Contrast classical conditioning.

origination site   The location from which a teleconference originates.

P

.pdf   A document designation used by Adobe's Acrobat software. Allows documents to be stored and downloaded, maintaining graphics and typesetting.

performance measure   Description of how the learning objectives will be measured, also referred to as *educational effectiveness*. Measurement tools can be objective, as in standardized tests, or subjective, as in assessments.

performance standards   A description of the level of demonstrable achievement(s) for each learning objective.

plug-in   A small software program that enhances functionality, usually downloaded from the Internet and installed on your own computer.

Point of Presence (POP)   Point of connection between an interexchange carrier and a local carrier to pass communications into the network.

portfolio   One measure of assessment, also referred to as 'authentic assessment', in which students create examples of their learning, writing samples, artworks, etc. to show what they are capable of.

post   A message contained on a discussion board or listserv.

PPP   A software package that allows a user to have a direct connection to the Internet over a telephone line.

preferences   Learning style indicators, used extensively in Gardner's theory of multiple intelligences.

prerequisite   A course that a student must take before he or she can enroll in another (usually more challenging) course.

prior learning portfolio or prior learning assessment   See 'assessment of prior learning'.

protocol   A formal set of standards, rules, or formats for exchanging data that assures uniformity between computers and applications.

R

residency   The time that academic programs set for required meetings on campus or at central locations, where students can interact and meet with faculty, plan, and participate in group activities.

S

scholarships   Awards that do not usually have to be paid back. They are given to students who demonstrate financial need and/or show promise of high achievement.

search engine   Interactive directories that enable users of the Internet to search for specific information.

semester   Calendar system used by colleges and universities. Classes and grade reports are divided into two periods in the spring and fall, each lasting about 16 weeks, and one period in the summer, usually lasting eight weeks.

server   A computer that provides information to client machines. For example, there are Web servers that send out Web pages, mail servers that deliver email, etc.

SQ3R   A popular study method. The initials stand for: Survey, Question, Read, Recite, and Review.

streaming audio   Web technology that allows you to hear audio files as they are downloading, reducing waiting time.

Student Aid Report (SAR)   The form students receive after filing a FAFSA application that notifies student of their eligibility for federal student aid.

syllabus   Information given to the students enrolled in a course. It includes objectives, textbooks, expectations, grading policies, and contact information for a specific course.

synchronous   Communication in which interaction between participants is simultaneous (contrast 'asynchronous').

T

telecommunication   The science of information transport using wire, radio, optical, or electromagnetic channels to transmit and receive signals for voice or data communications using electrical means.

teleconferencing   Two-way electronic communication between two or more groups in separate locations via audio, video, and/or computer systems.

thesis   In master's degree study, the culminating project or paper of the program. In research paper writing, the statement or main idea on which the paper is based.

thread   A subject area within an on-line discussion, under which messages are posted. Discussions usually contain many threads.

transcript   Official record of courses taken at an educational institution.

transfer   (education) The act and process of moving from one learning institution to another. (technology) The rate at which information moves between sender and receiver(s).

Transmission Control Protocol (TCP)   A protocol that makes sure that packets of data are shipped and received in the intended order.

transponder   Satellite transmitter and receiver that receives and amplifies a signal prior to retransmission to an earth station.

trojan horse   An insidious and usually illegal computer program that masquerades as a program that is useful, fun, or otherwise desirable for users to download to their system. Once the program is downloaded, it performs a destructive act.

U

undergraduate   A student who has not yet received a bachelor's degree, or the courses such a student takes.

Universal Resource Locator (URL)   The address of a home page on the WWW.

university   Higher education institution that usually offers four-year degrees, as well as degrees beyond the baccalaureate level (i.e., graduate and professional degrees). They may also offer two-year degrees.

uplink   The communication link from the transmitting earth station to the satellite.

V

videoconferencing   Often refers to one-way video and two-way audio, in which audience members can see presenters, but cannot be seen by them. Two-way videoconferencing links two or more locations with equipment that allows voice and viewing by all parties.

virtual university   Higher education institution that does not have a physical presence, using technology to connect educators and learners. Contrast 'brick and mortar' institutions.

virus   An insidious piece of computer code written to damage systems. Viruses can be hidden in executable program files posted on-line.

W

Wide Area Network (WAN)   A network composed of Internet connections.

World Wide Web (WWW)   A graphical hypertext-based Internet tool that provides access to home pages created by individuals, businesses, and other organizations.

worm   An insidious and usually illegal computer program that is designed to replicate itself over a network for the purpose of causing harm and/or destruction. Whereas a virus is designed to invade a single computer's hard drive, a worm is designed to invade a network.

SELECTED BIBLIOGRAPHY AND REFERENCES

It would be impossible and quite beyond the scope of this book to provide a complete bibliography of all the sources that have informed what is written in its pages. Listed here, instead, are references that I have found particularly indispensable over the course of my twenty-plus years working with adults and being an adult learner. These texts are also accessible to the average reader. They are offered as suggestions for further exposure for those who are interested in learning more about the field of adult learning and in their own development.

Following are texts that every successful student should have in their library. Finally, a selection of the more comprehensive directories to opportunities available through distance learning and other specialized resources is supplied. All of these texts are given as a convenience to those who are interested in learning more.

Cross, K. *Adults As Learners: Increasing Participation and Facilitating Learning*. Jossey-Bass. 1992.

Davis, J. *Better Teaching, More Learning: Strategies for Success in Postsecondary Settings*. American Council on Education. 1993.

Gross, R. *Peak Learning: How to Create Your Own Lifelong Education Program for Personal Enlightenment and Professional Success*. J. P. Tarcher. 1999.

Kegan, R. *In over Our Heads: The Mental Demands of Modern Life*. Belknap Press. 1995.

Knowles, M. *Self-Directed Learning: A Guide for Learners and Teachers*. Cambridge Book Co. 1988.

Merriam, S. and Caffarella, R. *Learning in Adulthood: A Comprehensive Guide*. Jossey-Bass. 1999.

American Council on Education publications on receiving credit for learning outside of the classroom include:

ACE *National Guide to Educational Credit for Training Programs*

Guide to Educational Credit by Examination, 5th edition. ACE (Available at: <*http://www.acenet.edu/calec/corporate/guides-S.html#CBEGuide*>.)
Everyone who undertakes college-level learning, whether anticipating a degree or not, should have in their possession a good dictionary and thesaurus. Beyond that, the following guides, or others suggested by your school, are essential to success at the college level and beyond.

Guide to the Evaluation of Educational Experiences in the Armed Services

Style and writing guides:

Sebraneck, P., Meyer, V. and Kemper, D. *Writers Inc: A Student Handbook for Writing & Learning*. Write Source. 2000.
Especially helpful for those just starting college at any age; also includes study tips, tables of weights and measures, maps, a glossary of college terms, and more.

Strunk, W. and White, E. B. *The Elements of Style*. Allyn & Bacon. 2000.
A short, indispensable guide to writing well.

Turabian, K. L. *A Manual for Writers of Term Papers, Theses, and Dissertations*. University of Chicago Press. 1996.
Provides comprehensive, detailed, superior guidance to writers of research papers.

Distance learning directories and source books:

Bear, M. and J. *Bears' Guide to Earning Degrees Nontraditionally (13th ed)*. Ten Speed Press.
The title says it all: Includes listing of all accredited night and weekend colleges, foreign medical schools, degrees by Internet and other e-mail avenues, and every other way of earning any degree without becoming a 'traditional' on-campus student. Published annually.

Bear, M. and J. *College Degrees by Mail & Internet 2000*. Ten Speed Press.
Easy-to-use format and listing of accredited-only colleges. 2000.

Criscito, P. *Barron's Guide to Distance Learning: Degrees, Certificates, Courses (Barron's Guide to Distance Learning, 1999)*. Barrons Educational Series.
Good if you are looking for distance options outside of degree programs. 1999.

Petersen's Guides. *Petersen's Guide to Distance Learning Programs, 2000.*
A giant text (708 pages) with a wealth of information, including individual course lists that help you see the differences between similar programs. 2000.

Phillips, V. *The Best Distance Learning Graduate Schools: Earning Your Degree Without Leaving Home (Serial).* Princeton Review. 2000.
Includes everything you need to know about 195 programs, including prerequisites, admissions, tuition, campus visit requirements, and delivery methods.

The International Association of Universities' (UNESCO) *International Handbook of Universities.* Palgrave/St. Martin's Press.
The most comprehensive, authoritative, and up-to-date reference for international university-level programs, offering detailed, in-depth information and statistics on more than 6000 university-level institutions in 174 countries around the world. 2000.

Additional specific resources:

Bear, J. and M. *Bear's Guide to Finding Money for College.* Ten Speed Press.
Unusual advice beyond the 'regular' financial aid sources; includes tips on bargaining with schools and other entrepreneurial approaches. Full foundation list. 1997.

Lamdin, L. *Earn College Credit for What You Know.* Kendall-Hunt. 1997.

Forms and Worksheets

FIGURE 3–1

Online Learning Self-Assessment

Here are questions you should ask yourself about your skills, abilities, and resources before trying computer-based distance learning.

Check off the areas where you feel you could use some help, and you will have a roadmap for skills improvement before you begin, instead of a frustrating experience that is educational in more ways than one!

Do I have good skills in...	*Y/N*	*Skills Good*	*Need Work*
Reading?			
Writing?			
Effective note taking?			
Mathematics?			
Library usage and research?			
Test taking?			
Studying?			
Memory?			
Time management?			
Do I possess the characteristics of. . .			
Self-confidence?			
Patience?			
Persistence?			
Self-motivation?			
Do I have. . . .			
A support network?			
Access to a good library?			
A specific goal that education will meet?			

My educational goal is: _____

My greatest studying strength is: _____

_____

My weaknesses are: _____

Review your responses and list below those areas that need improvement. Then note your plans to increase your abilities in those skills. Be specific. Give yourself deadlines. Visit the Online Resources™ for updated lists of helpful resources.

My plans to improve the weaknesses are:

Skill: _____   Plan:_____

Skill: _____   Plan:_____

Skill: _____   Plan:_____

Skill: _____   Plan:_____

FIGURE 3-2

Time and Activity Analysis Worksheet

Fill in the blanks below to determine how much time you spend now on the many tasks of daily living and how much time you can make available for learning. Feel free to make multiple copies to compare different ways of allocating your available time resources. Share this worksheet with your family and others when discussing how priorities may change.

	M	T	W	Th	F	Sa	Su	Total
WORK TIME								
Time at Work								
Commuting								
At-home work tasks								
Total Work Time								
LEISURE TIME								
Socializing								
Hobbies/crafts								
Movies, cultural events								
Travel/vacation								
Fitness/outdoor								
Spiritual								
Volunteer/community								
Other								
Total Leisure Time								
LIVING TIME								
Relationship time								
Cooking/eating								
Shopping								
Sleeping								
Personal grooming								
Housekeeping								
Home/car maintenance								
Managing finances/taxes								
Childcare								
Other								
Total Living Time								
TOTAL TIME NEEDED								

FIGURE 6-1

Search Reminder Worksheet

Date _____   Subject/Course _____

Search criteria	Engine used	Useful results (URLs, X bookmarks)

Learning Journal Template

Directions: Choose a concept or idea from class readings and record your thoughts, feelings, opinions, or personal experiences about them. Include reasons for your reactions, supporting your points. As possible, your entries should contain ideas for applying what you have learned to your daily life. Write in a descriptive way, and as freely as possible. Do not limit or censor yourself. This is not a research paper! Be yourself.

Include:

- observations
- descriptive examples
- realizations
- reflections on the realities of your life
- other reactions you feel are important

Make journal entries at least once a week. Keep them in separate folder or notebook. At the end of the class, read through all of your entries and complete the journal by summarizing them in a final entry. Feel free to construct a learning journal for more than one class.

Name of class: _____   Date:_____

Concept or idea:_____

How I feel about it: (Write as much as you wish.)

Describe why you feel this way. Use examples, if applicable:

Tell how this concept or idea may influence your behavior in the future:

FIGURE 11-1

School Decision Checklist

School Decision Checklist

Name of school_____   Date contacted_____
Web site URL_____   Name of contact_____

School

Offers program I want to study?

Accreditation—Regional assn.: _____   Program:_____

How long in existence?_____ How long accredited?_____

Credentials of faculty: %PhD_____ % that hold degree from this school:_____

How many students are enrolled?_____ Graduated?_____

Name, phone/e-mail of enrolled students or graduates to contact: _____

When are students admitted (i.e., January/Sept., rolling) _____

Program - Degree/Major: _____

What are the prerequisites for admission?_____

Any tests required?_____ Other documentation:_____

Letters of recommendation?_____ How many?_____ Who from?_____

What are the application deadlines? _____

Number of credits to graduate: _____ Allowed in transfer: _____

What are the transfer criteria? _____

How many courses can I take before applying? _____

Can I complete a certificate and later use those credits toward a degree?_____

Credit given for prior learning? How? _____

Graduation requirements: _____

Who teaches courses; what credentials do they have?_____

Will I have an assigned advisor?_____ Can I change advisors?_____

Are there residency requirements?_____

What is average length of time to complete program?_____

Is there a time limit to complete the program?_____ For each course?_____

Can I take time off if I need to? How?_____

What is the time limit before I have to reapply?_____

Is there a "real" graduation, where I can march down the aisle?_____

Courses

How are courses structured? (tutorial, classes, etc.)_____

How long before a class starts can I enroll?_____

Is class size limited? If so, to how many?_____

What happens if too many?_____

What are grading policies? (Pass/Fail, etc.)_____

How are students assessed (projects, exams, etc.)?_____

What are the policies on incompletes?_____

Support

How do I obtain textbooks?_____

How do I access a library?_____

Is there an on-line writing center?_____ Other assistance?_____

Is the Student Handbook on-line? URL:_____

Is there an on-line student directory?_____ Faculty directory?_____

Are there any career services?_____

Technical

What are the recommended technical requirements?_____

Is there a tutorial I can try out? URL:_____

How are technical problems handled?_____

What about an on-line support manual? URL:_____

Costs

How much does each course/program cost?_____

What is the application fee?_____

What is the average cost of books and materials?_____

Are there other fees (graduation, residency, travel, etc.)?_____

Is financial aid available?_____ What kind?_____

How do I apply?_____ What are the deadlines?_____

What credit cards do you accept?_____

Other Questions:

_____

_____

_____

_____

Action	Date received/Sent
Requested application materials	
Mailed application	
Requested recommendations	
Requested transcript(s):	
Accepted	

Notes:

FIGURE 12-4

Time and Task Adjustments

Write down the tasks or activities that can be adjusted to provide time for your studies. You may make multiple copies of this worksheet as the demands of your school schedule fluctuate. Be sure to share this worksheet with your family and others when delegating responsibilities!

Activities/tasks to delegate	Person responsible	Time saved
Activities to change	**How to change**	
Activities to delete temporarily	**When to resume**	
	Total time saved →	

INDEX